Making Instit Repositories Work

"*Making Institutional Repositories Work* sums it up very well. This book, the first of its kind, explains how IRs work and how to get the greatest results from them. As many of us know, numerous IRs launched with high hopes have in fact languished with lackluster results. Faculty have little interest, and administrators see little promise. But the many chapter authors of this very well edited book have made their IRs successful, and here they share their techniques and successes. This is a necessary book for anyone contemplating starting an IR or looking to resurrect a moribund one."

—Richard W. Clement
Dean, College of University Libraries & Learning Sciences
University of New Mexico

"This volume presents an interesting cross-section of approaches to institutional repositories in the United States. Just about every view and its opposite makes an appearance. Readers will be able to draw their own conclusions, depending on what they see as the primary purpose of IRs."

—Stevan Harnad
Professor, University of Québec at Montréal
& University of Southampton

"Approaching this volume as one of 'those of us who have been furiously working to cultivate thriving repositories,' I am very excited about what this text represents. It is a broad compilation featuring the best and brightest writing on all the topics I've struggled to understand around repositories, and it also marks a point when repository management and development is looking more and more like a core piece of research library work. Callicott, Scherer, and Wesolek have pulled together all the things I wished I'd been able to read in my first year as a scholarly communication librarian. As I tweeted while reading a review copy: 'To my #scholcomm colleagues—the forthcoming *Making Institutional Repositories Work* will be essential.'"

—Micah Vandegrift
Digital Scholarship Coordinator
Florida State University Libraries

"Whether your IR is new, you are new to an IR, or you want to learn how other institutions are successful in specific areas, *Making Institutional Repositories Work* offers valuable and practical guidance. Each topic is addressed from multiple angles, as 39 authors share a range of varied experiences with selecting platforms, adopting policies, recruiting content, understanding metrics, and more. All readers are likely to see their own academic library within these pages. *Making Institutional Repositories Work* is a book I wish had been available when I launched an IR a few years ago."

—Janelle Wertzberger
Assistant Dean and Director of Scholarly Communications
Gettysburg College

"*Making Institutional Repositories Work* should be required reading for any librarian involved in the establishment of an institutional repository. Covering fundamental topics such as platform selection and policy creation, this book can help new repositories start with a clear plan for success. It will also be a welcome addition to the shelves of seasoned IR managers, as its thoughtful thematic sections and case studies provide real-world approaches to assess, sustain, and improve repositories on any campus."

—Andrea Wright
Science & Outreach Librarian, University Copyright Officer
Furman University

"Institutional repositories manage and provide access to the results and products of research. And, when networked, repositories collectively represent a key component of the evolving global open science infrastructure. As the momentum for open access grows and universities take on greater responsibility for managing their research outputs, the role of repositories is, equally, gaining in importance. This book provides a valuable overview of the current trends in institutional repository services and offers helpful guidance in terms of addressing challenges and adopting best practices from key North American experts in the field."

—Kathleen Shearer
Executive Director, Confederation of Open Access Repositories

Making Institutional Repositories Work

Edited by Burton B. Callicott, David Scherer, and Andrew Wesolek

Charleston Insights in
Library, Archival, and Information Sciences

Purdue University Press
West Lafayette, Indiana

Library of Congress Cataloging-in-Publication Data

Names: Callicott, Burton B., 1968- editor. | Scherer, David, 1984- editor. |
    Wesolek, Andrew, 1983- editor.
Title: Making institutional repositories work / edited by Burton B.
    Callicott, David Scherer, and Andrew Wesolek.
Description: West Lafayette, Indiana : Purdue University Press, [2016] |
    Series: Charleston insights in library, archival, and information sciences
    | Includes bibliographical references and index.
Identifiers: LCCN 2015035810 | ISBN 9781557537263 (pbk. : alk. paper) | ISBN
    9781612494227 (epdf) | ISBN 9781612494234 (epub)
Subjects: LCSH: Institutional repositories. | Institutional
    repositories—United States—Case studies.
Classification: LCC ZA4081.86 .M35 2016 | DDC 025.04—dc23 LC record
    available at http://lccn.loc.gov/2015035810

Contents

Foreword: A Few Reflections on the Evolution of Institutional Repositories

Clifford Lynch

With institutional repositories well into their second decade of deployment, the sort of examination of where we have been, where we are, and where we might be going represented by the essays in *Making Institutional Repositories Work* feels very timely.

In early 2003 I published an article titled "Institutional Repositories: Essential Infrastructure for Scholarship in the Digital Age," where I tried to make the case that such services most essentially provide a framework (often, perhaps, of last resort) to manage, provide access to, and preserve new forms of digital scholarship otherwise at risk, to nurture innovation in forms of scholarly communication, and to facilitate the preservation and reuse of evidence underlying scholarly work. This vision stands in contrast to a well-articulated alternative view that casts institutional repositories first and primarily as mechanisms to support a transition of the traditional scholarly journal literature to open access models.

This dialectic—still unresolved—is well illustrated in the chapters of this volume. There is much coverage of the relationships between repositories and various developments that have advanced the cause of open access. One very nice property of this approach is that it's actually possible to measure progress toward success quantitatively, as opposed to the subjective assessments and very long view of nurturing new forms of scholarship. I was delighted to see coverage of the repositories in the context of electronic theses and dissertations (ETDs), but this discussion also underscores how long it takes for changes in practice to enter the mainstream in the academy: ETDs are now well into their *third* decade.

The importance of research data has only really received the serious attention it demands in the last decade, and various funder mandates surrounding the availability and reuse of data are just now taking hold, at least in the United States. It remains to be seen how we will ultimately find balances between the roles of disciplinary and institutional repositories in managing research data, discipline by discipline. For many purposes, I continue to suspect that disciplinary approaches are superior *when they are available and can be relied upon over time.* But it's clear they aren't always going to exist when scholars need them, and I continue to worry about the long-term financial commitments to repositories at all levels.

Other kinds of new digital materials continue to attract interest, including, for example, open educational resources (OERs) and how they relate to both the future of textbooks and various kinds of online instruction delivery. Institutional repositories are going to play an important role here.

There continue to be opportunities and compelling reasons to more systematically document and share the contributions to intellectual and cultural life that arise from our educational and cultural institutions. I have made this argument at length elsewhere[1] and was delighted to see developments in institutional repositories placed firmly in this context in the opening to Part 6. This is about institutional mission and the way that repositories can help to advance that mission.

There are very interesting convergences taking place between library publishing programs, university presses, repositories, and the digital humanities; here it has finally become very clear to scholars that a reliable, stable (institutionalized), credible management framework for new digital forms of scholarship is absolutely critical to legitimizing these new forms as core work rather than fringe experiments. Some of these developments are covered here, and I hope this helps to give them broader visibility and consideration.

It still feels to me like we are doing too much to try to "sell" the use of institutional repositories to all faculty simultaneously; this makes sense mainly in the context of responding to various open access mandates. I think we need to much more carefully explore and understand the potential roles and contributions that an institutional repository can make to faculty members over the full arc of their professional careers.

Finally, let me note one more highlight from this collection of essays, which we might view as a recognition of the growing maturity of institutional repositories. This is the increased attention to thinking about institutional repositories as a *system,* and perhaps even more importantly as components and subsystems in broader national and international systems that support scholarship. The final part of the book frames these opportunities well, and major current programs like the Association of Research Libraries–led SHARE initiative also build on this kind of thinking. I believe it will be an important future direction, accommodating an increasing interest in not only managing the huge and ever-expanding body of scholarship, but of also trying to actively understand its shape and growth analytically.

NOTE

See Lynch, C. A. (2008). A matter of mission: Information technology and the future of higher education. In R. Katz (Ed.), *The tower and the cloud* (pp. 43–50). Boulder, CO: EDUCAUSE. Corrected version is available online at www.educause.edu.

Introduction

Burton Callicott, David Scherer,
and Andrew Wesolek

HISTORY OF REPOSITORIES: HOW WE GOT WHERE WE ARE

Institutional repository initiatives consist of a suite of services intended to support the preservation and organization of, and access to, the intellectual output of the institution in which they are housed. The institutional repository (IR) itself typically refers to the software infrastructure on which these initiatives depend. More than that, though, institutional repositories were developed to be a solution to some of the problematic aspects of scholarly communication in a digital age. Specifically, they were and continue to be seen as a way to introduce competition to a monopolistic traditional publishing system by offering the possibility of immediate publication, long-term preservation, and barrier-free global access to those publications.

The promise of repositories in general was immediately apparent with the launch of the disciplinary-specific repository arXiv in 1991. On its debut, electronic communication of scholarly literature via this preprint server was rapidly embraced by high-energy physicists, and this has since expanded to include related areas of physics and mathematics while hosting more than one million EPrints. The revolutionary potential of this new mode of communication was recognized and embraced soon after its launch, and as early as the mid-1990s, some began recognizing the broader potential of such repositories to revolutionize traditional scholarly communication systems (Ginsparg, 1997).

Beginning in the early 2000s, the potential of disciplinary repositories to disseminate scholarship immediately and openly began to be applied at the institutional level. The year 2002 marked a watershed, seeing the first public release of the open source institutional repository software DSpace, along with the publication of the Scholarly Publishing and Academic Resources Coalition (SPARC) position paper, *The Case for Institutional Repositories* (Crow, 2002). These two events provided broadly accessible software support for institutional repositories, as well as a compelling case which tied institutional repository initiatives to institutional visibility and prestige. As a result, institutional repository programs began to grow at an exponential rate, now numbering in the thousands.

GROUNDING THE VISION

Although institutional repositories had lofty goals and intentions, the actual practice of repositories, and the activities undertaken to populate them, did not match the zeal of the library community. In her canonical 2008 article, Dorothea Salo (2008) stated that academic libraries were enticed into the wind and that the whole project might have been a waste of time. Many institutional repositories encountered unforeseen problems and a surprising lack of impact. Clunky or cumbersome interfaces, lack of value and use by scholars, fear of copyright infringement, and the like tended to dampen excitement and adoption.

Even today, libraries that have repositories (or those considering whether or not to take the plunge) have been questioning:

- What are the best containers/platforms?
- Should we host or not host?
- What are the best ways to make content visible and discoverable?
- What is the role of IRs in providing "green" open access to work published elsewhere?
- What should go in (and what should be kept out)?
- What is the role of IRs in being publishing platforms for original and unique institutional publications?
- What measures of success matter? Which measurements matter to whom?
- How are access and use measured—downloads, altmetrics, and so on?
- What is the impact of an institutional repository?

While repository initiatives have had to fight an uphill battle, widespread adoption and use indicates that they are here to stay and will have an impact in the evolution of scholarly communication. Libraries and those within the libraries who manage repositories have learned through their experiences and have demonstrated that the initial problems that they encountered can be overcome and that successful institutional repository initiatives are possible and replicable.

STRATEGIES FOR SUCCESS

Making Institutional Repositories Work takes newcomers as well as seasoned practitioners through the practical and conceptual steps necessary to have a successful IR customized to the goals and culture of their home institutions. Over the course of the last 10-plus years, much digital ink has been spilled discussing and debating the more technical aspects of IRs including platform design, methods of integrating datasets, open access initiatives, copyright considerations, and so forth. The result is a lack of practical and straightforward literature available to those considering an IR initiative at their institutions and for current practitioners seeking to increase the success of their current repository initiatives in a holistic way.

Making Institutional Repositories Work intends to fill this void. We asked several established and highly regarded experts in the world of institutional repositories to take a step back from the theoretical and highly technical details surrounding repository initiatives and share their real-world experiences, observations, and premonitions about the practice and shape of repositories. This volume contains their experiences, case studies, and strategies for success, as well as their perceptions on the future of institutional repositories and their role within the scholarly communication landscape.

THE STRUCTURE OF THE VOLUME

This volume is arranged in four thematic parts intended to take the pulse of institutional repositories—to see how they have matured and what can be expected from them, as well as to introduce what may be their future role. To keep the content grounded and practical, the volume also contains a series of case studies in which librarians at institutions of different sizes, repository platforms, and research focuses describe how and why they initially created IRs and how the role of the IR has evolved. The work concludes with a vision of the future of IR initiatives by detailing some of the challenges they face and strategies for sustained success.

PART 1: CHOOSING A PLATFORM

In the broadest sense, an institutional repository initiative seeks to capture the intellectual output of an institution and make it openly available in perpetuity. Launching such an initiative requires specialized software. Part 1 will focus on the many repository platform options available and the desired outcomes that influence software decisions. Does the institution wish to invest in the technical staff to develop its own repository or support an open source solution? Or would it be better suited to an "out of the box" proprietary option? In addition, Part 1 covers content and how these decisions will impact platform choice: what types of items will the repository hold? Articles, theses and dissertations, datasets, library-published materials? Finally, to what degree is discoverability important? If it is, what are some steps that the institution can take to enhance the discoverability of its repository's content?

Chapter 1, "Choosing a Repository Platform: Open Source vs. Hosted Solutions," by Hillary Corbett, Jimmy Ghaphery, Lauren Work, and Sam Byrd, lays out the major considerations that go into selecting an institutional repository platform. Those new to repositories will discover that what may appear to be a murky and even scary array of factors to consider can become quite clear with a simple assessment of key components. The chapter also offers insights and advice to readers who have an existing repository but are considering a platform change. The authors outline the major differences between open source and proprietary systems using DSpace/Fedora and Digital Commons to illustrate the relative advantages of each system. Drawing from the experience of Virginia Commonwealth and Northeastern University, separate sections detail the processes and considerations that go into switching from an open source to a proprietary system as well as the reverse.

These initial platform decisions will also have an impact on the types of data storage services that may be offered as part of a repository initiative. The use and sharing of research data is of increasing interest to funders and publishers, but repositories are often responsible for the long-term storage of and access to this information. Chapter 2, "Repository Options for Research Data," by Katherine McNeill, discusses the relationship between research data and repositories, in light of the experiences of the Massachusetts Institute of Technology (MIT) library system. McNeill examines the various types of data repositories currently available to academic institutions, noting key differences on several important characteristics. She suggests that institutions need to consider several questions when either developing a stand-alone data repository service or accepting research data into an existing institutional repository. She points out that there is no single solution, and for the foreseeable future, institutions will choose between varying repository models that will best fit the needs of their local context, and enable the best models of data storage and sharing.

The most beautiful and intuitive repository interface is functionally useless if its content is not discoverable by researchers. In Chapter 3, "Ensuring Discoverability of IR Content," Kenning Arlitsch, Patrick OBrien, Jeffrey K. Mixter, Jason A. Clark, and Leila Sterman explore the key factors that will reliably enhance search engine optimization. They start with metadata and provide tips that can enhance efficiency as well as effectiveness. The authors then provide suggestions for structuring IR sites that will enable search engine crawlers to more readily index content. In addition to providing useful approaches to data maintenance and cleanup, the authors outline best practices that will minimize overhaul work as search engines evolve, and as repositories become more integrated into various databases and new modes of research strategy.

PART 2: SETTING POLICIES

After selecting a platform to support an institutional repository, one must consider which policies are to be put in place. Part 2 examines the theoretical aspects and practical applications of two important policy decisions: institutional open access policies and published theses and dissertations.

Due in large part to the advent of repositories, many colleges and universities have passed or are in the process of passing open access policies. In Chapter 4, "Open Access Policies: Basics and Impact on Content Recruitment," Andrew Wesolek and Paul Royster explore the different types of open access policies currently in place and discuss steps and methodologies that can lead to development and passage. Wesolek served as scholarly communication librarian at an open access policy institution and as the chair of the Coalition of Open Access Policy Institutions (COAPI), while Royster manages the remarkably successful institutional repository at the University of Nebraska–Lincoln, an institution that made the conscious decision not to pursue passage of an open access policy. From these differing perspectives, Wesolek and Royster seek to answer the question, "Are open access policies necessary for successful repositories?"

In Chapter 5, "Responsibilities and Rights: Balancing the Institutional Imperative for Open Access with Authors' Self-Determination," Isaac Gilman makes a broader investigation of the ethical dimensions of an open access policy. Gilman makes the case that institutions have a clear and often explicitly stated goal of making locally created knowledge openly available to the world, while faculty and students, as rights holders, have an equally clear right to self-determination. He concludes that institutional repositories should play an essential role in fulfilling an institution's mission to share knowledge as broadly as possible while respecting faculty rights.

We then focus on the more concrete aspects of open access policy implementation with Chapter 6, "Campus Open Access Policy Implementation Models and Implications for IR Services," by Ellen Finnie Duranceau and Sue Kriegsman. In this chapter, the authors offer a snapshot of the institutional open access policy implementation landscape in an effort to build a roadmap for others moving forward in this "nuanced" environment. The authors report on a survey conducted by the COAPI that was designed to discover and chart the scope of the coalition membership's policies and their methods of implementation. Based on the data from this survey, Duranceau and Kriegsman provide a suite of strategies modeled on institutions with open access policies in place that have been employed to both meet faculty needs and successfully populate institutional repositories.

Gail McMillan then covers the most fundamental content of institutional repositories, electronic theses and dissertations (ETDs), in Chapter 7, "Electronic Theses and Dissertations: Preparing Graduate Students for Their Futures." Here, McMillan outlines some of the policy considerations associated with integrating an ETD program into an institutional repository. Institutional missions and ETD stakeholders as well as the impact these policy decisions may have on student-authors are discussed and contextualized.

Finally, Megan Banach Bergin and Charlotte Roh discuss key aspects of the ETD policy decisions made at the University of Massachusetts Amherst in Chapter 8, "Systematically Populating an IR with ETDs: Launching a Retrospective Digitization Project and Collecting Current ETDs." Ultimately, both chapters recommend empowering student-authors through educating them about their rights as authors in a landscape that is rapidly shifting toward open access.

PART 3: RECRUITING AND CREATING CONTENT

Once a platform is in place and policies have been adopted, institutional repository managers can begin to focus on content. From previously published materials, expanding forms of gray literature and other existing works, to the emerging field of repository-based publishing programs, the chapters in Part 3 cover the array of content that can potentially be added to an IR. This part also outlines challenges that institutions can face in terms of marketing IR services and soliciting scholarship while presenting strategies to meet and rise above real and perceived recruitment barriers.

In Chapter 9, "Faculty Self-Archiving," Stephanie Davis-Kahl identifies faculty resistance to self-archiving journal articles in institutional repositories. Davis-Kahl argues that while open access has become increasingly accepted, and IRs have contributed to that acceptance, there are still many points of confusion and concern regarding repository self-archiving practices including (but not limited to) repository awareness, copyright, time, perceptions of self-archived materials, and disciplinary culture and practices. She suggests that faculty use and perceptions of research may shift with the use of social media programs, such as ResearchGate and Academia.edu, to engage with faculty by enhancing the activities and practices faculty use to interact and communicate with colleagues and disciplinary counterparts.

As many early adopters have demonstrated, a repository cannot become successful by simply being built, regardless of the quality of the platform. In Chapter 10, "Incentivizing Them to Come: Strategies, Tools, and Opportunities for Marketing an Institutional Repository," David Scherer discusses that while repositories continue to emerge, they have not lived up to their expectations for growth and coverage. Based on his experience at Purdue, Scherer provides tried and true methods that can lead to a diverse, active, and constantly evolving marketing plan that emphasizes benefits and incentives to stakeholders, repository offerings, and additional resources that increase participation and use.

As libraries begin to collaborate with university presses at an ever expanding rate, institutional repositories are staged to play an important and active role in these new and budding programs and partnerships. In Chapter 11, "Repository as Publishing Platform," Simone Sacchi and Mark Newton discuss why institutional repositories are in a position to provide opportunities for current and future researchers to better understand the scholarly communication/publication process, how the institutional repository can be utilized as a publishing platform, and what may be the future of repository-based publishing.

Not only can repositories serve as new venues for publishing models, they can also serve as new training grounds to inform and educate those involved in the publication process, ranging from students becoming acclimated to academic activities and dissemination, to academic journal editors interested in new publishing models. Chapter 12, "Publishing Pedagogy: The Institutional Repository as Training Ground for a New Breed of Academic Journal Editors," by Catherine Mitchell and Lisa Schiff, explores the role of the institutional repository as a pedagogical tool and resource for campus stakeholders on several publishing topics and activities, including copyright, licenses, types and quality of peer review, and journal sustainability and business models. Mitchell and Schiff also discuss how their interactions with campus stakeholders have informed the California Digital Library (CDL) development plans and policies for the University of California's institutional repository, eScholarship.

PART 4: MEASURING SUCCESS

This final thematic part attempts to encapsulate all the tools and data that can reliably measure IR success for managers, contributors, users, departmental and institutional administrators, and other stakeholders. It seeks to answer the question, "So, I have an IR; now, how do I know that it is effective?"

In Chapter 13, "Purposeful Metrics: Matching Institutional Repository Metrics to Purpose and Audience," Todd Bruns and Harrison W. Inefuku tackle IR metrics that can be generated through repository platforms as well as third-party sources such as Google Analytics and Altmetrics. They provide methods of turning raw metric data into useful information parsed to the appropriate audience and purpose. The authors outline the ways that metric data captured and presented correctly can provide an avenue for establishing institutional repositories as an integral technology in the research enterprise of the institution.

Kim Holmberg, Stefanie Haustein, and Daniel Beucke introduce readers to the rapidly evolving and increasingly important realm of altmetrics. Chapter 14, "Social Media Metrics as Indicators of Repository Impact," inventories and assesses the various means of measuring impact through social media. They show how these measures can bring to light potentially more timely, granular, and nuanced measures of use and impact than what has been used previously. The chapter presents concrete examples from institutions that currently employ altmetrics as well as a likely future of this burgeoning approach to assessment.

Tacking away from raw numbers and metrics, "Peer Review and Institutional Repositories" (Chapter 15), by Burton Callicott, addresses the potential impact IRs may have on the peer-review system and the ways in which IRs may begin to play a significant role in credentialing and assessing scholarship. By exploring the ways in which gray literature has risen in prominence, availability, and legitimacy due to its inclusion in IRs, this chapter charts the ramifications this may have for "white" or more traditional scholarly publications—journal articles and monographs. Due to the radical increase in production of scholarship and the role of the repository in the process, this chapter also describes publishing trends and avenues of scholarly communication that are affected by repositories and the concomitant effect this will likely have on the peer-review system.

Marianne A. Buehler's "Defining Success and Impact for Scholars, Department Chairs, and Administrators: Is There a Sweet Spot?" (Chapter 16), the final chapter in Part 4, attempts to bring all the various assessment measures together such that they have value and resonance for all the major institutional constituents. Buehler outlines the ways that the primary interests of scholars and administrators may seem at odds on some levels but when viewed holistically can be seen to have shared goals that can be documented and graphed when success measures are implemented and reported in a way that reveals the "sweet spot" that has resonance and value for all involved.

PART 5: INSTITUTIONAL REPOSITORIES
IN PRACTICE: CASE STUDIES

Part 5 presents four case studies from institutions of varying size and mission that describe the implementation and application of the concepts and activities described in the previous parts.

Princeton University

In "Creating the IR Culture" (Chapter 17) Anne Langley and Yuan Li present a case study that maps out the creation of the institutional repository culture at Princeton University. Langley and Li describe how their experience was unique due to the fact that, unlike at most schools, an open access policy predated their repository. They emphasize the creation of a strong base of support across campus by telling the story of open access, while also being careful how the message was created to fit the needs of their audience.

College of Charleston

James Tyler Mobley takes readers through the decision-making process that led to an open source (DSpace) repository at the College of Charleston in "On Implementing an Open Source Institutional Repository" (Chapter 18). The case study illustrates the realities that many mid-sized state schools face when they want to play a part of the IR movement. Based on his experience, Mobley outlines what is required and what can be expected when the choice is made to go with a "free," open sourced platform with a limited number of staff members who have various levels of expertise and coding skills. As anyone who has attempted to employ open source software knows, unlicensed applications invariably come with unexpected cost expenditures in terms of staff time and training. Mobley provides an invaluable case study that can greatly impact a major IR decision both in terms of creating an IR from scratch or switching from a proprietary to an open source platform.

Purdue University

David Scherer, Lisa Zilinski, and Kelley Kimm's case study, "Interlinking Institutional Repository Content and Enhancing User Experiences" (Chapter 19), focuses on the connection and linkage of published research findings available in Purdue's textual-institutional repository, Purdue e-Pubs, to published datasets available in the Purdue University Research

Repository (PURR). They discuss a partnership with the Joint Transportation Research Program (JTRP) to develop these two repositories to further enhance two intersecting publishing workflows to account for enhancements and presentation of content, and to further develop the user's experience with an overall goal of increasing access and visibility of published technical report publications and published datasets.

Utah State University

Betty Rozum and Becky Thoms describe a strategy of populating an institutional repository through relying on subject librarians and cultivating grassroots efforts in Chapter 20, "Populating Your Institutional Repository and Promoting Your Students: IRs and Undergraduate Research." In coordination with its subject librarian, the Physics Department at Utah State University recognized the opportunity of the IR, DigitalCommons@USU, to showcase the department by combining student and faculty research and organizing it by research area. As a result, many student and faculty works that might not ordinarily receive a great deal of attention, such as posters and conference proceedings, have been discovered and utilized by scholars inside and outside of the Utah State system. Utah State's story demonstrates the potential of IRs for all schools.

PART 6: CLOSING REFLECTIONS AND THE NEXT STEPS FOR INSTITUTIONAL REPOSITORIES

The main purpose of Part 6 is to provide a better understanding of the priorities and challenges institutional repositories will face in the coming years by highlighting the broader factors that will most likely affect the development of repositories, repository services, and the roles of those directly involved including scholarly communications librarians, repository managers, and the library administrators in charge of making resource decisions.

CONCLUSION

The number of institutional repositories established and the total amount of content they hold has exploded in recent years. While institutional repositories are entering their second decade with rapid growth, they are still in their infancy and have yet to reach their fullest potential. We hope that this volume offers a bird's-eye view of the scholarly communication landscape and a clear picture of where IRs have been, where they are today, and where they will be in the future.

With this book, we hope that you will find one source that will allow you to gain a fuller grasp of the concept of institutional repositories as well as introduce you to strategies that have worked to make IRs relevant, useful, and vital at institutions nationally as well as internationally. We hope that those looking to launch a repository will find this volume helpful and that those of us who have been furiously working to cultivate thriving repositories will find new ideas and models for collaboration, innovation, and success within the following pages.

REFERENCES

Crow, R. (2002). The case for institutional repositories: A SPARC position paper. *ARL Bimonthly Report, 223.* Retrieved from http://www.sparc.arl.org/resources /papers-guides/the-case-for-institutional-repositories

Ginsparg, P. (1997). Winners and losers in the global research village. *Serials Librarian, 30,* 83–96.

Salo, D. (2008). Innkeeper at the roach motel. *Library Trends, 57*(2), 98–123. http://dx.doi.org/10.1353/lib.0.0031

Part 1

CHOOSING A PLATFORM

Selecting a platform for an institutional repository requires a host of decisions that should be considered within the context of one's unique campus environment. In the following chapters we see the distillation of these considerations into three major themes: staffing, purpose, and goals. First, Hillary Corbett, Jimmy Ghaphery, Lauren Work, and Sam Byrd weigh the benefits and disadvantages of several popular repository platforms, as well as discuss the process of migration from one to another. Katherine McNeill then explores the data repository ecosystem while offering insights into the role of the repository in this diverse landscape. Finally, Kenning Arlitsch and colleagues delve into strategies to effectively enhance the findability of the content hosted on an institutional repository through search engine optimization.

Corbett and colleagues outline the wide array of repository platforms and the major considerations that go into choosing one over another. One of the key themes in this evaluation is the type of investment an institution is willing or able to make in a repository initiative. Several open source platforms are evaluated that allow for flexibility in their implementation, at the cost of staff time to develop, maintain, and update them. Conversely, hosted repository platforms may be launched with as little as .25 FTE, but come with more rigid structures and limits on customizability.

Prior to selecting an institutional repository, one must consider the type of repository it is intended to be. Major funding agencies are requiring researchers to manage, and often openly share their data at a rapidly increasing rate. Is this a service an institutional repository initiative is intended to support? If so, should support come in the form of institutional repository infrastructure, or through ancillary services such as guiding researchers in the selection and deposit of materials in existing and external data-specific repositories? Katherine McNeill explores this nuanced and fluid ecosystem of repositories. Ultimately, she suggests a multifaceted approach of leveraging an institutional repository for research publications, while integrating them with datasets stored in a variety of external data-specific repositories.

Finally, what are the goals of a proposed institutional repository initiative? Is it enough for an IR to serve as an archive of the scholarly output of the institution, or does the repository initiative intend to disseminate that scholarly output broadly and openly? Kenning Arlitsch and colleagues argue in support of the latter: "discoverability of content through Internet search engines is paramount to the success and impact of institutional repositories." The authors then outline a variety of search engine optimization techniques that librarians may apply to their institutional repositories in order to increase discoverability.

Ultimately, platform decisions for institutional repositories are highly dependent on individual institutional contexts. However, Part 1 offers a framework for selection built on the themes of the staffing, purpose, and goals of a repository initiative. This framework may then be built upon further after a careful survey of the needs, values, and culture of the institution, thus providing the first step toward a successful repository initiative.

1 | Choosing a Repository Platform: Open Source vs. Hosted Solutions

Hillary Corbett, Jimmy Ghaphery, Lauren Work, and Sam Byrd

Platform selection is a concept that will be familiar to many who work in libraries, regardless of whether they have worked with an institutional repository. Selection and implementation of a new integrated library system (ILS) or discovery platform are experiences that most library staff will generally encounter more than once in their careers, and they are processes that typically represent a significant, long-term time commitment for staff across the organization. The stakes are high because so many library employees' day-to-day work involves active and extensive use of the system that is chosen. Because of this common experience, it naturally follows that library staff tasked with choosing an institutional repository platform may approach the job with trepidation. But in reality, the selection process doesn't have to be time-consuming or fraught with anxiety. (Indeed, a common pitfall may be to overplan for the process.)

While it's essential to include representatives of different areas of expertise, the group tasked with selection can be fairly compact. This will help the process move more smoothly. Who should be included in this group? If there is an existing repository, its manager should be involved, of course. Staff from metadata and systems units should also be included. Even with a hosted platform, where no on-site technical expertise would be needed, the systems representative will likely be best able to evaluate its architecture and interoperability. Someone with an archival background can also provide valuable perspective on the preservation aspects of the repository platforms under consideration. Your Web developer or user experience expert can be very helpful in evaluating interfaces and their potential customizations. Above all, the repository must be usable. It can have great metadata support and elegant architecture, but if the interface is clunky, no one will use it. A team member who knows how users interact with the library's other online resources is essential. Finally, you may also wish to seek input from a power user of your current repository, or someone who is likely to be an active user of a repository under development. If including them during the selection process isn't feasible, such users should certainly be asked to help later with usability testing.

Your library may already have an existing repository, but try to evaluate prospective new platforms independently of whether or not they are "better" or "worse" than your current platform. In many ways, a new platform will likely just be different—and that's going to be a combination of positive and negative. Of course, it's important to consider your current platform in the context of how you will migrate its contents! But you've already made the decision to move to a new platform—strive to evaluate your choices on their own merits. The goal in your selection process is to compare new platform with new platform, not new platform with current platform (or with the absence of a platform, if you don't currently have a repository). If your library already hosts a repository and you're looking for a new platform, you should certainly make a list of your current platform's pros and cons—but don't let them influence your process too much or get bogged down with too much discussion of the current platform. Likewise, keep in mind that platforms are constantly under development, and specific features you note as absent or less well developed may be slated for future releases. Most importantly, remember this evaluation is not a mere side-by-side comparison, but needs to be tied to your institution's repository goals and ambitions.

While this chapter discusses selection of a locally hosted, open source system (DSpace/Fedora) vs. a cloud-hosted, proprietary system (Digital Commons), it is important to note that these examples are merely illustrative. Libraries have a range of choices for repository software that includes open source and proprietary in any number of support environments, and exemplary repositories are flourishing on a variety of systems, both open source and proprietary. This chapter focuses on the differences between proprietary and open source solutions, but also demonstrates how and why libraries choose a repository system. In writing about this process, we realized that it was important to acknowledge that there are two different audiences for this chapter: those who may just be starting out with building a repository at their institution, and those with an established repository who are considering a platform change. Thus, this chapter addresses the challenges and opportunities of platform selection in both circumstances.

SELECTIVE LITERATURE REVIEW

The library literature regarding open source software has dealt with a variety of systems, including integrated library systems (ILS) and repository platforms. Pruett and Choi's (2013) article comparing select open source and proprietary ILS software includes a thorough review of previous research, including welcome background from fields other than library science. Palmer and Choi's (2014) descriptive literature study is also an important touchstone for an understanding of previous research on library open source software. In this review, the authors found that almost 35% of the library literature regarding open source has dealt with digital repository software, and they posit that this concentration is largely due to a preponderance of open source repository platforms (DSpace, Fedora, EPrints). Indeed, the repository market is almost an opposing image of the open source ILS market since open source solutions have defined repository solutions from the outset.

Library literature concerning the choice between open source or proprietary repository platforms reflects the multifaceted and unique circumstances that individual institutions face. Burns, Lana, and Budd (2013) reflect this reality in the conclusion of their survey of institutional repositories, stating that "the most important lesson learned from this survey is that not all institutional repositories are alike" (Discussion, section 5, para. 1). Though widely applicable evaluation methodologies and parameters for choosing an institutional repository are well documented (Fay, 2010; Giesecke, 2011; Rieger, 2007), final decisions for open source vs. proprietary platforms are most often unique to the circumstances of each institution and emerge from university-level needs assessments. Common factors cited in the case studies for choosing proprietary solutions include costs of technical infrastructure and staffing, the need for swift implementation to allow for a focus on repository population and promotion, interface branding and customization, electronic publishing options, and online discoverability of scholarly research (Bluh, 2009; Mandl & Organ, 2007; Younglove, 2013). Libraries that select open source repository platforms also note customization as a positive factor, but include extensibility, flexibility to ingest varied formats, and interoperability (Fay, 2010; Marill & Luczak, 2009). In line with these cost-benefit issues of open source, Samuels and Griffy's (2012) case study in evaluating open source publishing solutions includes a comparative methodology that includes total cost of ownership.

Salo's tongue-in-cheek essay "How to Scuttle a Scholarly Communication Initiative" (2013) is required reading, both for its insightful look into library culture and its very well-developed bibliography for anyone interested in starting or improving a scholarly communication program. In discussing platform choice, Salo encourages usability and beta testing as well as reaching out to colleagues who are current or former users of the systems under consideration. Salo makes her point about the pitfalls of focusing solely on platform without consideration of the larger scholarly communication goals of the organization in a particularly humorous manner: "It is particularly important to fixate on a software package before the initiative's mission, milestones, and workflows have been decided . . . to maximize the discrepancies between necessary work and the software's capabilities" (p. 3).

VIRGINIA COMMONWEALTH UNIVERSITY: FROM OPEN SOURCE TO PROPRIETARY

Virginia Commonwealth University (VCU) launched a DSpace instance in 2007 as a platform to support its electronic theses and dissertations (ETD) program. All systems and database administration, server maintenance, and application support were handled by library technical staff. There were no additional staff allocated for the ongoing support of the repository. The initial installation and support were carried out by the Web systems librarian, who relied heavily on the DSpace-tech listserv[1] for support and advice. Shortly after launching DSpace, the library sought clarification of its goals for the repository. A Statement of Direction was developed that intentionally limited use of DSpace to deposit of ETDs for several reasons: anticipated difficulty in supporting an expanded DSpace repository, environmental scans of difficulties that other fledgling repositories were facing, and a sense that focusing on digitization of local library collections would yield greater impact.

Once DSpace was installed and launched, support did not entail any significant work beyond routine operating system patches. The ETD collection grew without incident. In 2010, VCU's Web systems librarian, who served as the lead support person for DSpace, left the university for another position. It was not possible to find a replacement who had the same level of DSpace expertise, which was problematic due to an anticipated need to upgrade both hardware and software. Migration of embargoed ETDs while preserving their security was of particular concern. While VCU had previously received help for some issues on the DSpace-tech listserv, this type of assistance was not always consistent or sufficient to support what was becoming a larger and more mission-critical collection of ETDs. For all of these reasons, the library contracted with a vendor to provide support services specifically for upgrading the software.

This upgrade process was a significant task. It included vendor support in testing the new version on a hosted sandbox server as well as local work in writing custom SQL code to move retrospective embargo data to new database fields. After the successful migration, the decision was made to continue vendor support. On January 9, 2014, it was announced on the DSpace-tech listserv that, consistent with the DSpace Software Support Policy,[2] the version of DSpace being used at VCU would no longer be supported with security patches. Even though VCU had already made the decision to move to Digital Commons at that point, issues with local upgrades of DSpace were one of the factors that encouraged us to move to a cloud-hosted solution. While VCU did face some technical challenges with DSpace, we were by no means dissatisfied. An official software support policy is an excellent step toward keeping software moving forward, and the software was very stable with only minor issues. We achieved this consistency of performance without major staff investments. And like other enterprise-level library software, DSpace was not unique in requiring significant effort in testing and deploying upgrades.

Meanwhile, the library had been making modest steps toward expanding the scope of the repository. In 2013, two collections were published on the DSpace platform: *British Virginia,* a peer-reviewed series of scholarly editions from and about the Virginia colonies, and an annual series of undergraduate research posters. Both of these projects engaged external departments at VCU who saw great benefit in partnering with the library in these publishing endeavors. The field of scholarly communication and library publishing had likewise shifted dramatically since our cautious 2007 assessments, with a number of successful models.

The desire to expand the library role in publishing was also surfacing as a new need. Based on our own research and previous experiences running DSpace, we felt that DSpace would not be adequate as a journal publishing platform. As such, if we remained on DSpace for our anticipated repository growth, we were also looking at implementing another system to support journal publishing such as Open Journal Systems (OJS). We considered various combinations of local and hosted implementations of DSpace and OJS. We did find the open source virtues of these systems, and the natural alliance of open source and open access, to be compelling. However, after much discussion across the organization, and against the backdrop of recent successes with migrating our other major library systems to the cloud, we decided that Digital Commons was our best path forward to quickly meet our ambitions.

Beyond the vendor-supported cloud platform and its integrated repository and publishing systems, there were a number of other enticing features of Digital Commons that led to our decision to migrate. We were drawn to the marketing and outreach features of Digital Commons and were excited about features such as automated author notifications, federated networking of all customer content, and search engine optimization. These functions seemed difficult to reproduce with open source solutions, especially given VCU's systems staffing. And because of recent experiences with other cloud-based systems, we knew that the process of implementing new releases would likely come with less overhead than we were used to on a locally supported system.

VCU's implementation of Digital Commons was rapid, enabled by a number of factors. During a two-month period, design decisions and IR policy outlines were established—library administration wanted to move the project along quickly, and a task force was established that helped accelerate this progress. VCU signed its contract with bepress at the beginning of February 2014, the repository went live in March, and it accepted its first submission in the new system in April.

The migration of VCU's data from DSpace highlighted structural differences between the two systems and the importance of portability of repository data. In certain areas we ran into difficulty reconciling differences between the two platforms. One had to do with how supplemental files are handled; another was representation of special characters and diacritics in the metadata. The actual handling of the Dublin Core metadata was significantly different for each system, particularly for the date and creator fields. A number of bulk loads, revisions, and finally some targeted manual editing were needed to complete the project. Bepress customer support was extremely helpful during this process, but in the final analysis it was our responsibility to migrate, test, and accept data.

There are a number of features from DSpace that we certainly miss. We obviously do not have direct database access and must depend upon the vendor for certain reports, including quarterly backups. Many things require vendor intervention, such as setting up a new collection. Fortunately, bepress provides an exemplary level of customer support to turn our requests around quickly. We have embraced the limitations of the user interface design templates with an understanding that common design patterns across all customer sites enhance the ability for agile product improvements.

We have been impressed thus far with new features and strategic directions of bepress, including more intentional support for datasets and images. A few other qualities of Digital Commons have also been affirming our platform decision. We have seen initial evidence that the author notification and search engine optimization features that appealed to us in the selection process also appeal to our users at VCU and are fostering greater acceptance of the repository. The road toward establishing mature repository and publishing services, however, is long, and we are admittedly at the start of the journey. Our current confidence in and excitement with the Digital Commons platform is enabling us to offer these services to the university community in a way that seemed out of reach to us before.

NORTHEASTERN UNIVERSITY: FROM PROPRIETARY TO OPEN SOURCE

As an early developer of an institutional repository, the Northeastern University Libraries have perhaps had a wider range of experience with IR platforms than many institutions. Northeastern began building its first repository instance in 2004 in a development partnership with Innovative Interfaces. The repository, called IRis, was launched in 2006 using Innovative's Symposia platform. While a proprietary system, Symposia was mounted locally and required a significant commitment from library staff. In 2009, the library decided to move to a hosted repository platform in order to free up staff to work on other strategic priorities, and migrated to bepress's Digital Commons solution.

A hosted solution is an excellent long-term option for many institutions that do not have the local resources to develop and sustain a repository built using open source software. A hosted solution can also serve as a first step during the time that a local repository is being developed. However, the amount of time needed to develop the local platform may end up being significantly greater than originally anticipated. We found this to be true at Northeastern. When Northeastern transitioned to Digital Commons at the end of 2009, we already expected that it would be a medium-term solution until the library had the resources to build and support a Fedora-based repository. In fall 2014, our Fedora-based Digital Repository Service (DRS) entered a soft-launch phase after two full-time staff years of concerted effort from our Web developers. Full release of the DRS took place in July 2015.

Northeastern chose to model the DRS after Pennsylvania State University's Fedora- and Hydra-based ScholarSphere repository.[3] Converting the ScholarSphere engine for our purposes and removing its existing dependencies was challenging, although the developers at Penn State extracted functionality from ScholarSphere into a new open source Web application called Sufia,[4] which our developers were able to make use of. Another challenge in development of the DRS was the need to support a prototype model that had gone into production earlier than planned in order to support immediate on-campus needs that could not have been met by the Digital Commons–based repository.

Our goal when developing the DRS was to have all our digital assets—faculty-authored materials, electronic theses and dissertations, learning objects, digital special collections, and archival materials—managed by a single architecture. Most importantly, a local repository, built with open source software, gives an institution total control over its content and how it is organized and displayed. Open source software like Fedora offers flexibility for local customization to an extent not possible with a hosted platform with hundreds or thousands of clients. With a locally developed repository, it becomes easier to meet the specific needs of local users, as opposed to offering a product that has been developed to meet the more commonly encountered needs of the average repository user. The types of materials being deposited in the repository may also drive development—at Northeastern, a department wanted to deposit large quantities of images directly from digital cameras, and have thumbnails automatically generated while preserving the original large files. We were able to customize the deposit interface to make this possible for them, and for future users with a similar need. Understandably, the providers of a hosted IR solution would not be likely to take on this type of customization work for a single client.

At institutions where the majority of IR deposits are PDFs, an "out-of-the-box" solution that requires little customization works very well. While its infrastructure can certainly accommodate other types of materials, the manner in which non-PDF materials are arranged and presented can be limiting. However, with an open source solution like Fedora, another open source tool like WordPress or Omeka may be used to create a "discovery layer" that exposes content from the repository in a manner that is more meaningful and appropriate, especially for nontextual materials. We recently worked on such a project for a group on campus who wanted to store videos in the repository, but make them available through a site that could also present other content in a flexible interface. A WordPress instance was a good solution for this need and created a strong use case for future projects. The ability to make use of a robust repository infrastructure while exposing content in non-"repository-like" ways will certainly serve to make the repository a more attractive solution for potential campus clients.

While choosing to build a repository based on open source software offers many opportunities for development and customization, it also comes with challenges. Aside from the time and technology costs required to get the repository from day one of development to a full production instance, there are also important ongoing workflow considerations. With a hosted repository platform, the library pays for customer support as part of the annual maintenance fee. With open source, there are online communities of developers using the same platform who can offer advice, but bug squashing may definitely be more challenging.

Academic libraries sometimes have trouble retaining skilled developers, simply because they aren't able to compete with the salaries offered in the corporate or startup worlds. The library should thus not assume that the person on staff who originally built their repository is going to be around to sustain active development. We found this to be the case at Northeastern; in fact, a significant amount of the repository development has been done by a student who has worked with us for several years. Repository developers should fully document their work as they go so that new staff can take over without interruption. Beyond the developer, the library should also have someone on staff to serve as the repository manager. While this role is necessary in any library with a repository, regardless of the platform chosen, in a locally hosted repository it is vital that the repository manager is able to be highly responsive, as there is no customer service staff elsewhere. At Northeastern we have moved from having the hosted repository managed by the scholarly communication librarian, who has other duties, to having a dedicated digital repository manager for the DRS.

Ongoing support, both maintenance and continuing development, must not be overlooked as a cost when deciding to build a repository based on open source software. The library must be able to *fully* support the repository—"adequate" support for such a significant and high-investment resource is not enough. Northeastern estimates that support for the DRS will equal 1.5 FTE—a full-time repository manager, and half of our senior Web developer's time. This is in sharp contrast to the staff necessary to support the Digital Commons–based repository: 0.25 FTE of the scholarly communication librarian's position and a minimal amount of time (fewer than five hours per week total, on average) from two metadata staff.

For those who have worked with the repository at Northeastern, the transition from the Digital Commons platform to the open source DRS is bittersweet. We are excited about the new opportunities for providing an increased level of customization for our users, and feel positive that the direction our repository's development takes will be entirely under our control. However, bepress has been an excellent company to work with, and they made our use of Digital Commons a productive and important stage in the lifespan of our repository.

CONCLUSION

The VCU and Northeastern case studies are similar in their emphasis on choosing and implementing a repository platform to best serve local needs. Neither VCU nor Northeastern has found critical flaws in the systems from which they are migrating, and indeed both institutions' recent migrations were driven primarily by local priorities: VCU chose Digital Commons in response to an identified need to quickly provide enhanced repository and publishing services, and Northeastern decided to go open source in order to offer greater customization and maintain control over content. These decisions echo the literature on repository platform selection: a locally supported open source system allows maximum flexibility, whereas a proprietary system offers turnkey entry and support.

Both institutions' experience with migrating content from one repository system to another indicate an area for future research, as metadata and file standards can be implemented in different ways between systems. Planning for possible future migration is wise when considering how you implement and customize your current system. If repositories grow to include vast amounts of material, as we hope they will, it is not clear how existing migration strategies will scale.

It is also important to note that the distinction between open source and proprietary solutions has started to blur. Following the model in other industries, a number of commercial support services are available for open source systems, ranging from hourly vendor support to full software-as-a-service offerings. Likewise, some commercial firms provide a range of choices to libraries to either install software locally or host it offsite. In general, we feel that the repository system landscape will be brighter in the future as a result of competition between various service models. Finally, it cannot be overstated that the platform itself is not a panacea, but merely one component of the institution's repository service.

NOTES

1. See https://lists.sourceforge.net/lists/listinfo/dspace-tech.
2. See https://wiki.duraspace.org/display/DSPACE/DSpace+Software+Support +Policy.
3. See https://scholarsphere.psu.edu/.
4. See https://github.com/projecthydra/sufia.

REFERENCES

Bluh, P. (2009, July). *TCO and ROI: Assessing and evaluating an institutional repository.* Paper presented at the American Association of Law Libraries meeting, Washington, DC. Retrieved from http://digitalcommons.law.umaryland.edu/fac_pubs/796/

Burns, C. S., Lana, A., & Budd, J. M. (2013). Institutional repositories: Exploration of costs and value. *D-Lib Magazine, 19*(1–2). http://dx.doi.org/10.1045/january2013-burns

Fay, E. (2010). Repository software comparison: Building digital library infrastructure at LSE. *Ariadne, 64.* Retrieved from http://www.ariadne.ac.uk/issue64/fay

Giesecke, J. (2011). Institutional repositories: Keys to success. *Journal of Library Administration, 51*(5–6), 529–542. http://dx.doi.org/10.1080/01930826.2011.589340

Mandl, H. E., & Organ, M. K. (2007). Outsourcing open access: Digital Commons at the University of Wollongong, Australia. *OCLC Systems & Services—International Digital Library Perspectives, 23*(4), 353–362.

Marill, J. L., & Luczak, E. C. (2009). Evaluation of digital repository software at the National Library of Medicine. *D-Lib Magazine, 15*(5–6). http://dx.doi.org/10.1045/may2009-marill

Palmer, A., & Choi, N. (2014). The current state of library open source software research: A descriptive literature review and classification. *Library Hi Tech, 32*(1), 11–27. http://dx.doi.org/10.1108/LHT-05-2013-0056

Pruett, J., & Choi, N. (2013). A comparison between select open source and proprietary integrated library systems. *Library Hi Tech, 31*(3), 435–454. http://dx.doi.org/10.1108/LHT-01-2013-0003

Rieger, O. Y. (2007). Select for success: Key principles in assessing repository models. *D-Lib Magazine, 13*(7–8). http://dx.doi.org/10.1045/july2007-rieger

Salo, D. (2013). How to scuttle a scholarly communication initiative. *Journal of Librarianship and Scholarly Communication, 1*(4), eP1075. http://dx.doi.org/10.7710/2162-3309.1075

Samuels, R. G., & Griffy, H. (2012). Evaluating open source software for use in library initiatives: A case study involving electronic publishing. *portal: Libraries and the Academy, 12*(1), 41–62. http://dx.doi.org/10.1353/pla.2012.0007

Younglove, A. (2013). Rethinking the digital media library for RIT's The Wallace Center. *D-Lib Magazine, 19*(7–8). http://dx.doi.org/10.1045/july2013-younglove

2 | Repository Options for Research Data

Katherine McNeill

Data are fundamental in virtually all forms of research yet time-intensive to collect and generate. Many research questions can be answered by using secondary data (that collected by another researcher), and thus data sharing has become of growing interest to funders and publishers. Effective data sharing depends upon repositories for long-term storage of and access to research data. In the context of this volume on the role of institutional repositories (IRs), various types of repositories are available for locally produced data: institutional repositories, domain repositories for specific types of data, and more. What options are available? How do researchers select a repository for deposit? What might institutions recommend to their researchers? How does the IR fit into this landscape? This chapter will answer these questions and share the experience of the library system of one research-extensive university in the United States, the Massachusetts Institute of Technology (MIT).

CONTEXT AND LITERATURE REVIEW

Data repositories serve a pivotal role in the data life cycle. The secondary use of data, if shared, enables further investigation and is almost always more efficient than collecting one's own data. The past 10 years have seen a dramatic increase in attention to this issue in many fields, building on the robust and long history of data sharing in some disciplines; for example, ICPSR (the Inter-university Consortium for Political and Social Research) has been preserving and providing access to quantitative data in the social sciences since 1962.[1] Data sharing has become of growing interest to funders worldwide, who aim to extend the impact of their funding, and publishers, who desire reproducibility of the research that they publish. Requirements of these bodies have raised the profile of data sharing and the role of data repositories.

There are numerous long-term benefits and significant time saved by managing data well, yet researchers find it challenging to invest time in managing, documenting, and sharing their data, and need support (Akers & Doty, 2013; Carlson, Fosmire, Miller, & Nelson, 2011; Housewright, Schonfeld, & Wulfson, 2013; Tenopir et al., 2011). The investment of time in preparing data for deposit in a repository, largely spent preparing the data and documentation for public use, generally still outweighs the perceived benefits to researchers of sharing their data.

What can be done at the institutional level to enable researchers to most effectively manage and share their data? What is the role of repositories? While researchers are experts in their academic fields, librarians bring skills in the management, organization, and preservation of information (Erway, 2013; Tenopir, Birch, & Allard, 2012) and can provide services alongside those of other units at their institution (Fearon, Gunia, Pralle, Lake, & Sallans, 2013; Hofelich Mohr & Lindsay, 2014). Librarians experienced in the discovery and use of data are equipped to advise researchers about the form that data and documentation should take to make them independently understandable for public use at the end of the data life cycle (McNeill, 2011). In addition, librarians can provide services for checking and preparing data for sharing (Peer, Green, & Stephenson, 2014). Moreover, librarians generally have well-developed connections with academic departments across their universities and are well positioned to work upstream in the research life cycle and enable the "last mile" of the research data management infrastructure (Gabridge, 2009).

Despite the resources and support needed to prepare data for deposit in a repository, the benefits to researchers in the long run are significant: having a researcher's data in a repository makes it more readily discoverable, often relieves the data producer of the need to serve users, and can support a university's ability to comply with sharing requirements and verify its research results. Moreover, select repositories provide curation features to enhance access and long-term preservation of the data.

DATA REPOSITORIES

Repositories for research data fit within a broader set of institutional research data management (RDM) services. Institutional repositories designed specifically for research data are neither the sole answer to RDM services, nor required for robust data management, as discussed below. Rather, data repositories, whether based at one's university or elsewhere, are key components of technological services that, along with consultative services, contribute to a robust university RDM infrastructure (Rice et al., 2013; Rice & Haywood, 2011; Soehner, Steeves, & Ward, 2010; Tenopir et al., 2012).

What kinds of repositories are available for data? How do storage needs for data differ from those for other types of materials? Data, in their varied forms (e.g., quantitative, qualitative, geospatial, images, models, binary files, code, and more), have different requirements in archiving than do most textual publications. File format obsolescence can be a significant challenge, given varied, complex, and rapidly changing data formats. The quality of data must be verified for effective reuse (Peer et al., 2014). Simple access to data alone is insufficient for public use; research data in any form are rarely self-describing and thus must be accompanied by documentation that adequately states the provenance, context, and content of the data files (Mauer & Watteler, 2013).

Academic institutions have available a range of repository options in order to track, store, preserve, and share research data created by their researchers. Within those options, data repositories differ along several key characteristics:[2]

- Association with an institution
- Specialization in a particular type of data
- Business model
- Levels of professional curation and unmediated deposit models

This final characteristic merits some discussion. Repositories—within and among the categories listed below—vary widely in the extent to which staff members manage data through activities such as accepting, depositing, reviewing, enhancing, managing, and preserving data and associated documentation (Peer et al., 2014). As data storage does not equal preservation, differing repository procedures dictate how well the data can be used in the future. Some repositories have extensive professional involvement, whereas others have an entirely unmediated deposit process and rely exclusively on the depositor to check the quality of the data and documentation. Some such as Dataverse rely upon software features for their curation and preservation.[3] A process of data quality review enables data to be "independently understandable for informed reuse," yet many repositories lack the services necessary to do so, placing that burden upon the researcher (Consultative Committee for Space Data Systems, 2012; Peer et al., 2014, p. 264). Moreover, only some repositories provide for long-term preservation beyond bit-level management, through activities such as emulation or migration of formats, sustainability, technology watch, and activities for usability over time (Choudhury, Palmer, Baker, & DiLauro, 2013; Treloar, Groenewegen, & Harboe-Ree, 2007). Review procedures necessarily place greater requirements on the depositor (e.g., for thorough data documentation) but doing so assures more usable data into the future.

University Institutional Repositories (IRs)

IRs are designed to house the scholarly output of researchers based at that institution, including data, and are at a close distance to the researcher (Baker & Yarmey, 2009). The major use case for an IR is for researchers, and universities, looking for a single common location for data regardless of subject and format, especially in cases where a suitable domain repository does not exist. However, given that data require significantly more management than do publications, IR administrators must consider what if any resources will be deployed to ensure data usability over time. Many IRs have an unmediated deposit process for datasets, but some universities have dedicated workflows for depositing and managing data within their IR (Awre & Duke, 2013; Johnston, 2014; Pink, 2012; Tarver & Phillips, 2012).

Local Data Repositories

A few universities—such as Johns Hopkins, Princeton University, Purdue University, the University of Bristol, and the University of Edinburgh—have created dedicated repositories exclusively for locally produced data.[4] Some even have been custom-designed for the work of a particular research group (Peer & Green, 2012). The major use case for such a repository is for those universities that want local archiving of data and are able to invest additional resources in a system tailored for this format.

National or Government Data Repositories

Researchers in select countries and regions (particularly in Europe) can avail themselves of extensive government infrastructures for storing and sharing research data, such as ReShare from the UK Data Service or Zenodo from the European Union.[5] Some may be specialized in nature and function as domain repositories. The major use case for such repositories is for a researcher with an eligible national or funder affiliation.

Domain Repositories

Data in domain repositories[6] are housed with similar data deposited by researchers from many institutions, which often improves the discovery of data in a particular realm. Such repositories focus on data from a particular subject realm (e.g., ecology, astronomy) and/or format type (e.g., quantitative data, qualitative data, images). Moreover, some repositories may provide particular features for working with or analyzing the particular data type; examples include ICPSR, Research Collaboratory for Structural Bioinformatics Protein Data Bank, National Snow and Ice Data Center, U.S. Virtual Astronomical Observatory, and the Qualitative Data Repository.[7] Another characteristic that varies: the business model of domain repositories can influence who is eligible to deposit, how open the data are for public use, and the curation services the repository can provide (Marcial & Hemminger, 2010). The major use case for a domain repository is for researchers who would like their data to be collocated with those in their subject field and utilize additional features or services provided to manage, access, or preserve that particular type of data.

Self-Deposit Independent Repositories

An emerging type of repository is one designed around self-deposit and self-management models, such as Dataverse and Figshare.[8] Developed and maintained by Harvard University, Dataverse is an open source software system for storing and providing access to quantitative data; Harvard makes its local installation of Dataverse open to deposit by any researcher group worldwide.[9] Such repositories provide researchers with a high level of control of the deposit process and collections and place little if any requirements on depositors. Information professionals, however, caution that while systems for self-archiving may appear to the researcher to have great ease of use, the lack of professional review makes them likely to result in inadequate documentation and ultimately the loss of usable data (Peer et al., 2014). Therefore, the use case for such a system is the researcher who either is willing and able to do a thorough review of data and documentation in advance of deposit, or values the independence of such a system above the assurances of future usability that a more professionally managed system would provide.

Journal Replication Data Archives

Journals increasingly require sharing the data that underlie a publication, as well as the computer code to generate the findings, in order to enable replication and further research. Journals vary in how they direct researchers to store and share their data, including on-demand requests of authors, journal Web sites, established journal data repositories, or deposit in a subject or domain repository.[10] Journal requirements thus necessarily influence the researchers' chosen mechanism for data sharing. Moreover, the policies and practices, and the method by which they are enforced, significantly affect the availability and ultimate usability of such data (McCullough, McGeary, & Harrison, 2008). In addition, journals with policies generally only require sharing of the data to reproduce tables in the paper and do not foster access to the full set of data generated in the research.

Staging Repositories

Complementing the options above, a select number of institutions have established formal systems for researchers to store, document, and work with data more systematically during the active phase of research, in order to facilitate ultimate deposit into a preservation repository (Steinhart, 2007; Smithsonian Institution, n.d.; Treloar et al., 2007). Similarly, scientific workflow systems are used by some researchers to structure their information during the active phase of research and could potentially be deployed in a centralized way (Littauer, Ram, Ludäscher, Michener, & Koskela, 2012; Lyle, Alter, & Green, 2014). Such systems have great potential value to institutions that have the resources and the organizational culture that would benefit from centralization of data management during the active phase of research.

The Role of the IR

What is the role of an IR in the context of this array of repositories? University IRs can serve as a fallback location for storing their researchers' data in the absence of a domain repository. Promoting the IR as the preferred repository for locally produced data can provide simplicity for researchers and service providers alike and potentially enable a more systematic transfer of data from active data storage. If universities have formal policies for RDM, they can align the characteristics of an IR with those policies and local user needs. In addition, universities leveraging their IR to meet funder requirements for open access to publications can examine its suitability to support data sharing requirements as well. Universities wanting to ensure long-term access and usability of their researchers' data, however, will need to consider what combination of services, policies, and quality assurance will be required.

SUPPORTING DATA REPOSITORY SELECTION: EXPERIENCES AT THE MASSACHUSETTS INSTITUTE OF TECHNOLOGY (MIT)

The main components of the MIT Libraries' RDM service are a Web guide,[11] instruction workshops, consulting, and repositories for long-term data storage and access. Our consultants advise researchers on a range of issues, including writing funder-required data management plans; storing, organizing, and documenting data files during the active phase of research; creating data documentation for public use; managing and sharing sensitive data; and selecting a repository for long-term public access to data.

REPOSITORIES AVAILABLE TO MIT RESEARCHERS

For data storage in the earlier phase of the data life cycle, MIT has no systematic centralized system and no services or tools for moving data from active storage to long-term repositories. Anecdotal evidence shows that MIT researchers store active data in centralized or departmental research computing systems, hard drives and other removable media, commercial cloud services, and Git-based repositories, among others. If and when they choose to share their research data and store it long-term after the conclusion of the research,[12] MIT researchers, like those at other institutions, have at their disposal a number of possible repositories, discussed in the following paragraphs.

DSpace@MIT

MIT's IR is based on the DSpace software that the MIT Libraries codeveloped (Smith, 2002). Like many IRs, DSpace@MIT[13] can house any file or material type produced or sponsored by MIT faculty, including data in any form (e.g., quantitative, images, audial, textual, and more), and the MIT Libraries have created policies for accepting datasets.[14] While staff involvement is required to create a collection, subsequent deposit by local researchers is unmediated, and library staff members do not review the data or documentation for completeness. In addition, assurances of long-term access depend upon the file format provided by the depositor. MIT researchers who have selected DSpace as their data repository of choice have stated reasons such as the association with the institution and collocation with other of their publications that may end up in the IR.

Harvard Dataverse Network

MIT researchers have selected Dataverse as their repository of choice for features such as public access to data, deposits accepted from any researcher based at any institution, collections can be individually branded, researchers maintain a high level of control of both the deposit process and their collections, and the historic relationship between MIT and Harvard.

Domain Repositories

As with researchers at other institutions, those at MIT can deposit in domain repositories. MIT researchers have selected such repositories for features such as collocation and discovery along with similar data, added features for their data type(s) (e.g., tailored metadata, analysis features, and preservation services), and specialized services that are beyond the expertise or resources of most university IRs or self-publishing systems (e.g., ICPSR can enable restricted access to sensitive data).[15]

THE SELECTION PROCESS

Given these various options, the MIT Libraries' RDM consultants, knowledgeable librarians, play a key role in assisting researchers who need a repository to select one, as part of broader data management conversations. Consultants provide each researcher with a menu of options, rather than suggesting a generally preferred repository. This practice arose from the experience of service providers, rather than being formally established. Library staff members articulate to the researcher differences among repositories and the risks and benefits of each, as the optimal choice depends upon the needs and preferences of the researcher. Even universities that have established a dedicated institutional data repository present it as one option among others (Johns Hopkins University Libraries, 2014; McGinty, 2014).

The MIT Libraries' research data management consultant will consider the data at hand and perform activities such as the following:

- Present the leading repository options, their most significant differences, and any requirements for preparing the data for deposit.
- Communicate with a potential repository to better understand its services.
- Coach the researcher to select a repository.
- At times, facilitate deposit of the researchers' data through activities such as these: communicate with repository staff to help the user prepare for the deposit process, advise on file formats, and review and provide feedback on data documentation for public use (McNeill, 2011). Services for quality review of data and documentation have not been widespread or integrated into most MIT consultations; doing so would be more involved and improve the quality of data deposited (Peer et al., 2014).

In summary, data repository technology, however essential, is not a service that can stand on its own. Local consultants, who can help the researcher select a repository and prepare appropriately, are critical to what researchers have termed the consultative and technological infrastructure required for RDM (Tenopir et al., 2012, p. 3).

NO SINGLE SOLUTION

For the foreseeable future, researchers at MIT and elsewhere will continue to choose varying repositories for their needs; some like the assurance that their data are being stored at their institution, others prefer the control and flexibility of self-archiving models such as Dataverse, and still others opt for a more full-service domain repository providing curation services to ensure that the data will be usable into the future. Some institutions will choose to prefer and urge deposit in their IR, whereas others will guide researchers through the optimal selection on a case-by-case basis. In this context, enabling data discovery among different repositories is of growing importance. Some institutions have developed formal mechanisms to track the data assets created at their university, regardless of location of deposit (Rice et al., 2013; Rice & Haywood, 2011; Rumsey & Neil, 2013; Wright et al., 2013). Such registries also are being created at the national level (Australian National Data Service, 2014; Molloy, 2014). RDM professionals also are working to develop complex solutions for interoperability among repositories in order to both facilitate data discovery across locations and link publications with their underlying data; efforts include the DataCite Metadata Search and activities of the Research Data Alliance/ World Data System Publishing Data Services Working Group (Plale et al., 2013).[16] Moreover, repositories need not necessarily be in competition with one another for researchers' deposits, but rather could engage in complementary partnerships in support of data discovery, access, and preservation (Green & Gutmann, 2007; Lyle et al., 2014).

CONCLUSION

Future developments will influence the array of repository options at MIT. The MIT Libraries are collaborating more with departments on campus whose services relate to RDM, which may spawn new projects related to data repositories; for example, working with IT to streamline the storage and movement of data throughout the life cycle, partnering with our scholarly publication department to advance repository services for supporting federal public access requirements and linking data and publications, and more. In addition, future services and activities at MIT certainly will be influenced by developments in the field at large. It is vital to look outward at how other institutions are enabling long-term data storage and access and use those ideas to continually evolve local services.

Institutions considering developing or enhancing data repository services should consider several important issues. Universities should not assume that they must have a single solution for housing their researchers' data, or even that a university must house the data produced by its researchers, but local repositories can play key roles. If an institution is to accept data in its IR, or consider the creation of a local data repository, it must decide how data will be accepted and processed, what level of mediation will be suitable for the deposit process, what level of quality assurance of data and documentation are desired, and what workflows and nications to establish with researchers. When considering repositories as a service, institutions should spend equal effort considering the consultative services that will enable researcher selection and preparation for deposit into local or remote repositories. How will this process work and how can one best communicate the array of options to researchers? Will services (beyond guidelines and consultation) be provided to help researchers prepare data for sharing and long-term preservation?

In conclusion, data repositories play a vital role in enabling the storage, sharing, and secondary use of research data. Data repository options vary, and individual researchers need support finding the appropriate solution for their needs. Institutions must consider what array of options works best in their local context.

NOTES

I would like to thank Patsy Baudoin, Ellen Duranceau, and Ann Green for reviewing and providing helpful feedback and ideas for this chapter.

1. See http://www.icpsr.umich.edu/icpsrweb/content/membership/about.html.
2. The re3data.org schema describes repositories along a range of characteristics, including subject, content types, countries, type (disciplinary/institutional), terms of use and deposit, and more. See http://www.re3data.org/schema/2-1/ and Pampel et al. (2013).
3. See http://thedata.org/.
4. See https://archive.data.jhu.edu, http://dataspace.princeton.edu/jspui, https://research.hub.purdue.edu, http://data.bris.ac.uk/data, http://datashare.is.ed.ac.uk.
5. See http://reshare.ukdataservice.ac.uk/, https://zenodo.org/. Note: Zenodo now is open to researchers worldwide.
6. For a directory, see http://www.re3data.org/ and Pampel et al. (2013).
7. See http://www.icpsr.umich.edu, http://www.rcsb.org, http://nsidc.org/, http://www.usvao.org/, and https://qdr.syr.edu/
8. See http://figshare.com/.
9. Software: http://thedata.org; Harvard's installation: http://thedata.harvard.edu/
10. For examples of these respective practices, see AEA Journal Data and Program Archives: https://www.aeaweb.org/rfe/showCat.php?cat_id=9; Dryad journal integration: http://datadryad.org/pages/journalIntegration; American

JournalofPoliticalScience(AJPS)Dataverse:http://dvn.iq.harvard.edu/dvn/dv
/ajps; PKP-Dataverse Integration Project: http://projects.iq.harvard.edu/ojs
-dvn; and Nature: http://www.nature.com/sdata/data-policies/repositories or
BioMed Central: http://www.biomedcentral.com/about/supportingdata

11. See http://libraries.mit.edu/data-management.

12. For those who chose to do so. Not all researchers—even those under data sharing requirements—formally share their data via repositories; many continue to
engage in very limited data management and sharing practices.

13. See http://dspace.mit.edu.

14. See http://libguides.mit.edu/content.php?pid=456907&sid=3741704.

15. See http://www.icpsr.umich.edu/icpsrweb/content/ICPSR/access/restricted.

16. See http://search.datacite.org and https://rd-alliance.org/group/rdawds-pub
lishing-data-services-wg.html.

REFERENCES

Akers, K. G., & Doty, J. (2013). Disciplinary differences in faculty research data
management practices and perspectives. *International Journal of Digital Curation, 8*(2), 5–26. http://dx.doi.org/10.2218/ijdc.v8i2.263

Australian National Data Service. (2014). Data discovery and access. Retrieved
from http://www.ands.org.au/discovery/discoveryandaccess.html

Awre, C., & Duke, M. (2013). *Storing and sharing data in an institutional repository Hydra@Hull*. Edinburgh: Digital Curation Centre. Retrieved from http://
www.dcc.ac.uk/resources/developing-rdm-services/storing-sharing-data-hull

Baker, K. S., & Yarmey, L. (2009). Data stewardship: Environmental data curation
and a web-of-repositories. *International Journal of Digital Curation, 4*(2),
12–27. http://dx.doi.org/10.2218/ijdc.v4i2.90

Carlson, J., Fosmire, M., Miller, C. C., & Nelson, M. S. (2011). Determining data
information literacy needs: A study of students and research faculty. *portal: Libraries and the Academy, 11*(2), 629–657. http://dx.doi.org/10.1353
/pla.2011.0022

Choudhury, G. S., Palmer, C., Baker, K., & DiLauro, T. (2013, January). *Levels of
services and curation for high-functioning data*. Presented at the Eighth International Digital Curation Conference, Amsterdam, Netherlands. Retrieved
from http://www.dcc.ac.uk/webfm_send/1093

Consultative Committee for Space Data Systems. (2012). *Reference model for an
open archival information system (OAIS)* (No. Magenta Book CCSDS 650.0

-M-2). Retrieved from http://public.ccsds.org/publications/archive/650x0m2
.pdf

Erway, R. (2013). *Starting the conversation: University-wide research data management policy*. OCLC Research. Retrieved from http://www.conference-center
.oclc.org/content/dam/research/publications/library/2013/2013-08.pdf

Fearon, D., Gunia, B., Pralle, B. E., Lake, S., & Sallans, A. L. (2013). Research data management services: SPEC Kit 334. Retrieved from http://publications.arl
.org/Research-Data-Management-Services-SPEC-Kit-334

Gabridge, T. (2009). *The last mile: Liaison roles in curating science and engineering research data* (No. 265; pp. 15–22). Retrieved from http://www.arl.org
/bm~doc/rli-265-gabridge.pdf

Green, A., & Gutmann, M. P. (2007). Building partnerships among social science researchers, institution-based repositories and domain specific data archives. *OCLC Systems & Services, 23*(1), 35–53. http://dx.doi.org/10.1108
/10650750710720757

Hofelich Mohr, A., & Lindsay, T. (2014, June 4). *It takes a village: Strengthening data management through collaboration with diverse institutional offices*. Presented at the International Association for Social Science Information Services & Technology Annual Conference, Toronto, ON, Canada. Retrieved from http://www.library.yorku.ca/binaries/iassist2014/2H/2014_2H
_HofelichMohr.pptx

Housewright, R., Schonfeld, R. C., & Wulfson, K. (2013). *Ithaka S+R US faculty survey 2012* (p. 44). Retrieved from http://www.sr.ithaka.org/research-pub
lications/us-faculty-survey-2012

Johns Hopkins University Libraries. (2014). About storing & archiving your research data. Johns Hopkins University Libraries. Retrieved from http://dmp
.data.jhu.edu/preserve-share-research-data/preserve-archive/

Johnston, L. (2014). *A workflow model for curating research data in the University of Minnesota Libraries: Report from the 2013 data curation pilot*. University of Minnesota Digital Conservancy. Retrieved from http://hdl.handle
.net/11299/162338

Littauer, R., Ram, K., Ludäscher, B., Michener, W., & Koskela, R. (2012). Trends in use of scientific workflows: Insights from a public repository and recommendations for best practice. *International Journal of Digital Curation, 7*(2), 92–100. http://dx.doi.org/10.2218/ijdc.v7i2.232

Lyle, J., Alter, G., & Green, A. (2014). Partnering to curate and archive social science data. In J. M. Ray (Ed.), *Research data management: Practical strategies for information professionals* (pp. 203–221). West Lafayette, IN: Purdue University Press.

Marcial, L. H., & Hemminger, B. M. (2010). Scientific data repositories on the Web: An initial survey. *Journal of the American Society for Information Science and Technology, 61*(10), 2029–2048. http://dx.doi.org/10.1002/asi.21339

Mauer, R., & Watteler, O. (2013, May 30). *Data are like parachutes: They work best when open.* Presented at the International Association for Social Science Information Services & Technology Annual Conference, Cologne, Germany. Retrieved from http://www.iassistdata.org/downloads/2013/2013_pechaku chao4_mauer_watteler.pdf

McCullough, B. D., McGeary, K. A., & Harrison, T. D. (2008). Do economics journal archives promote replicable research? *Canadian Journal of Economics/Revue Canadienne d'Économique, 41*(4), 1406–1420. http://dx.doi.org/10.1111 /j.1540-5982.2008.00509.x

McGinty, S. (2014, February 6). Feedback on data storage. Retrieved from http:// www.iassistdata.org/topic/other-topics/digital-repositories

McNeill, K. (2011, October 6). *Role of libraries in data stewardship: A view from one university.* Presented at the ICPSR Biennial Meeting of Official Representatives, Ann Arbor, MI. Retrieved from http://libraries.mit.edu/data-man agement/files/2014/05/role-of-libraries-in-data-stewardship.pdf

Molloy, L. (2014). *JISC research data registry and discovery service phase 1 final report.* JISC. Retrieved from http://www.dcc.ac.uk/webfm_send/1736

Pampel, H., Vierkant, P., Scholze, F., Bertelmann, R., Kindling, M., Klump, J., . . . Dierolf, U. (2013). Making research data repositories visible: The re3data .org registry. *PLoS ONE, 8*(11), e78080. http://dx.doi.org/10.1371/journal .pone.0078080

Peer, L., & Green, A. (2012). Building an open data repository for a specialized research community: Process, challenges and lessons. *International Journal of Digital Curation, 7*(1), 151–162. http://dx.doi.org/10.2218/ijdc.v7i1.222

Peer, L., Green, A., & Stephenson, E. (2014). Committing to data quality review. *International Journal of Digital Curation, 9*(1), 263–291. http://dx.doi .org/10.2218/ijdc.v9i1.317

Pink, C. (2012). *Building a data repository to meet an institution's needs.* Presented at the Institutional Data Repositories Workshop—Roles and Responsibilities, Open Repositories. Retrieved from http://www.dcc.ac.uk/webfm_send/870

Plale, B., McDonald, R. H., Chandrasekar, K., Kouper, I., Konkiel, S., Hedstrom, M. L., . . . Kumar, P. (2013). SEAD virtual archive: Building a federation of institutional repositories for long-term data preservation in sustainability science. *International Journal of Digital Curation, 8*(2), 172–180. http://dx.doi .org/10.2218/ijdc.v8i2.281

Rice, R., Ekmekcioglu, Ç., Haywood, J., Jones, S., Lewis, S., Macdonald, S., & Weir, T. (2013). Implementing the research data management policy: University of Edinburgh roadmap. *International Journal of Digital Curation, 8*(2), 194–204.

Rice, R., & Haywood, J. (2011). Research data management initiatives at University of Edinburgh. *International Journal of Digital Curation, 6*(2), 232–244. http://dx.doi.org/10.2218/ijdc.v6i2.199

Rumsey, S., & Neil, J. (2013). DataFinder: A research data catalogue for Oxford. *Ariadne* (71). Retrieved from http://www.ariadne.ac.uk/issue71/rumseyjefferies

Smith, M. (2002). DSpace: An institutional repository from the MIT Libraries and Hewlett Packard Laboratories. In *Research and advanced technology for digital libraries* (pp. 543–549). Springer. Retrieved from http://link.springer .com/chapter/10.1007/3-540-45747-X_40

Smithsonian Institution. (n.d.). SIdora. Retrieved from http://www.fedoracom mons.org/node/60

Soehner, C., Steeves, C., & Ward, J. (2010). E-science and data support services: A study of ARL member institutions. *Association of Research Libraries*. Retrieved from http://www.arl.org/storage/documents/publications/escience -report-2010.pdf

Steinhart, G. (2007). DataStaR: An institutional approach to research data curation. *IASSIST Quarterly, 31*(34), 34–39.

Tarver, H., & Phillips, M. (2012). Integrating image-based research datasets into an existing digital repository infrastructure. *Cataloging & Classification Quarterly, 51*(1–3), 238–250. http://dx.doi.org/10.1080/01639374.2012.732203

Tenopir, C., Allard, S., Douglass, K., Aydinoglu, A. U., Wu, L., Read, E., . . . Frame, M. (2011). Data sharing by scientists: Practices and perceptions. *PloS One, 6*(6), e21101. http://dx.doi.org/10.1371/journal.pone.0021101

Tenopir, C., Birch, B., & Allard, S. (2012). *Academic libraries and research data services: Currentpractices and plans for the future; an ACRL white paper.* Association of College and Research Libraries, a division of the American Library Association. Retrieved from http://www.ala.org/acrl/sites/ala.org.acrl /files/content/publications/whitepapers/Tenopir_Birch_Allard.pdf

Treloar, A., Groenewegen, D., & Harboe-Ree, C. (2007). The data curation continuum: Managing data objects in institutional repositories. *D-Lib Magazine, 13*(9/10). http://dx.doi.org/10.1045/september2007-treloar

Wright, S. J., Kozlowski, W. A., Dietrich, D., Khan, H. J., Steinhart, G. S., & McIntosh, L. (2013). Using data curation profiles to design the datastar dataset registry. *D-Lib Magazine, 19*(7/8). http://dx.doi.org/10.1045/july2013-wright

3 | Ensuring Discoverability of IR Content

Kenning Arlitsch, Patrick OBrien, Jeffrey K. Mixter,
Jason A. Clark, and Leila Sterman

Discoverability of content through Internet search engines is paramount to the success and impact of institutional repositories (IRs). Overwhelming evidence suggests that library and IR Web sites attract relatively little direct traffic, and instead the vast majority of users begin their research with search engines (DeRosa et al., 2010) and land at local Web sites only through referrals. Americans conduct 18 billion searches per month in Internet search engines (comScore, Inc., 2014), so the potential market for visitors is deep, but library Web sites and repositories typically see only a minuscule fraction of that traffic. Libraries find themselves struggling to become effective in a discovery environment that "means syndication to search engines, to disciplinary resources, or to other specialist network-level resources" (Dempsey, Malpas, & Lavoie, 2014). This directive speaks to making IR content available and usable to a variety of user agents on the Web through data interchange standards that are widely accepted and supported.

Search engines must be able to access IR metadata and make sense of its structure. Even the best repository software will fail if it offers metadata that is incomplete, lacks context, or is not understood by machines. The user experience is also a significant factor for search engines. Google is very concerned with delivering a superior experience to its customers and makes it clear that sites can improve ranking in search results by addressing the user experience (Google Inc., 2015b). This includes providing high-quality content with rich descriptive text that is useful, presented in a logical linking structure, and easily accessed by both users and Web crawlers (Google Inc., 2015a).

The extent to which IR content draws attention from search engines and ranks in search results is contingent on the search engine optimization (SEO) practices that are built into the repository. While SEO itself has been described in great detail elsewhere, this chapter discusses SEO issues unique to IR as well as several newer Semantic Web techniques that can help improve the discoverability and relevance ranking of IR content, including structured metadata, Semantic Web Identity, PDF cover sheets, and semantic description of content through Linked Data.

STRUCTURED METADATA

The Metadata Problem

Structured metadata is a fundamental underpinning of digital library work, and it can help address the lack of search engine attention to IR content. Metadata must be accessible and organized for machines as well as humans. Several types of user agents must be considered in the formula for discovering metadata in IR:

1. Commercial search engine crawlers (Google, Bing)
2. Specialized search engines (Google Scholar)
3. Intelligent software agents (Semantic Web bots)
4. Human users

Search engine crawlers don't actually crawl through repository databases. Instead, they systematically trigger the display of Web pages by following links, and when an HTML page is generated they harvest its contents. It is at the crucial point of page display that all the metadata necessary to represent the content must be simultaneously visible to the human and comprehensible to the crawler. Other potential obstacles to crawlers may include IR websites that don't provide clear and quick paths to content; overuse of graphics that crawlers can't decipher; conflicting sitemaps and robots.txt files; slow server response; and content that is moved without appropriate messaging to inform crawlers of the changes, whether tempo-rary or permanent (Arlitsch & OBrien, 2013).

In 2011 Google Scholar announced that institutional repositories should "use Dublin Core tags as a last resort" because the schema isn't ap-propriate for describing scholarly works (Google Scholar, n.d.a). Dublin Core doesn't include unambiguous fields for each part of a bibliographic citation: volume, issue number, first page, last page, or a field for the PDF URL. Nor are there appropriate fields that distinguish a published article from a preprint, a dissertation from a thesis, or a book chapter from a book. In short, Dublin Core cannot provide the parsed bibliographic information that Google Scholar gets from publishers who use other schemas such as Highwire Press, PRISM, EPrints, and bepress. Google Scholar's dismissal of Dublin Core has been a major factor in the poor visibility of open access IR content (Arlitsch & O'Brien, 2012).

Beyond the specific requirements that enable discovery in Google Scholar, there are broader possibilities in the areas of semantic markup and Linked Data that help to establish higher engagement and use of IR content. The content of an IR must be classified so that machines may understand the site in broad context. Schema.org, a collaborative project between Google, Bing, Yahoo, and Yandex, is a vocabulary for defining things on the Web. The vocabulary of Schema.org tends to skew toward description for e-commerce settings, but classes and properties are being actively defined and are increasingly applicable to scholarship and aca-deme. Active W3C Working Groups (WG), such as the Schema BibExtend WG (http://goo.gl/ZKbE4J), are open for participation in these defining activities. This growth in the vocabulary is key for accurate description in IR settings. Several Schema.org types help guide the semantic markup for IR content, including:

- schema.org/Article
- schema.org/Dataset
- schema.org/ScholarlyArticle

The work needed to establish Semantic Web Identity and convert leg-acy IR metadata into Linked Data is described in more detail below.

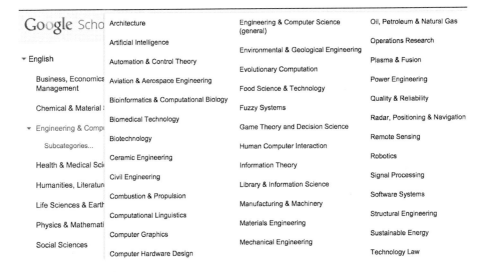

Figure 3.1. Google Scholar Metrics "Engineering & Computer Science" category and its subcategory taxonomy.

Consistency of Metadata

Much of the work of ensuring discovery of IR content has focused on machine-readable markup and semantic modeling practices, but providing consistent metadata for IR items is a core requirement. IRs are often part of the library ecosystem, and practices like applying Library of Congress Subject Headings may already be a part of the ingest process. It is important for both humans and machines that the application of terms is consistent. It may be obvious for items that have specific names (departments, colleges), but it is similarly important to apply consistent metadata in all fields. A machine may not know that "biology," "Biology," and "Biological sciences" could be synonymous in the organizational structure. There are a large number of other controlled vocabularies that IR managers can choose from, and most pertain to specific fields or domains. One possibility for assigning "Web-friendly" vocabularies are the facets that Google applies in its own systems. For example, Google Scholar citations (http://goo.gl/TejdTK) uses an academic taxonomy consisting of 8 broad categories and 253 subcategories that could provide a useful framework for organizing IR content (Figure 3.1).

DISCOVERY IN GOOGLE SCHOLAR AND OTHER SEARCH ENGINES

The ubiquity of Google and Google Scholar has established them as the paradigms of commercial search engines. Google's mission is to "organize the world's information and make it universally accessible and useful" (Google Inc., 1999). Google Scholar (GS) is a specialized search engine designed to find and index scholarly literature; it is a separate part of the Google organization and uses different algorithms and methods to analyze Web content. The different approaches of these two related search engines underscores the challenge to IRs trying for a presence in both: they must present content on a single Web page for various audiences. Below is an example of Modern Language Association, Seventh Edition (MLA) citation information presented for human readability:

> **Human-Readable MLA Citation Format**
> Arlitsch, Kenning, and Patrick S. O'Brien. "Invisible Institutional Repositories: Addressing the Low Indexing Ratios of IRs in Google Scholar." *Library Hi Tech* 30.1 (2012): 60–81.

Humans benefit from their ability to grasp context and parse a citation into its individual elements. We can determine the difference between title, journal, volume, issue, and page numbers, regardless of the various formats and styles that are available. But machines see only strings of characters and need help identifying the string of text as a bibliographic citation, parsing the citation's elements, and establishing relationships between fields.

The crawlers that gather information for search engines prefer each of these elements to be provided in defined fields. Figures 3.2 and 3.3 are respective examples of structures that help general search engines like Google and academic search engines like Google Scholar understand a bibliographic citation. They show the same citation with each element in specific Schema.org and Highwire Press tags.

Key information provided to general search engines via Schema.org:

- Lines 3 and 4 indicate this is a scholarly article as defined by Schema.org (i.e., http://schema.org/ScholarlyArticle).
- Lines 9–11 indicate the exact "Kenning Arlitsch" we are referring to per

```
1  <script type="application/ld+json">
2  {
3     "@context": "http://schema.org",
4     "@type": "ScholarlyArticle",
5     "name": "Invisible Institutional Repositories: Addressing the Low Indexing Ratios of IRs in Google Scholar",
6     "author": [
7        {"@type": "Person",
8           "name": "Kenning Arlitsch",
9           "sameAs":[ "http://viaf.org/viaf/294187294",
10          "https://scholar.google.com/citations?user=KWrhbCMAAAAJ&hl",
11          "http://www.lib.montana.edu/people/about.php?id=31" ] },
12       {"@type": "Person",
13          "name": "Patrick S. O'Brien",
14          "sameAs": ["http://viaf.org/viaf/306101244",
15          "https://scholar.google.com/citations?user=tWV-IE4AAAAJ&hl",
16          "http://www.lib.montana.edu/people/about.php?id=21" ] }
17    ],
18    "isPartOf": [
19       {"@type": "PublicationVolume",
20          "volumeNumber": "30" },
21       {"@type": "PublicationIssue",
22          "issueNumber": "1" },
23       {"@type": "Periodical",
24          "datePublished": "2012",
25          "name": "Library Hi Tech",
26          "issn": "0737--8831",
27          "publisher": "Emerald" } ],
28    "pageStart": "60",
29    "pageEnd": "81",
30    "associatedMedia":
31       {"@type": "MediaObject",
32          "encodingFormat": "PDF",
33          "contentUrl":
34          "http://scholarworks.montana.edu/xmlui/bitstream/handle/1/3193/Arlitsch-Obrien-LHT-GS-final-revised_2012-02-18.pdf"
35       },
36    "sameAs": [
37       "http://dx.doi.org/10.1108/07378831211213210",
38       "hhttp://scholarworks.montana.edu/xmlui/handle/1/3193" ]
39  }
40  </script>
```

Figure 3.2. General search engine markup applying Schema.org.

VIAF, Google Scholar, and Montana State University's URI Linked Data. This becomes very important when an author has a common name, such as "John Smith."

- Lines 18–27 indicate this scholarly article is part of the Library Hi Tech journal, Volume 30, Issue 1, published by Emerald.

- Lines 30–35 indicate that a PDF of the scholarly article is available via the MSU Scholarworks IR URL provided.

- Lines 36–39 indicate that the Web page containing the code above is about the same "thing" (i.e., schema.org/ScholarlyArticle) as the HTML page in the MSU Scholarworks IR and the doi.org URI.

```
 1  <!-- Title & Author -->
 2  <meta name="citation_title"
 3      content="Invisible Institutional Repositories: Addressing the Low Index Ratios of IRs in Google Scholar" />
 4  <meta name="citation_authors" content="Arlitsch, Kenning" />
 5  <meta name="citation_authors" content="O'Brien, Patrick" />
 6  <!-- Publisher & Journal -->
 7  <meta name="citation_journal_title" content="Library Hi Tech" />
 8  <meta name="citation_publisher" content="Emerald Insight" />
 9  <meta name="citation_date" content="2012" />
10  <meta name="citation_volume" content="30" />
11  <meta name="citation_issue" content="1" />
12  <!-- Article Location -->
13  <meta name="citation_firstpage" content="60" />
14  <meta name="citation_lastpage" content="81" />
15  <meta name="citation_pdf_url"
16      content="http://scholarworks.montana.edu/xmlui/bitstream/handle/1/3193/Arlitsch-Obrien-LHT-GS-final-revised_2012-02-18.pdf" />
17
```

Figure 3.3. Highwire Press tags for academic search engines like Google Scholar.

While these figures may look complicated, the markup is designed for machines to parse the information and provides a method, format, and syntax that both Google and Google Scholar understand.

IR SITE STRUCTURE

Content is more easily found by both humans and machines if there is a short and efficient pathway from the home page to item-level content (Google Inc., 2015a). IRs also benefit from providing a clear sitemap directing search engines to the most important content, such as item pages. In addition, libraries can structure the human-readable links on the IR entry Web site to match the organization of the institution, thereby ensuring consistent and clearly defined content. Matching the hierarchical structure of the institution (College > Department > Item) or providing a similar logical structure can assist human navigation.

Ranking algorithms are enormously important in the search engine business. One method of ranking "objectively and mechanically" (Page, Brin, Motwani, & Winograd, 1999), called "PageRank," was Google's first algorithm and still plays into the many factors that help Google give order to the vast World Wide Web. PageRank is largely based on the number of inbound links a site has from other Web sites, as they are interpreted by search engines as a vote of confidence. IRs can improve their rank in search results by encouraging organizations or centers on campus to link back to relevant sections of the IR from their own Web sites and social media profiles. Although many of Google's current 200+ "signals" (Dean, 2014) that rank search results are secret, they are largely based on the standards of SEO best practices and machine-readable markup, which are outlined in webmaster guidelines and tools that some search engines provide.

PDF Files and Cover Sheets

One goal of IRs is to ensure that the public has easy access to the content. The portable document format (PDF) is currently the most common way to deliver scholarly articles. Google Scholar recommends maximum PDF file sizes of 5 MB (Google Scholar, n.d.b), and the filename should be the article title, with words separated by hyphens.

A standardized PDF cover sheet may also be helpful to humans as it identifies the source of a downloaded file, and it is useful for machines because it provides another standard method of communicating citation information. Google Scholar makes recommendations for optimized IR PDF cover pages (Google Scholar, n.d.c). Some software generates cover sheets automatically, though it may be prudent to check the created page against Google Scholar's recommendations.

BEST PRACTICES FOR THE FUTURE

Establishing Semantic Web Identity

Although humans are good at inferring meaning from words and context, machines are not. Homonyms, or more specifically in this case, homographs, are a challenge to machines trying to discern varying definitions from the same string of characters and can cause them to deliver inaccurate search results. Does that "jaguar" on a Web site refer to the animal, car, sports team, supercomputer, or an old Macintosh operating system?

Things or concepts can be established as "entities," which helps search engines understand and trust them, and that in turn may help increase visitation and use. Google's Knowledge Graph is an effort to build a knowledge base of semantically related and vetted information about established entities. Using data collected through its Knowledge Graph, Google has thus far rolled out three enhancements to search results: Knowledge Card, Carousel, and Answer Box.

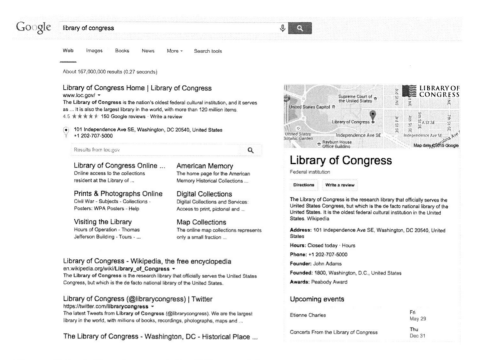

Figure 3.4. A Google search for "Library of Congress" displays a Knowledge Card for the organization.

The Knowledge Card (see Figure 3.4) is a panel that now often appears to the right of Google search results and displays information about specific entities (e.g., people and organizations). The Carousel (see Figure 3.5) is a group of instances that comprise a concept and appears across the top of the search results screen (e.g., sports teams, universities in a given state). The Answer Box (see Figure 3.6) provides facts about concepts or things that haven't necessarily been established as entities and is embedded at the top of traditional search results.

Each of these enhancements is populated with information that the Knowledge Graph compiles from certain sources on the Web that are trusted to establish entities. Chief among these sources is structured data generated from Wikipedia entries. Other sources may include Google My Places, Google+, Wikidata, and Schema.org markup consistent with the human-readable content in Web sites. Ensuring that these sources are populated with accurate information helps create Semantic Web Identity.

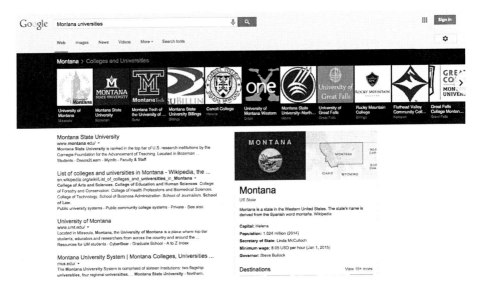

Figure 3.5. A Google search for "Montana universities" displays a Carousel with logos from each of the schools.

A Google search for "Montana State University Library" in 2013 demonstrated what happens when a thing (an organization in this case) doesn't have an established Semantic Web Identity. Instead of displaying the flagship library of the Montana State University (MSU) system, located in Bozeman, the Knowledge Card display showed another MSU campus in Billings, Montana (see Figure 3.7). The phrase "Montana State University Library" was simply a text string to Google, and it interpreted the organization incorrectly because the data sources contained erroneous information about the MSU Library. As a result, Google incorrectly identified the MSU Library as a building in Billings, Montana. A screenshot from 2015 demonstrates that the authors have successfully corrected the problem (see Figure 3.8).

There were several reasons why the MSU Library in Bozeman was misidentified in Google's Knowledge Card: (1) no one had claimed the property or verified facts about the library in the trusted data feeds to Google's Knowledge Graph; and (2) no article about the MSU Library had been created in Wikipedia.

The example of the Semantic Web Identity problem of the MSU Library can be extended to IRs as well. The concept of an institutional repository is currently not well understood by Google because it hasn't

Figure 3.6. A Google search for "biofilm" displays an Answer Box containing a definition from Wikipedia.

been carefully defined for machines by librarians in Google's trusted data sources. Currently, searching for "institutional repository" in Google brings an "Answer Box" based on a Wikipedia entry. The Wikipedia entry contains descriptive text, but it has no machine-understandable properties (i.e., parent institution, topics represented, languages, etc.). Moreover, there are zero *instances* of the "concept" of an institutional repository. In other words, the IR is a *described* concept only, and machines would be hard pressed to provide a list of IRs, let alone point to one. Wikipedia

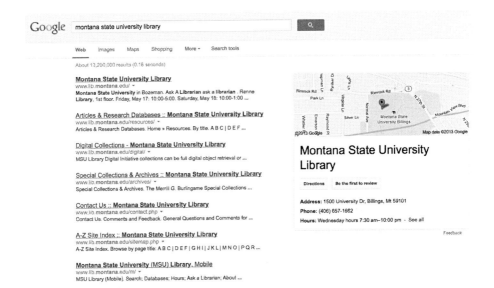

Figure 3.7. A Google search for "Montana State University Library" in 2013 displayed a Knowledge Card for a branch campus in Billings, Montana.

has a loosely related "List of Repositories" (http://en.wikipedia.org/wiki /List_of_repositories) containing fewer than 20 repositories, and none are from the United States.

Contrast that situation with a Google search for "Montana universities," where a rich Carousel display appears that includes a list (instances) of all the universities in Montana with their logos, as well as a robust Knowledge Card display about the state in which they are located. This kind of display makes it clear that Google has verified each of those organizations as "university" entities located in the entity of "Montana" and is anticipating that the searcher will have questions about the state of Montana. Currently, the Semantic Web lacks similarly structured data about individual IRs from trusted sources.

DESCRIBING ITEMS ON THE SEMANTIC WEB

An adequate description of a library organization on the Semantic Web must be followed by descriptions of the items held by the library. The process of describing library items in a way that is helpful to search engines is no trivial task, and given the current infrastructure used by most libraries (i.e., OPAC and content management systems), syndication of library data

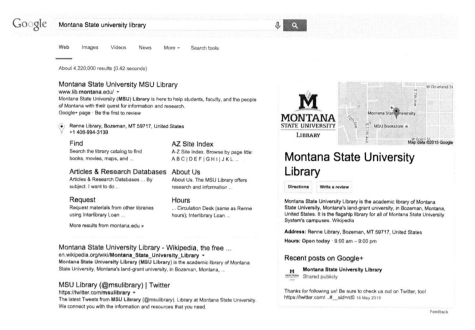

Figure 3.8. A Google search for "Montana State University Library" in 2015 displays a Knowledge Card with correct information about the organization.

can prove to be a difficult challenge. Libraries cannot just describe items on their Web sites using basic HTML because it is a markup language that is neither intended nor useful for semantic description. RDF (resource description framework) is a W3C standard designed to describe things on the Web in a way that allows machines to consume and understand the item. The model structures data in a simple sentence-like syntax (Mixter, 2014):

Subject => Predicate => Object

This framework allows for the structured description of things on the Web using domain-specific or general-purpose vocabularies. Domain-specific vocabularies tend to narrowly focus on a particular area of interest, such as bibliographic material, and have few ways of describing things outside of that domain. Domain-specific vocabularies are not always understood and consumed by search engines. General-purpose vocabularies, like Schema.org, were developed and published by search engines (Google, Yahoo!, Bing, and Yandex), so they were designed to describe a wide variety of things on the Web and to be understood by those machines. Since its release in 2011, Schema.org has become the lingua franca for describing things on the Web. Using RDF as the basic framework and Schema.org as the vocabulary, libraries can describe their items on the Web in a format that allows search engines to understand, consume, and index the data.

Data Cleanup

With a basic understanding of Semantic Web infrastructure for syndicating data, IRs can begin to clean up existing metadata. For the purposes of this discussion, data cleanup refers to the process of turning string values into URIs (uniform resource identifiers) that can be dereferenced online. For example, a URI for Aldous Huxley, the author, is http://dbpedia.org/resource /Aldous_Huxley. Machines that follow the URI link will be presented with more structured data about the thing, such as a class (e.g., person, book, place) and its properties (e.g., name, birthdate, birthplace, occupation, etc.). Some of these properties themselves will be URIs that machines can follow to learn even more. This chain reaction allows search engines to place the initial thing, in this case the author Aldous Huxley, into a much broader context and understand how he connects to other entities on the Semantic Web.

The following list presents a basic library use case:

- A search engine crawls a library Web page (with structured metadata) for the book Brave New World. That Web page describes Aldous Huxley as the author of the book.
- The search engine follows the URI for Aldous Huxley and learns that he was born in http://dbpedia.org/resource/Godalming (Godalming, United Kingdom). The DBpedia link provides the search engine with additional information about Godalming.
- The search engine can also learn that Aldous Huxley wrote http://dbpedia.org/resource/The_Doors_of_Perception (The Doors of Perception). This type of information is used by search engines to help users discover other relevant items.

Semantic Web graph theory is explained well in a blog post published by Google that describes the Google Knowledge Graph and how it is different from traditional search engines (Singhal, 2012).

Existing metadata in an IR can contain errors and inconsistencies, and improving the quality of that metadata is a prerequisite to giving it the structure that is appropriate for search engines. Data cleanup can be done a variety of ways, but open source tools will be sufficient for most IRs, given the limited number of metadata records that IRs typically contain. OpenRefine is a tool that can import a variety of data formats such as Excel spreadsheets, TSV (tab-separated value) or CSV (comma-separated value) documents, and JSON (JavaScript object notation). Most repository software allows for export of data into these common data formats, so there should not be any need for costly or difficult initial format conversion. Once the dataset is loaded into OpenRefine, built-in tools can be used to clean up the data (Verborgh, De Wilde, & Sawant, 2013). Of particular importance is the reconciliation tool, which can be used to query string labels in metadata fields, such as "Aldous Huxley" against trusted entity datasets such as DBpedia.org. The services will automatically match and pull over the entity URI or if there are multiple matches, the user will be prompted to select the correct one. Figure 3.9 illustrates the high-level theory behind the reconciliation process that turns text strings into defined entities understood by search engines.

One of the most difficult tasks in converting legacy metadata into RDF data is converting the strings that do not reconcile into unique entities. In instances where strings do not match existing entities, libraries may need to create their own entity descriptions (Mixter, OBrien, & Arlitsch, 2014a). Once the dataset is cleaned up, it is ready for conversion into RDF.

Data Conversion

An RDF vocabulary must be applied before data can be converted to RDF. As previously mentioned, the RDF framework can be broken down into three basic parts: Subject; Predicate; Object. When this syntax is applied to data, the result is a triple in which two entities are connected by a property:

> **Machine-Readable Serialization:**
> <http://www.worldcat.org/oclc/2457589>
> <http://schema.org/author>
> <http://viaf.org/viaf/71392434>

Human-Readable Serialization:

"Brave New World" => authored by => "Aldous Huxley"

In the example above, the two entities are the book "Brave New World" and the person, "Aldous Huxley." They are connected by a property that indicates that the book was authored by the person. At a very basic level, an RDF vocabulary is used to describe things and the relationships between them. Figure 3.10 is a diagram of how an RDF vocabulary can be used to describe theses and dissertations.

An RDF extension (http://refine.deri.ie/) for OpenRefine can be used to apply an RDF vocabulary to an existing dataset (http://refine.deri.ie /rdfExport). After the mapping is complete, the dataset can be exported as RDF, at which point it is almost ready for syndication on the Web.

Data Syndication

After the dataset has been cleaned up and converted into RDF, there is still a need to serialize it on the Web so that search engines can consume it. This can be somewhat difficult because RDF has a variety of serializations that are geared toward different audiences, such as databases, humans, or machines. RDF is the underlying framework for all of the serializations, and conversion between them is seamless/lossless. However, search engines do not consume all serializations. Search engines prefer RDFa and JSON-LD serializations of RDF, and consequently, it is important for libraries to use one of these two serializations when they syndicate their RDF data on Web

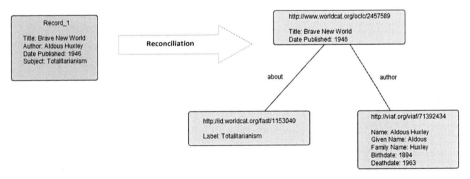

Figure 3.9. Converting records to entities.

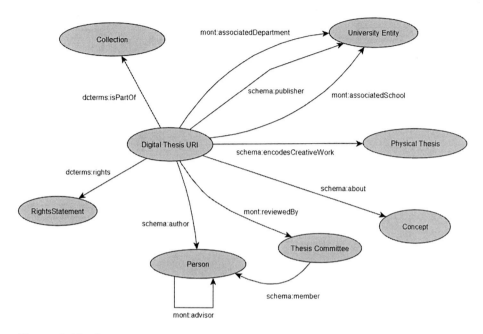

Figure 3.10. Concept map for theses and dissertations (Mixter, OBrien, & Arlitsch, 2014b).

pages (Google Developers, 2015). RDFa is a W3C recommendation seri-alization that uses HTML tags and attributes to encode RDF data. Since RDFa uses HTML, it is a natural choice for syndicating RDF on Web pages, but RDFa can be difficult to construct and debug. JSON-LD is a W3C rec-ommended serialization and can be embedded directly into Web pages the same way that JavaScript is embedded. Although JSON-LD is easier to em-bed on Web pages than RDFa, there is a concern that search engines will not trust all JSON-LD markup, since the semantic data are not visible to human users of the Web page. Google recommends using JSON-LD for spe-cific types of entities (e.g., Events) but otherwise recommends using RDFa for semantic markup (Google Developers, 2015). Regardless of which se-rialization is chosen for syndication, libraries will need to make sure that there is a mechanism in their content management systems for display-ing serialized data on Web pages. In addition to syndicating the RDF data about the bibliographic items, there is also a need to store and syndicate the data about entities that were locally created, such as students, faculty (that do not exist in VIAF, ORCID, or ISNI), local subject headings, and so on. These entities can be stored in a local triple store and syndicated using open source software such as Pubby (http://wif05-03.informatik.uni-mannheim.de/pubby/). Once the RDF is syndicated, it is prudent to check that items are described and displayed well and that the syndication is recognized and consumed by search engines.

SUMMARY

Although IRs preserve a wealth of knowledge, much of the content remains hidden to Internet users because of poor or inconsistent discovery by external search engines. This chapter has focused on some SEO techniques that can help improve discovery of IR content by search engines, and these include structured metadata applied consistently and accurately for a variety of user agents, user experiences, cover sheets, and accessible site structures. It also described some techniques IR managers can employ to participate in entity-based search on the Semantic Web. Librarians would do well to become familiar with Semantic Web Identity and be more active in helping to develop robust entity definitions of IR and related library concepts in data sources trusted by search engines. IR should add a layer of Linked Data, which will help improve comprehension for humans and machines.

Linked Data entities will grow organically as items in repositories are explicitly defined and linked to other data sets. As the ecosystem evolves, machines will more clearly understand what an IR is, what it contains, and the value in directing users to trusted information sources. Publishing IR content as Linked Data will increase the number of connected entities on the Semantic Web, increasing the value and meaning of each data point as it is connected to other entities on the Web. Consistent application and practice of these SEO and Semantic Web techniques will help ensure that IR content is discoverable on the Web.

REFERENCES

Arlitsch, K., & O'Brien, P. S. (2012). Invisible institutional repositories: Addressing the low indexing ratios of IRs in Google Scholar. *Library Hi Tech, 30*(1), 60–81. http://dx.doi.org/10.1108/07378831211213210

Arlitsch, K., & OBrien, P. S. (2013). *Improving the visibility and use of digital repositories through SEO*. Chicago, IL: ALA TechSource, an imprint of the

American Library Association. Retrieved from http://search.ebscohost.com /login.aspx?direct=true&scope=site&db=nlebk&db=nlabk&AN=578551

comScore, Inc. (2014, April 15). comScore releases March 2014 U.S. search engine rankings. Retrieved from http://www.comscore.com/Insights/Press-Releases /2014/4/comScore-Releases-March-2014-U.S.-Search-Engine-Rankings

Dean, B. (2014, August 8). Google's 200 ranking factors: The complete list. Retrieved from http://backlinko.com/google-ranking-factors

Dempsey, L., Malpas, C., & Lavoie, B. (2014). Collection directions: The evolution of library collections and collecting. *Portal: Libraries and the Academy, 14*(3), 393–423. http://dx.doi.org/10.1353/pla.2014.0013

DeRosa, C., Cantrell, J., Carlson, M., Gallagher, P., Hawk, J., & Sturtz, C. (2010). *Perceptions of libraries, 2010: Context and community* (p. 108). OCLC, Inc. Retrieved from http://www.oclc.org/reports/2010perceptions.htm

Google Developers. (2015). About Schema.org. Retrieved from https://developers .google.com/structured-data/schema-org

Google Inc. (1999, November 5). Google: Company info. Retrieved from https:// web.archive.org/web/19991105194818/http://www.google.com/company .html

Google Inc. (2015a). Steps to a Google-friendly site. Retrieved in 2014 from https:// support.google.com/webmasters/answer/40349?hl=en

Google Inc. (2015b). Webmaster guidelines: Quality guidelines. Retrieved in 2014 from https://support.google.com/webmasters/answer/35769#quality _guidelines

Google Scholar. (n.d.a). Inclusion guidelines for webmasters. Retrieved in 2011 from http://scholar.google.com/intl/en/scholar/inclusion.html

Google Scholar. (n.d.b). Inclusion guidelines for webmasters: Content guidelines. Retrieved in 2011 from https://scholar.google.com/intl/en-US/scholar/inclu sion.html#content

Google Scholar. (n.d.c). Inclusion guidelines for webmasters: Troubleshooting. Retrieved in 2014 from http://scholar.google.com/intl/en-US/scholar/inclu sion.html#troubleshooting

Mixter, J. (2014). Using a common model: Mapping VRA core 4.0 into an RDF ontology. *Journal of Library Metadata, 14*(1), 1–23. http://dx.doi.org/10.1080 /19386389.2014.891890

Mixter, J., OBrien, P., & Arlitsch, K. (2014a). Describing theses and dissertations using Schema.org. In *Proceedings of the International Conference on Dublin*

Core and Metadata Applications. Austin, TX. Retrieved from http://dcev ents.dublincore.org/public/dc-docs/2014-Master.pdf

Mixter, J., OBrien, P., & Arlitsch, K. (2014b, October). Describing theses and disserations using Schema.org. In *Proceedings of the International Conference on Dublin Core and Metadata Applications.* Austin, TX. Retrieved from http://dcevents.dublincore.org/IntConf/dc-2014/paper/view/269/313

Page, L., Brin, S., Motwani, R., & Winograd, T. (1999). *The PageRank citation ranking: Bringing order to the Web* (No. SIDL-WP-1999-0120). Stanford InfoLab. Retrieved from http://ilpubs.stanford.edu:8090/422/1/1999-66.pdf

Singhal, A. (2012, May 16). Introducing the Knowledge Graph: Things not strings [Google Official Blog post]. Retrieved from http://googleblog.blogspot.com /2012/05/introducing-knowledge-graph-things-not.html

Verborgh, R., De Wilde, M., & Sawant, A. (2013). *Using OpenRefine.* Birmingham, UK: Packt Publishing.

Part 2

SETTING POLICIES

Once a repository has been selected, practitioners may turn their attention to the next set of decisions geared toward cultivating success: setting policies. Two major policy decisions, the pursuit of an institutional open access policy and the inclusion of theses and dissertations, may have a significant impact on the success of an institutional repository initiative, particularly at the very early stages of its development. The authors in Part 2 explore the nuances and ramifications of each of these policy decisions.

Wesolek and Royster begin by examining the basic concepts and implications of institutional open access (OA) policies, specifically those of the Harvard-style rights retention model. Wesolek argues that these policies expand the rights of an institution's faculty authors, provide clarity to the often-murky permissions environment, and open pathways to systematically collect and upload content for a repository. Royster, however, argues that institutional OA policies fundamentally transform the relationship between a repository initiative and its community from one based on mutual cooperation and respect to one based on coercion. Moreover, as the highly successful repository initiative at the University of Nebraska–Lincoln demonstrates, open access policies are unnecessary for a successful repository.

While Wesolek and Royster allude to the tension between the individual rights of faculty authors and the collective good of openly available research inherent in open access policies, Gilman explores this issue in greater depth. Gilman makes the case that universities have a responsibility, or perhaps even an obligation, to share the knowledge they create for the public good, while remaining aware of the fact that they are composed of individual researchers who typically hold the copyrights in the works they create. Due to the faculty-led nature of open access policies, their individual opt-out options, and broad support for green open access via institutional repositories, Gilman sees these policies as striking a balance between the imperatives of the university and the rights of the faculty.

Open access policies are not a panacea for content recruitment and where they are to be pursued, their pursuit must proceed thoughtfully and with careful consideration given to one's unique campus culture. That said, the passage of open access policies is increasingly widespread. But, once a policy is passed, how does one implement it successfully? Duranceau and Kriegsman offer us a roadmap for successful open access policy implementation. Drawing on the collective knowledge and experience of the Coalition of Open Access Policy Institutions, the authors offer a suite of strategies for successful OA policy implementation that allow practitioners to effectively recruit or harvest content for an institutional repository.

Gail McMillan also supports the claim that universities have a responsibility to disseminate the knowledge they produce, which she applies to our second major policy decision: electronic theses and dissertations (ETDs). Decisions on policies related to ETDs, though, have an impact on numerous stakeholders on campus, perhaps most importantly on graduate students. McMillan addresses the ways in which these stakeholders are impacted by ETD decisions while emphasizing the importance of education and data. Specifically, graduate students should be made fully aware of an institution's policies on ETDs from the outset—not on the eve of graduation. And, since policy decisions are often impacted by concerns that open ETDs damage publication potential, these concerns should be explored through research and hard data, not anecdotes or assumptions.

Finally, Bergin and Roh explore some of the practical aspects of ETD policies through a detailed case study of the ETD and retro ETD digitization projects undertaken at the University of Massachusetts Amherst. They find that digitizing current and retrospective theses and dissertations is hugely beneficial to the institution, students, and the success of their institutional repository.

In Part 2 we see the policy decisions on open access policies and the inclusion of theses and dissertations dissected. In each of these, we begin at the higher levels by exploring the tension between individual rights and the public good and how that tension manifests itself in both OA policies and theses and dissertations. We then drill down to the more concrete implications of these policy decisions, offering strategies for success in both OA policy implementation and ETD digitization projects.

4 | Open Access Policies: Basics and Impact on Content Recruitment

Andrew Wesolek and Paul Royster

The allure of passing an institutional open access (OA) policy as a strategy to populate an institutional repository is clear. After all, educating faculty to retain their rights to their scholarly publications through passage of such a policy, then requiring them to make those publications available through an IR seems a sure path to success. However, this approach of "if you pass it, they will comply" rings eerily similar to the early and decidedly misplaced optimism of populating institutional repositories through a "build it and they will come" proposition (Salo, 2007).

The Registry of Open Access Repositories Mandatory Archiving Policies (ROARMAP) reports, though, that 73 campuses now have some form of institutional, departmental, or school open access policy in place. Additionally, the Coalition of Open Access Policy Institutions (COAPI) consists of more than 60 institutions that have OA policies in place or are actively working to pass them. Some of the most dramatic growth in COAPI membership and ROARMAP registration occurred in 2013, indicating that open access policies are increasing in popularity and have been implemented with success (Duranceau & Kriegsman, 2013; Kipphut-Smith, 2014).

So, while OA policies are not a panacea for obtaining repository content, with the right approaches in development and implementation they can provide content, educate campus communities, and enhance faculties' academic freedom through rights retention. This chapter will explore some of the types of open access policies and discuss whether or not an OA policy may be right for every institution.

POLICY BASICS

Though methods of implementing open access policies vary greatly (Duranceau & Kriegsman, 2013; Kipphut-Smith, 2014), the type of policies institutions have passed can be broken into two distinct categories, with some variation seen within them: open access resolutions and permission-based policies. Both of these demonstrate a grassroots-led institutional or departmental commitment to the values of open access and institutional repository initiatives while providing an important catalyst for the educational efforts of IR managers and scholarly communications librarians. However, the critical difference is that the latter has a solid legal foundation, the implementation of which can enhance the author's rights of faculty members and expand the corpus of openly available scholarship at the institution (Priest, 2012). The former is not a policy in a strict sense, but more of a sentiment that can provide some support for the educational efforts of institutional repository staff, but cannot be implemented with the same degree of latitude as a permission-based policy. For that reason, we will focus on permission-based policies here.

Permission-based policies generally rely on the Harvard model OA policy and as such, consist of very similar language. The scope of these policies, though, can vary greatly. The OA policy passed at the University of Kansas, for example, applies to the entire institution, stating, "all scholarly peer-reviewed journal articles authored or co-authored while a faculty member of KU" (*Open Access Policy,* 2009). Conversely, Brigham Young University has taken a unit-based approach, passing a policy of very similar structure, but applicable only to faculty in the Harold B. Lee Library and the Department of Instructional Psychology and Technology (Wiley, 2009).

While the scope of policies such as these varies, the structure of each deviates little from the Harvard model open access policy. Voted into effect by the Faculty of Arts and Sciences at Harvard University in February 2008, this permission-based policy set the precedent for subsequent policies at MIT, University of Kansas, BYU, and others. The author of the policy, Stuart Shieber, has done the important work of making an annotated version of it available online, which clearly articulates the reasoning behind the exact language of the model policy so that it can be adopted on other campuses with the desired effect (Shieber, 2009).

There are three aspects of the Harvard model that are important for this discussion: the grant of rights, the opt-out options, and deposit requirements, if any. First, the faculty *grants* to the university the nonexclusive right to exercise copyright in their scholarly articles and to authorize others to do the same. Use of the word "grants" is important, as it ensures that the policy only applies to articles published after the passage of the policy, and it requires no action on the part of faculty for it to take effect. Second, the provost or a designate *will* waive this license if expressly directed to do so by the faculty author, typically on a per article basis. Third, each faculty author will provide accepted author manuscripts to the Provost's Office or a designate, and the Provost's Office or designate may make the article openly available in an institutional repository.

While on the surface it appears that an OA policy of this type imposes additional rules on faculty, unpacking the legal language reveals an enhanced freedom for faculty to do what they like with their own scholarly works. First, the automatic grant of rights ensures that by doing nothing, faculty always have a green open access option for their scholarly works available to them. While many publishers currently allow authors to self-archive their accepted author manuscripts, this is not always the case. Scholarly communications librarians may work with faculty to encourage them to submit author addenda along with their publication agreements to ensure that they have the right to self-archive, or encourage them to publish in journals that have such language in place as part of their standard agreements, but faculty authors often find the legal agreements difficult or too time consuming to navigate. A grant of rights as outlined survives any publication agreement that faculty authors may enter into and removes the work of researching and negotiating publication agreements from their shoulders.

Second, Harvard-style policies typically contain language that allows authors to opt out of the policy at their sole discretion. In many cases, waivers to the policy are issued via online Web forms that automatically generate a waiver at a faculty author's request. There is no administrative oversight of this process, and authors may not be required to provide any sort of reason for the waiver request. So, rather than having to "opt in" to open access through negotiation with one's publishers, OA becomes the default, but the faculty member is completely at liberty to "opt out" of OA if he or she chooses.

BENEFITS

Institutional open access policies drafted in the Harvard style have positive implications for the scholarly communications landscape, institutional culture, and expanded rights for individual faculty members. At the broadest level, the increase in number of passed OA policies sends a powerful and unified message that green OA is important to an increasing number of institutions and the faculty researchers affiliated with them. This message then increases pressure to universalize green open access options for published articles.

If the OA policy is passed as a faculty-led grassroots initiative, as recommended by the guide *Good Practices for University Open-Access Policies,* then it can be used as an effective educational tool to facilitate a more open campus environment (Shieber & Suber, 2015). In many cases, the institution's library is designated by the provost to implement the OA policy. The combination of this designation along with the grassroots aspects of policy passage can give libraries a degree of political capital, allowing them to meet stakeholders and departments across campus, which they may not otherwise have been able to do. This bit of leverage also allows scholarly communications librarians or others in the library to continue to have conversations with their community about the broader issues in the current scholarly communications environment and the services the library may be offering to support faculty authors.

Arguments have been made that OA policies create additional burdens for the faculty subjected to them in exchange for the perceived greater good of a reformed scholarly communications system. If OA policies simply required faculty deposit of scholarly material in an institutional repository, this might be the case. But the granting of license inherent in the policy lays the necessary foundation to make deposit of material in an institutional repository a much more streamlined process, and due to the opt-out option, still essentially voluntary. When the grant of license in the OA policy takes effect, faculty no longer have to conduct burdensome investigation and negotiation to determine whether or not they have the rights to make a manuscript copy of their works available in an institutional repository. Unless that faculty member has requested a waiver of the policy for that particular article, he or she always has the right to make it openly available.

This is where institutional open access policies can be highly effective in populating institutional repositories. The early "if you build it, they will come" supposition did not lead to successful institutional repositories, nor will "if you pass it, they will comply" lead to successfully implemented open access policies. If institutional open access policies can be implanted in ways that streamline the deposit of content into an institutional repository, though, both the IR and the deposit process can be mutually successful. This can be achieved through automated opt-out processes, employing subject librarians to facilitate deposit of the research produced in their areas of responsibility, or partially automating the process by linking faculty activity reporting systems with institutional repositories (Wesolek, 2014).

Much has been written about strategies for successfully developing and implementing an institutional open access policy. The Berkman Center's guide to *Good Practices for University Open-Access Policies* is an excellent starting point (Shieber & Suber, 2015). In addition to this guide, those interested in developing a policy on their own campus may find a wealth of information through the members of the Coalition of Open Access Policy Institutions (COAPI, 2015). COAPI exists to both educate and advocate for OA and OA policies, and COAPI leadership is happy to connect those interested in developing OA policies with members that have experience doing so in similarly sized institutions.

The ease, or lack there of, of passing an institutional open access policy will likely depend greatly on the culture and organizational structure of a particular university. When developed and implemented well, policies can have a significant impact on institutional repository success. They are by no means a panacea, though, and likewise a successful institutional repository is not a sufficient or necessary condition for the development of an OA policy. Both Harvard and Princeton, for example, passed open access policies without the benefit of an existing IR at the time of their passage. From the Nebraska perspective, outlined below, we will see that at least one highly successful institutional repository made the conscious decision not to pursue development of an OA policy.

WHY I DON'T WANT A MANDATORY OPEN ACCESS DEPOSIT POLICY: A NEBRASKA PERSPECTIVE

The University of Nebraska–Lincoln (UNL) Libraries have operated an institutional repository (IR) since 2005. As of November 2014, it holds more than 75,000 items and has been furnishing downloads at the rate of 500,000 per month for the past several years. Yet faculty have never been required to deposit there, and the IR managers have not pursued passage of a rule mandating deposit by faculty. This contravenes the wisdom and advice from numerous bodies, organizations, and experts. In my opinion, however, a mandatory deposit policy is not merely unhelpful in populating an institutional repository, it is also positively harmful to its growth, acceptance, and functioning. I will enumerate my reasons for believing this at some length, but they might be summed up by the following "thought experiment" (with apologies to Jackson Galaxy):

> Imagine the faculty as a population of cats. You can make it a rule that they have to bring you the bodies of all the birds and small animals they kill. But obedience among cats is spotty and entirely voluntary, so the real challenge is making them want to. You can only succeed by establishing a trust relationship and providing rewards—chicken, tuna, milk—and perhaps grooming. Then you may soon be awash in dainty little carcasses. But since the rule won't work without the rewards, why have the rule?

The popularity of deposit policies may be said to have begun around the time that Harvard University's Faculty of Arts and Sciences passed their first such resolution in February 2008, at which time they had neither a repository nor an office for scholarly communications. The event was well publicized, and it drew public attention to the campaign for "open" access to scholarly materials. Frankly, I was surprised that university faculty would vote to impose an additional requirement upon themselves, but I took it as a measure designed to encourage (or force) their university to set up an infrastructure for the open sharing and dissemination of scholarship—something we already had ongoing at Nebraska, where recruitment of IR content was, and remains, my primary responsibility.

I discussed the Harvard resolution with the UNL Dean of Libraries at the time, Joan Giesecke (who had been mainly responsible for starting the IR here), and we agreed that, while it was helpful to bring the issues of access and repositories to public attention, there was no reason for us to imitate that example and to seek a campus-wide mandate or policy of required deposit (Giesecke, 2011). For one thing, our IR was already growing at a healthy rate of 400 to 500 items per month on a strictly voluntary basis, and we felt that securing passage of a faculty resolution to mandate deposits would expend time and political capital that we did not care to invest. We also felt, moreover, that conversion of our voluntary program to one that was required by rule would place our efforts and our relationship with faculty on a fundamentally different footing. Here on the Great Plains, in the western United States, a culture that celebrates libertarian values and abominates government regulation is not necessarily inclined to "take orders"; moreover, university faculty generally fall somewhere between cats and cowboys on the spectrum of independent-mindedness.

In April 2010, our faculty senate did pass a resolution endorsing the IR and recommending its services to faculty, but there was never any discussion or suggestion of a requirement. The senate resolved:

> that the participating faculty are to be congratulated for their support and use of the institutional repository and that all faculty are to be encouraged to take advantage of these services.

That is where we stand today, and, with more than half of all faculty represented by some amount of content and a steady flow of new recruits, the absence of a deposit requirement has not demonstrably limited the growth or acceptance of the IR. Quite the contrary, it has contributed to an atmosphere of mutual cooperation and respect. Our depositors have become our best ambassadors and recruiters; and faculty are free to participate on whatever terms and to whatever extent they choose.

Meanwhile, it has seemed that a good many scholarly communications professionals have settled on a two-pronged approach—either to purchase or to compel deposits. I believe that purchasing content by using library resources to pay open access (OA) fees is not a good idea; but that is a subject for a different essay. The other road for recruiting content—by requiring, mandating, or compelling deposits—is similarly unattractive for reasons that fall into roughly three categories: passion, pragmatism, and proprietary rights.

PASSION

One of the core values of the Montessori program is "The child does something because of an inner desire to do it, not because the teacher said so." Can we not extend this same courtesy to our faculty colleagues? Or do we regard them as manipulatable objects, as experimental subjects for social or academic engineering—all, of course, in the name of a good cause?

How can we claim to be helping faculty when we are imposing additional rules and requirements on them? Who, then, are we really helping—repositories that cannot otherwise get the cooperation of academic authors, or perhaps gold and hybrid OA publishers whose sales of paid licenses make for convenient solutions to the deposit requirements? My philosophy of the IR has been: "The repository belongs to the faculty, not to the library, not to the university, not to the public." The repository serves the needs of the faculty as they see them, on their terms, at their convenience. The universities and world at large have no rights to access or reissue their research, unless the faculty authors choose to specifically transfer or share those rights.

On a larger scale, I have come to believe there are too many rules already, and I doubt the usefulness of most of them, and especially distrust those instituted for people's "own good." I do not want to work with faculty under compulsion; ours is strictly a voluntary effort. I can be enthusiastic about offering a service that disseminates faculty research across the Internet; I have no stomach for enforcing further rules on a class of employees already laboring under so many constraints. "Great news! Now you are supposed to make bricks without straw! Isn't that exciting?" The university is a soulless corporation, and the "public" an amorphous abstraction; but the faculty is a body of living individuals with whom one can have actual human relationships and bonds (even) of friendship. Our voluntary IR arrangement fosters this feeling on both sides; a compulsory arrangement—even one self-imposed—places the parties on a different standing. I have spoken with IR managers from institutions with mandatory policies who say that they don't ever tell faculty that it's a requirement, for fear of spoiling their willingness to participate.

Mandatory deposit policies put the libraries or scholarly communications officers in an enforcement role, for which they lack the means and the will. I have seen posts recently about "putting teeth" into mandate policies, and I can only surmise this involves inventing some form of punishment (biting?) for faculty members who fail to comply. Personally and karmically, I want no part of that. The institution–employee relationship for faculty is already one-sided, and the library is fortunate not to be involved in administering discipline. The difficulty librarians face in getting faculty to return overdue books or pay library fines suggests that they may not be the proper agents for policing and enforcing deposit mandates.

Overall, I believe it is more beneficial and effective to instill a *passion* for the benefits of using an IR than to seek rules or procedures designed to prescribe participation. If we cannot make repositories attractive, easy, and rewarding to use, no amount of ordinance or regulation will produce the desired results.

At Nebraska we seek potential depositors, welcome them with open arms, shower them with service, and above all make it easy to participate. I realize none of this is inconsistent with a deposit mandate or policy, but it makes the policy unnecessary.

PRAGMATISM

When the idea of mandated deposit policies first became widespread, it was suggested to our dean by others that we pursue a deposit resolution by referendum or edict, but to her (and to her credit), the effort and political capital involved seemed to outweigh any possible benefit. A binding resolution would have required action by the library dean, the faculty, and the campus administration. Multiple committees would have been created, convened, and consulted; the issues discussed, considered, and subjected to recommendations. Surveys or polls would probably have been taken, stakeholders identified, rubrics and procedures defined. And all this would have happened in "academic time." The campaign would have raised issues of power and control over research output, involving the expectations and reward structure among the various participating (as well as the merely observing) bodies. And the library would have been in the middle, trying to broker accommodations and steer developments toward a concrete goal. It is extremely challenging to get numbers of faculty to agree on anything—I don't think this qualifies as a discovery; it's more of an axiom. Let's just say that any proposal would have been considered from a wide range of perspectives and subjected to intense analysis from multiple viewpoints, and these would have needed either to be harmonized or facilely glossed over. In addition, complexities increase exponentially with the numbers of academics involved.

As mentioned, we were already up and running at this time, and this (hypothetical) resolution campaign would have reduced time spent on the primary goal of populating the repository with faculty content—an activity that I personally found more rewarding than canvassing for votes at the hustings. The idea of lobbying for passage of a new university rule was not attractive to me—I am just not evolved temperamentally for that sort of campus political activity.

Furthermore, a mandatory deposit rule had no obvious rewards to tempt the faculty in favor of passage. The existence of a requirement would not by itself produce wider dissemination; it would not lead more people to read your stuff once deposited. A mandatory deposit policy has no dangling "carrot" to lure the faculty into depositing; and its punitive "stick" is frail or nonexistent and held in the wrong hands. Most mandated deposit policies have all the force of a New Year's resolution—leaving one free to "opt out" at will. So I remain perplexed at the utility of working to implement a rule that can be observed or ignored at the discretion of the subjects.

Pragmatically speaking as well, a deposit mandate does not even apply to the vast majority of scholarship, that is, previously published material. So its efficacy in filling a repository is entirely prospective (and hypothetical). Repositories, however, have a mission to collect and disseminate the entire corpus of published (and unpublished) scholarship, including everything from the development of the clay tablet to the invention of the Nook. For example, more than 80% of Nebraska's IR contents were published before 2010 (see Table 4.1); and among the "most downloaded" items, documents from the 2000s, from before 1900, and from the 1950s predominate. We observe that usage of documents in the repository is related to relevancy much more than recency; and if traffic is an indicator of IR success, then the large corpus of scholarship untouched by deposit mandates is a critical component. I have not heard of any deposit policy that makes a retroactive stipulation, and have no idea how one would work.

Table 4.1. UNL repository contents and past-year downloads by decade of publication.

Decade	No. of Items	Percent of Total Downloads	Top 30* Downloads 2013–2014	Percent of Top 30 Downloads
2010s	13,730	18.2%	41,937	10.6%
2000s	26,286	34.8%	125,427	31.7%
1990s	13,272	17.6%	46,710	11.8%
1980s	7,972	10.6%	13,547	3.4%
1970s	5,574	7.4%	—	
1960s	3,102	4.1%	—	
1950s	1,917	2.5%	55,620	14.0%
1940s	946	1.3%	—	
1930s	889	1.2%	—	
1920s	625	0.8%	—	
1910s	600	0.8%	—	
1900s	229	0.3%	—	
Pre-1900	304	0.4%	112,672	28.5%
Total	**75,446**	**100%**	**395,913**	**100%**

*The top 30 items represent 6.24% of the 12-month total of 6,344,419 downloads.

Finally, on the pragmatic front, adoption of a mandated policy would seem to me to threaten the IR manager with loss of control over the workflow. I have been fortunate to be able to proceed at my own pace in a semiorganized manner. We have been generally proactive in seeking content, but there have been times when the faculty response has threatened to overrun our defenses, and we struggle to deliver promised services on an appropriate timetable. The prospect of 2,000 researchers all dropping versions of their latest accepted manuscripts is actually frightening. I realize that, in theory, the IR manager does little more than punch their ticket and send them down the information highway, but the practical aspects of managing a faculty archive have little to do with theory. Self-deposited materials are rarely suitable for posting as submitted. Most often, there are permissions issues related to what version of an article may be allowed, as well as issues related to presentation and usability, clarification of rights, and the relation of the deposit to the version of record. I do not believe our faculty here are unique in having a varied assortment of misunderstandings about the deposit policies of all the different publishers; and the differences among preprints, postprints, and author-revised and peer-reviewed manuscripts are often more than a little esoteric and ineffable.

PROPRIETARY RIGHTS

The most pernicious effect of some of the mandatory deposit policies I have seen is the assertion by the institution of preexisting publication and distribution rights to the content. Under some mandates, the depositor surrenders to the institution a part-ownership interest—granting the right to distribute and *to exercise all rights under copyright and to authorize others to do so.* This assertion is said to precede and survive any subsequent grant of publication rights to a publisher; it is not limited by term or specific media or format. I feel this is a slippery slope, trending downward toward a future where the institution controls the distribution of the research output of the faculty as though it were a work for hire.

I am familiar with the justification—that this preserves the faculty author from the ruthless domination of the publisher, by establishing a prior claim to allow open distribution via the repository; but to me, the cure is nearly worse than the disease. I have attended or worked for six different universities (three Ivy, two Big Ten); there is not one of them that I would trust to administer publication rights to an article of mine. I will grant that there exists an inequality of power between the single author and the giant multinational publisher, but there is an even more one-sided relationship with the university, which already controls the author's working conditions, income, health care, housing, and so on. An author may fall out with John Wiley or the American Chemical Society and never publish with them again. Falling out with one's home institution is a much more dangerous situation. This blanket assertion of a license to distribute is a paternalistic incursion on the rights of faculty, albeit "for their own good," but it is unnecessarily heavy-handed. (See Table 4.2 for a comparison of author vs. institutional rights under two types of deposit policies.)

The deposit requirement, as I see it, presents faculty authors with a dilemma: they may opt out, rendering the whole question of mandates moot;

Table 4.2. Author deposits, rights, and permissions under two regimes.

	Nebraska-type[a]	**"Harvard"-type**[b]
Deposit requirement	No	Yes
Posting agreement	Permission	License
Effective term	At will	95 years
Deposit is revocable	Yes	No
Other formats/media	no	yes
Deposit is transferable	no	yes
University can authorize derivatives	no	yes
Opt-out provision	*n/a*	yes

[a] Voluntary one-time permission to post in IR.

[b] Mandated deposit, exercise all rights under copyright and authorize others to do so.

or they may misrepresent to publishers their capacity to convey unencumbered publication rights, because, in fact, the mandating institution has already established what is essentially a 95-year easement on the use of the intellectual property. An alternative might be to pay for gold or hybrid open access, in which case everyone is covered; though the authors must then secure the extra funds for the publisher and release under OA license any exclusive proprietary rights they might have wished to retain.

For those institutions that already have and love their deposit requirements, I have only good wishes. If it works for you, well, great; but it's not a club I am interested in joining. Some promoters of the idea seem to be looking far beyond the operation of the individual repositories, using them, in fact, as counters in the campaign for universal "open" access. Yet the justification seems more often focused on the rights of the public to use and repurpose the faculty's content than on the interests of the faculty or their rights to control their own intellectual property. I believe the repositories can and will be major factors in the growth and ultimate triumph of common access to academic and scientific research; but I believe this will be achieved by pumping huge amounts of content onto the Internet rather than by putting a net of deposit requirements over working researchers to capture their budding output between conception and publication.

REFERENCES

COAPI: Coalition of Open Access Policy Institutions. (2015). Retrieved from http://www.sparc.arl.org/COAPI

Duranceau, E. F., & Kriegsman, S. (2013). *Implementing open access policies using institutional repositories.* American Library Association. Association for Library Collections and Technical Services.

Giesecke, J. (2011, July 1). Institutional repositories: Keys to success. *Journal of Library Administration, 51,* 529–542.

Kipphut-Smith, S. (2014). "Good enough": Developing a simple workflow for open access policy implementation. *College & Undergraduate Libraries, 21*(3–4), 279–294. http://dx.doi.org/10.1080/10691316.2014.932263

Open access policy for University of Kansas scholarship. (2009). Retrieved from http://policy.ku.edu/governance/open-access-policy

Priest, E. (2012). Copyright and the Harvard open access mandate. *Northwestern Journal of Technology and Intellectual Property, 10.* Retrieved from http://papers.ssrn.com/sol3/papers.cfm?abstract_id=1890467

Salo, D. (2008). *Innkeeper at the roach motel.* Johns Hopkins University Press and the Graduate School of Library and Information Science. University of Illinois at Urbana-Champaign.

Shieber, S. M. (2009). *A model open access policy.* Retrieved from https://osc.hul.harvard.edu/sites/default/files/model-policy-annotated_0.pdf

Shieber, S. M., & Suber, P. (2015). *Good practices for university open-access policies.* Retrieved from bit.ly/goodoa

Wesolek, A. (2014, January 1). Bridging the gap between digital measures and Digital Commons in support of open access: Or, how I learned to stop worrying and love human mediation. *Collection Management, 39*(1), 32–42.

Wiley, D. (2009). Two units in BYU adopt open access policies. *Iterating Toward Openness.* Retrieved from http://opencontent.org/blog/archives/1137

5 | Responsibilities and Rights: Balancing the Institutional Imperative for Open Access With Authors' Self-Determination

Isaac Gilman

From their inception, open access[1] institutional repositories have been presented in largely utilitarian and pragmatic terms. Initially, institutional "archives" were conceived as a means of quickly and efficiently sharing scholarship whose dissemination was delayed by the traditional journal model (Okerson & O'Donnell, 1995; Tansley & Harnad, 2000). As the rationale for institutional repositories evolved, two parallel roles coalesced: the repository as a response to "the inertia of the traditional publishing paradigm" and the repository as a tool for building "institutional visibility and prestige" (Crow, 2002, p. 6). While accurately reflecting the current use of repositories, this framing is inherently problematic—it situates the institutional repository as the solution to a problem. Whether that problem is the broken economic model of scholarly journal publishing, or the need for an institution to extend its brand and impact, presenting the institutional repository as a solution implies that other solutions may also exist—and immediately undercuts the unique institutional imperative for building and sustaining an open repository of scholarly work. Such an imperative *does* exist; however, it is not a pragmatic consideration, but rather a moral obligation rooted in the nature of created knowledge and in the purpose and mission of universities. Aligning a repository program with this basic missional obligation can further strengthen the case for institutional repositories beyond any considerations of promotional value or impact on the scholarly publishing system. However, institutions that seek to frame their repositories in this way must also be mindful of a competing ethical responsibility—the respect for, and protection of, authors' intellectual property rights and agency in exercising those rights. The following discussion will explore the moral responsibility of academic institutions to freely share locally created scholarship and the tension between this obligation and the rights of academic community members to determine how and where their created knowledge should be shared.

KNOWLEDGE AS A COMMONS

As a precursor to examining the specific heritage and mission that compels universities to share the work of their scholars, it is helpful to consider whether there exists any general expectation for individual authors and researchers to share their work freely and openly with the public. Scholars have argued that knowledge should be considered a "commons"—a "resource shared by a group of people" (Hess & Ostrom, 2005, p. 4) or a "kind of property in which more than one person has rights" (Hyde, 2010, p. 27). This view of knowledge as a commons available to all is based on two basic ideas. First, knowledge is necessary for basic human functioning; Willinsky (2006) states that there is "a human right to know" (p. 3). Second, the evolution of knowledge essential for advances in society, culture, and science "is almost always cumulative and collaborative" (Hyde, 2010, p. 179) and requires that knowledge be shared.

This shared nature of knowledge is privileged even when the commons is "stinted"[2]—when knowledge is converted by law into intellectual property and exclusive rights are given to a limited number of individuals (i.e., authors and creators) (Hyde, 2010). The copyright and patent clause of the U.S. Constitution (Article 1, §8, Clause 8) states that authors' exclusive rights in their original works are created and protected *for the purpose* of "promot[ing] the Progress of Science and useful Arts"—a construction that introduces the idea that knowledge is created to serve the public good. This position is plainly stated in a U.S. House of Representatives report from 1988:

> Under the U.S. Constitution, the primary objective of copyright law is not to reward the author, but rather to secure for the public the benefits derived from the author's labors. By giving authors an incentive to create, the public benefits in two ways: when the original expression is created and . . . when the

limited term . . . expires and the creation is added to the public
domain. (as cited in Hyde, 2010, p. 54)

It is evident both from the Constitution itself, and from this legislative interpretation, that a first principle of intellectual property law in the
United States is that such laws are created to ensure that knowledge is accessible to the public. As Supreme Court justice Louis Brandeis wrote, "The
general rule of law is that the noblest of human productions—knowledge,
truths ascertained, conceptions, and ideas—became, after voluntary communication to others, free as the air to common use" (*International News
Service v. Associated Press*, 1918).

Clearly, there is a general expectation—however subverted it may be
by the current application of intellectual property law—that, by its nature,
knowledge is created as a contribution to the public good, not simply to
serve its creator. And the most efficient way for knowledge to serve the public is for that knowledge to be made freely accessible.

FEEDING THE COMMONS: REVIVING THE UNIVERSITY'S MISSION

Although intellectual property law creates opportunities to sell knowledge
(or individual rights associated with the use of that knowledge), there remains at least one sector of society in which the common, free nature of
knowledge is respected and protected—or in which it *should* be. While the
prevalence of technology transfer offices that facilitate licensing research
discoveries and the willingness of faculty to author textbooks that students
are unable to afford would indicate otherwise, colleges and universities
have historically maintained a strong commitment to the open dissemination of knowledge created within their walls. Renewing the focus on this
core attribute of higher education should provide institutions with substantial impetus to build and sustain open repositories.

Endowed for the Common Good

The collegiate ethos of promoting public access to knowledge saw some of
its most profound expression in the United States in the 19th century. As
the American education system had evolved from its predominately ecclesi-
astic and classical influences to embrace science and scholarship, a parallel
emphasis developed on the public responsibility of colleges and universities

(Rudolph, 1962). Joseph McKeen, the first president of Bowdoin College, declared in his 1802 inaugural address that "literary institutions are founded and endowed for the common good, and not for the private advantage of those who resort to them for education" (Rudolph, 1962, p. 58). The specific contribution that universities can make to the common good was later described by Daniel Coit Gilman, the second president of the University of California and the first president of Johns Hopkins University: "Apply the double test, what is done for personal instruction, and what is done for the promotion of knowledge, and you will be able to judge any institution which assumes [the name of "university"]" (1898, p. 52). Gilman was an especially ardent believer in universities' responsibility to disseminate knowledge, reflecting on this obligation in multiple public addresses:

> Universities distribute knowledge. The scholar does but half his duty who simply acquires knowledge. He must share his possessions with others. This is done, in the first place, by the instruction of pupils. . . . Next to its visible circle of pupils, the university should impart its acquisitions to the world of scholars. . . . But beyond these formal and well-recognized means of communicating knowledge, universities have innumerable less obvious, but not less useful, opportunities of conveying their benefits to the outside world. (*The Utility of Universities,* 1885 [Gilman, 1898, pp. 57–58])

> The fourth function of a university is to disseminate knowledge. The results of scholarly thought and acquisition are not to be treasured as secrets of a craft; they are not esoteric mysteries known only to the initiated; they are not to be recorded in cryptograms or perpetuated in private notebooks. They are to be given to the world, by being imparted to colleagues and pupils, by being communicated in lectures, and especially by being put in print, and then subjected to the criticism, hospitable or inhospitable, of the entire world. . . . Publication should not merely be in the form of learned works. The teachers of universities, at least in this country, by text-books, by lyceum lectures, by contributions to the magazines, by letters to the

daily press, should diffuse the knowledge they possess. Thus
are they sowers of seed which will bear fruit in future genera-
tions. (*Higher Education in the United States,* 1893 [Gilman,
1898, pp. 297–298])

Though Gilman was a firm proponent of formally published scholarship, he notes above that universities (and their faculty) should use *all*
available means of communication to "diffuse the knowledge they possess."
This need for alternative forms of dissemination outside of scholarly books
and journals was recognized by the U.S. Congress in the Smith-Lever Act
(1914), which required land grant institutions to develop "extension" programs "in order to aid in diffusing among the people of the United States
useful and practical information." While the act called for "development of
practical applications of research knowledge," "giving of instruction," and
"imparting information . . . through demonstrations, publications, and otherwise," it seems reasonable that, were it written today, it would recommend the creation of online institutional repositories as one means of sharing knowledge created at these institutions. Indeed, prominent land grant
institutions like Oregon State University (http://ir.library.oregonstate.edu
/xmlui/) and Purdue University (http://docs.lib.purdue.edu/) host robust
institutional repository collections that openly share work not only from
their extension programs but from faculty and researchers across their
universities. Even though they represent a small percentage of all higher
education institutions, the 75 current land grant institutions in the United
States are a significant example of the positive impact on the public good
that universities can have by actively sharing the knowledge they create.

Mission-Driven Dissemination

Lest the responsibility of universities to openly disseminate knowledge
be deemed either the sole province of agricultural schools or an artifact
of 19th-century idealism, it is helpful to examine current positions—both
collective and individual—regarding the role and responsibilities of the
university. In 2009, the Association of American Universities (AAU), the
Association of Research Libraries (ARL), the Coalition for Networked Information (CNI), and the National Association of State Universities and
Land Grant Colleges (NASULGC) issued a report, *The University's Role in*

the Dissemination of Research and Scholarship—A Call to Action, which included this "vision statement":

> *The creation of new knowledge lies at the heart of the re-search university* and results from tremendous investments of resources by universities, federal and state governments, industry, foundations, and others. *The products of that enter-prise are created to benefit society.* In the process, those prod-ucts also advance further research and scholarship, along with the teaching and service missions of the university. Reflecting its investments, *the academy has a responsibility to ensure the broadest possible access to the fruits of its work* both in the short and long term by publics both local and global.
>
> Faculty research and scholarship represent invaluable in-tellectual capital, but the value of that capital lies in its effective dissemination to present and future audiences. *Dissemination strategies that restrict access are fundamentally at odds with the dissemination imperative inherent in the university mis-sion.* (p. 1, emphasis added)

This statement directly echoes the themes present both in the consti-tutional construction of intellectual property and in early American educa-tors' declarations of purpose for their institutions: created knowledge as a public benefit and open knowledge dissemination as a core component of a university's identity.

Examining the mission statements of individual American universities reveals parallel themes. For example, the Massachusetts Institute of Tech-nology (2014) mission includes a commitment to "generating, disseminating, and preserving knowledge, and to working with others to bring this knowl-edge to bear on the world's great challenges." Brown University (n.d.) uses similar language—"The mission of Brown University is to serve the commu-nity, the nation, and the world by discovering, communicating, and preserv-ing knowledge and understanding . . ."—while Columbia University (n.d.) makes explicit its responsibility to give its knowledge to the world: "[Colum-bia] expects all areas of the university to advance knowledge and learning at the highest level and to convey the products of its efforts to the world."

Certainly, not every institution includes specific language in its mission about its responsibility to disseminate knowledge to the world. For example, it is understandable that a university with a robust research program would be more likely to emphasize the external dissemination of knowledge than would a liberal arts college with a more inward focus on undergraduate teaching. However, even when a college or university's mission does not explicitly oblige it to freely share its knowledge with the global community, there is often a strongly stated moral imperative that—if committed to fully—would compel the institution to do just that.

This implicit obligation is expressed differently by each college or university, but it usually includes similar themes: global citizenship, social justice, equality, and service. The California Institute of Technology's (Caltech) mission, for example, describes a responsibility "to expand human knowledge and benefit society through research integrated with education" (n.d.). The mission of an institution with a different overall scope, Earlham College, includes comparable language that stresses a responsibility to society at large—"At Earlham College this education is carried on with a concern for the world in which we live and for improving human society"—as well as an emphasis on "equality of persons" (n.d.).

For institutions similar to Earlham with a strong focus on undergraduate liberal arts education, the mission statement's moral themes are often framed in terms of student outcomes or attributes. Pacific University "inspires students to think, care, create, and pursue justice in our world" (n.d.), while Denison University (n.d.) "envision[s] our students' lives as based upon rational choice, a firm belief in human dignity and compassion unlimited by cultural, racial, sexual, religious or economic barriers, and directed toward an engagement with the central issues of our time." Even though the emphasis is on students, it seems reasonable to presume that if an institution wishes to instill specific values in its students—to "pursue justice" or to display "compassion unlimited by cultural, racial, sexual, religious or economic barriers"—the best way to do so would be for the institution and its faculty to tangibly model such behaviors.

Given universities' identity as centers of knowledge and learning, one of the obvious areas for an institution to look to when seeking to improve human society, or to model justice, or to remove cultural or economic barriers, is the issue of access to knowledge. Even if the basic idea of access to knowledge as a human right does not compel a university to move to address inequities in access, it is impossible to deny that knowledge is a necessary prerequisite to individuals' abilities to "defend, as well as advocate for, other rights" (Willinsky, 2006, p. 143). If a university, or its faculty, supports gender equality, or intellectual freedom, or access to health care, or political freedom, or is engaged in the struggles against food insecurity or religious intolerance or *any* of the compelling human issues that confront its local, regional, and global communities, then it is impossible for that institution to *not* support equitable access to the knowledge that is needed in order for individuals who face these challenges to advocate for themselves in an informed manner. And if necessary knowledge is being *created* at a university, it should ensure that access to that knowledge is provided in a way that is just and does not present economic barriers to those who could benefit from it.

Universities may, of course, dismiss calls for such engagement by observing that a mechanism already exists for sharing the knowledge created by faculty and researchers: the scholarly journal. However, not only do traditional scholarly journals offer a flawed, anachronistic means of sharing scholarship (Preim & Hemminger, 2012), but subscription-based journals introduce economic barriers to access for millions of scholars and public citizens in developing nations (Dickson, 2012; Ezema, 2011). Although programs like *Research4Life,* which partners with journal publishers to "provid[e] affordable access to critical scientific research" to developing nations in the form of free or low-cost journal subscriptions (Elan & Masiello-Riome, 2014), are helping to address this issue, the very existence of such programs is a tacit acknowledgment that scholarly knowledge is economically inaccessible to many people. Even academic libraries in some nations are unable to afford a fraction of the resources that are available to similar-sized institutions in the United States: the University of the West Indies, an institution comparable to ARL member institutions, is able to spend only 20% of what the average ARL library does per student on journals (Papin-Ramcharan & Dawe, 2006).

While knowledge sharing solely through traditional scholarly journals clearly damages universities' support for equal rights and desire to benefit human society, it also has a dampening effect on the open, broad exchange of knowledge that is vital for the progress of science. As Willinsky (2006) notes of traditional publishing, "scholars everywhere need to question their assumptions about what constitutes an adequate circulation of their and others' work" (p. 109). Even faculty who are publishing in reasonably priced journals should consider whether *any* subscription fee introduces an unnecessary barrier to wide visibility for their work. If the ultimate goal of scholarship (absent the tenure system)—and of universities—is to share knowledge, it would seem prudent to actively support mechanisms that best facilitate that goal. Open access publications offer one alternative to traditional journals, but the inherent issues of all scholarly journals are not altogether absent from open access journals—and the cost of author fees for some journals may be prohibitive for some scholars (and institutions). Institutional repositories offer a locally controlled means of ensuring rapid, persistent dissemination of various forms of scholarship—whether white papers, article preprints, datasets, reports, and so on—and are a logical way for universities to meet their missional and moral obligations to share knowledge. Indeed, the 2009 AAU/ARL/CNI/NASULGC report recommends: "Where local dissemination infrastructure exists (such as institutional repositories), promote its use and expand its capabilities as required" (p. 4).

AN INSTITUTION OF INDIVIDUALS

Whether as historically founded, or as currently stated in their missions, universities clearly have a responsibility—even an obligation—to widely share the knowledge that they create. However, universities as monolithic entities do not create this knowledge; it is the product of communities of dozens or even hundreds of individual faculty members and researchers. And while their scholarship is made possible by virtue of their employment at a university, faculty scholars retain individual rights—especially intellectual property rights—that must be considered and respected when a university endeavors to make all faculty scholarship openly available through an institutional repository.[3]

Faculty members' rights in the intellectual property that they create are well established and similarly circumscribed across most colleges and universities. While many institutions claim an interest (in the legal sense) in patentable intellectual property created by their faculty employees, faculty usually retain ownership and control over copyrightable works (Nelson, 2012). Beyond the legal assignment of copyright to faculty as the authors of their own original works, the standard of faculty ownership of "traditional academic works" (i.e., course materials and scholarly or creative works) is also grounded in the principle of academic freedom (American Association of University Professors [AAUP], 1999). As noted by the AAUP *Statement of Principles on Academic Freedom and Tenure,* "the free search for truth and its free exposition" are necessary attributes of higher education and, as such, faculty and researchers should be "entitled to full freedom . . . in the publication [of their scholarship]" (AAUP, 1940).

Implicit in the idea of "full freedom" in the distribution of their scholarly work are two faculty rights: the right not to be censored in sharing their knowledge and the right to choose how and where their knowledge will be shared. In practical terms, this latter right gives faculty the ability to select where and under what terms their scholarship will be published. These choices will vary by individual and are influenced not only by personal preferences but also by disciplinary norms: every disciplinary culture has accepted modes of discourse, which include the ways in which ideas are argued and presented (Hyland, 2000). These cultural approaches to information sharing extend beyond accepted rhetorical practices to include modes of sharing knowledge. For example, within the physics community, sharing prepublication research manuscripts in the arXiv disciplinary repository is a commonly accepted (and even expected) practice. As universities develop institutional repositories, they must be mindful of the fact that institutionally based dissemination may conflict with existing disciplinary practices that are important to faculty (Cullen & Chawner, 2011)—whether those focus on centralized subject repositories like arXiv or on more traditional forms of communication.

Modeling Balance: Open Access Policies

Perhaps the predominant traditional form of scholarly communication—and the example most frequently mentioned here—is the scholarly journal article. While certain disciplines prize the scholarly monograph as the ultimate expression of knowledge, all disciplines participate in journal publishing to some extent. This, coupled with the fiscal issues created by commercial journal publishers, has led to a conflict between the broad dissemination mission of universities and the narrower distribution of subscription journals. An increasingly common response to this conflict is an institutional open access policy. Open access policies (or "mandates") offer an excellent model for how an institution can respect faculty authors' individual agency while also pursuing the comprehensive dissemination of knowledge created within the institution.

An important attribute of most university open access policies is that they are faculty-driven and faculty-approved. Unlike a top-down approach, with the institution decreeing that all faculty must contribute their articles to an open access repository, a faculty-driven policy that is debated and approved through a faculty governance system recognizes the importance of faculty rights. Beyond this procedural aspect, most open access policies include three key elements that balance the institution's ability to disseminate knowledge with authors' rights to choose where their work is published. First, the policy requires a nonexclusive license from faculty to allow the institution to distribute their articles through an institutional repository. This license acknowledges faculty ownership of their work (Harvard Open Access Project [HOAP], 2014), allows them to retain all rights associated with that work, and yet makes it possible for the institution to openly share the work. Second, the policy is an "opt-out" rather than an "opt-in" policy; this places the emphasis on open dissemination of knowledge, but still respects faculty agency by providing a way to decline participation if necessary. Finally, the "opt-out" nature of the policy is made possible by offering waivers—exemptions to the default action of sharing an article—if a faculty member's publisher will not permit it. The waiver option ensures that authors have the ability to publish in whatever journal they choose, not just those that are amenable to the terms of the institution's open access policy (HOAP, 2014). By framing open dissemination of scholarly articles as the default action, while at the same time ensuring faculty authors' continued ability to choose publishing venues that are appropriate for them as individuals and members of a discipline, universities are effectively using open access policies to both fulfill their missions and respect faculty rights.

Finding Balance Beyond the Article

While open access policies and publicly available repository collections of scholarly articles are a significant contribution to universities' obligation to share their knowledge, they do not on their own meet an institution's responsibility to the common good. As Daniel Coit Gilman noted, there are many modes of publication and "innumerable less obvious" forms of "communicating knowledge"—and this is even truer today than in the 19th century. If a university wishes to openly disseminate the entirety of the knowledge created within its bounds, it needs to think beyond the article to consider the other ways in which its faculty communicate their knowledge. And, of course, it must explore the dissemination of these other forms of scholarship—and any proposed open alternatives—with the same respect for individual rights that is present in open access policies for journal articles.

The guiding principle when considering how to encourage (if not compel) faculty to openly share knowledge that might otherwise be constrained by economic or technological barriers should be the same balance present in the copyright and patent clause of the Constitution: knowledge is created for the common good, and knowledge creation is stimulated by offering scholars a certain (delimited) control over what they create. This balance recognizes that, while knowledge is a public good that should be shared freely, authors and creators are often motivated not simply by an altruistic desire to contribute to common knowledge, but by the assurance that they will receive some benefit—whether reputation, compensation, or advancement—for having made the contribution. By applying this principle, rather than simply compelling faculty to release their work to common use (or for the profit of the university, as is sometimes the case with online curricular materials [Butrymowicz, 2014]), universities are more likely to receive broader faculty support—and ultimately are more likely to come closer to the goal of sharing all knowledge created within the institution.

With that principle in mind, universities should examine the other traditional "closed" forms of scholarship outside of the journal article: scholarly monographs and textbooks. Similar to scholarship published in subscription-based journals, these forms of scholarship present economic (and sometimes technological) barriers to access. It would be unreasonable, of course, to suggest that faculty stop authoring scholarly books and textbooks. As noted earlier, there are strong disciplinary traditions that are centered on the monographic argument—not to mention the educational value of many books. There are also questions of economic, not simply academic, freedom that accompany books and textbooks. While it is not common for a faculty member to earn substantial sums from a scholarly text, some authors do earn a small royalty from sales of their work—and authors with a popular textbook may earn much more. Universities need to acknowledge this reality and propose methods of openly sharing the knowledge contained in faculty-authored books that will provide alternative incentives for faculty. Such incentives could include, for example, special recognition in the promotion and tenure process for publishing a monograph under an open access model, or stipends that would encourage faculty to create open textbooks that can be distributed through the institutional repository rather than authoring expensive commercial textbooks. Whatever incentives are offered, however, faculty must remain free to share and publish their knowledge as they see fit. This means that even if a particular press doesn't publish open access monographs, or allow self-archiving of chapters in a repository, the faculty member must be free to choose that publisher—just as with the waiver in open access article policies. Even in such cases, though, there are options a university can pursue to make a book's content freely available. For example, adopting the model recently proposed by AAU/ARL (2014) in their *Prospectus for an Institutionally Funded First-book Subvention* would see an institution underwrite the costs of a faculty publisher of choice in order to make "a basic digital edition" of the book openly available (including through the university's institutional repository). These types of strategies—whether providing faculty incentives to create open resources or funding the open publication of faculty work through the allocation of resources—will signal the university's commitment both to promoting knowledge and to respecting the expertise and rights of their faculty.

CONCLUSION: CLARITY AND COMPLEXITY

While universities' inherent imperative to share knowledge for the common good is clear, the complexity of both the scholarly communication system and the intellectual property laws that govern it make meeting that responsibility much more challenging than it was in a predigital era. Open institutional repositories should form the backbone of universities' knowledge dissemination efforts, but creating the capacity to distribute (and ideally preserve) scholarly works is only the beginning. Institutions must carefully examine the types of scholarship that are created within each of their schools and departments and determine—in consultation with faculty and researchers—how that knowledge can be best shared for public benefit. "Best" in this sense may not always equal the same degree of openness across all disciplines. Certainly, economic and technological barriers to access for students, independent scholars, and the general public both domestically and internationally should be removed. But when contributing work to the commons, institutions have a responsibility to ensure that their authors' rights—particularly their moral rights—are protected; this may entail licensing some works more restrictively than others. Similarly, sometimes certain rights must be asserted (and legally protected) when sharing knowledge with the public in order to ensure that work intended for the common good is not unduly commoditized by commercial interests (Hyde, 2010). By sharing knowledge in ways that make it available to the public in perpetuity, and that respect the rights of its creators, universities will ensure that their communities of scholars are encouraged to contribute to the "common stock of knowledge"[4] for years to come.

NOTES

1. For the purposes of this chapter, "open access" is used in the most inclusive sense—that is, it includes content that is publicly and freely accessible but may carry the full restrictions of copyright law with regard to use/reuse. While the 2012 Budapest Open Access Initiative recommendations call for content to be licensed using a Creative Commons—Attribution license or equivalent in order to be considered open access, there is legitimate debate as to whether it is necessary or appropriate to license all openly available institutional repository content in this way. (For further discussion, see: Poynder, R. (2014, August 31). The open access interviews: Paul Royster, Coordinator of Scholarly Communications, University of Nebraska–Lincoln. Open and Shut? Retrieved from http://poynder.blogspot.com/2014/08/the-open-access-interviews-paul-royster.html.)

2. For an excellent discussion of intellectual property as a stinted commons, see Hyde (2010).

3. It is worth noting here that, while institutional repositories are also commonly used as a mechanism for the mandatory deposit and dissemination of student work (Kennison, Shreeves, & Harnad, 2013), such work (especially in the form of theses and dissertations) has a long and accepted history of compulsory distribution by the student's institution, often as a degree requirement. Given this, the issues surrounding the dissemination of student work are not addressed here.

4. With gratitude to Benjamin Franklin for this evocative turn of phrase.

REFERENCES

American Association of University Professors (AAUP). (1940). *Statement of principles on academic freedom and tenure.* Retrieved from http://www.aaup .org/report/1940-statement-principles-academic-freedom-and-tenure

American Association of University Professors (AAUP). (1999). *Statement on copyright.* Retrieved from http://www.aaup.org/report/statement-copyright

Association of American Universities (AAU) & Association of Research Libraries (ARL). (2014). *Prospectus for an institutionally funded first-book subvention.* Retrieved from http://www.arl.org/publications-resources/3280-aau-arl-pro spectus-for-an-institutionally-funded-first-book-subvention

Association of American Universities (AAU), Association of Research Libraries (ARL), Coalition for Networked Information (CNI), & National Association of State Universities and Land Grant Colleges (NASULGC). (2009). *The university's role in the dissemination of research and scholarship—A call to action.* Washington, DC: Association of Research Libraries. Retrieved from http:// www.arl.org/bm~doc/disseminating-research-feb09.pdf

Brown University. (n.d.). Brown's mission. Retrieved from http://www.brown .edu/about/mission

Butrymowicz, S. (2014, March 1). Professors peeved to learn they don't own what they teach online. *Time.* Retrieved from http://nation.time.com/2014/03/01 /online-courses-moocs-ownership/

Caltech. (n.d.). Mission statement. Retrieved from http://www.caltech.edu/content /mission-statement

Columbia University. (n.d.). Mission statement. Retrieved from http://www .columbia.edu/content/mission-statement.html

Crow, R. (2002). *The case for institutional repositories: A SPARC position paper.* Washington, DC: Association of Research Libraries.

Cullen, R., & Chawner, B. (2011). Institutional repositories, open access, and scholarly communication: A study of conflicting paradigms. *Journal of Academic Librarianship, 37*(6), 460–470.

Denison University. (n.d.). Vision and values. Retrieved from http://denison.edu /campus/about/our-values

Dickson, D. (2012, September 3). Developing world gains open access to science research, but hurdles remain. *The Guardian.* Retrieved from http:// www.theguardian.com/global-development/2012/sep/03/developing -world-open-access-research-hurdles

Earlham College. (n.d.). Mission statement. Retrieved from http://www.earlham
.edu/about/mission-beliefs/mission-statement/

Elan, S., & Masiello-Riome, C. (2014). *Unsung heroes: Stories from the library.*
Research4Life. Retrieved from http://www.research4life.org

Ezema, I. J. (2011). Building open access institutional repositories for global visibility of Nigerian scholarly publication. *Library Review, 60*(6), 473–485.

Gilman, D. C. (1898). *University problems in the United States.* New York: The
Century Co. [Reprint edition, 1969. New York: Arno Press & The New York
Times].

Harvard Open Access Project (HOAP). (2014, October 27). Talking about a policy.
Berkman Center for Internet Studies. Retrieved from http://cyber.law.harvard
.edu/hoap/Talking_about_a_policy

Hess, C., & Ostrom, E. (Eds.). (2005). Introduction: An overview of the knowledge
commons. In C. Hess & E. Ostrom (Eds.), *Understanding knowledge as a
commons: From theory to practice* (pp. 3–26). Cambridge, MA: MIT Press.

Hyde, L. (2010). *Common as air: Revolution, art, and ownership.* New York: Far-
rar, Straus and Giroux.

Hyland, K. (2000). *Disciplinary discourses: Social interactions in academic writing.* Harlow, England: Longman.

International News Service v. Associated Press, 248 U.S. 215 (1918).

Kennison, R., Shreeves, S. L., & Harnad, S. (2013). Point & counterpoint: The
purpose of institutional repositories: Green OA or beyond? *Journal of Librarianship and Scholarly Communication, 1*(4), eP1105. http://dx.doi.org
/10.7710/2162-3309.1105

Massachusetts Institute of Technology. (2014). Mission. *MIT Facts 2014.* Retrieved
from http://web.mit.edu/facts/mission.html

Nelson, C. (2012, June 12). Whose intellectual property? *Inside Higher Ed.* Retrieved from https://www.insidehighered.com/views/2012/06/21/essay-fac
ulty-members-and-intellectual-property-rights

Okerson, A. S., & O'Donnell, J. J. (1995). *Scholarly journals at the crossroads: A
subversive proposal for electronic publishing: An Internet discussion about
scientific and scholarly journals and their future.* Washington, DC: Association of Research Libraries.

Pacific University. (n.d.). Origins, mission and vision. Retrieved from http://www
.pacificu.edu/about-us/who-we-are/origins-mission-and-vision

Papin-Ramcharan, J. I., & Dawe, R. A. (2006). Open access publishing: A developing country view. *First Monday, 11*(6). Retrieved from http://firstmonday.org/ojs/index.php/fm/article/view/1332/1252

Priem, J., & Hemminger, B. M. (2012). Decoupling the scholarly journal. *Frontiers in Computational Neuroscience, 6*(19). http://dx.doi.org/10.3389/fncom.2012.00019

Rudolph, F. (1962). *The American college and university: A history.* New York: Alfred A. Knopf.

Smith-Lever Act (Agricultural Extension Act) of 1914. Stat. 372, 7 U.S.C. 341 et seq. (1914).

Tansley, R., & Harnard, S. (2000). Eprints.org software for creating institutional and individual open archives. *D-Lib Magazine, 6*(10).

Willinsky, J. (2006). *The access principle.* Cambridge, MA: MIT Press.

6 | Campus Open Access Policy Implementation Models and Implications for IR Services

Ellen Finnie Duranceau and Sue Kriegsman

Implementation of campus open access policies in the United States is still a relatively new—though increasingly widespread—activity. According to the Registry of Open Access Repositories Mandatory Archiving Policies (ROARMAP), U.S. campus policies have grown to include 73 campuses[1] (Figure 6.1), with steady increases since 2009, when the Harvard Faculty of Arts and Sciences adopted the first such policy in the United States. There was particularly dramatic growth in 2013, the last complete year measured.

While short summaries of some individual libraries' approaches to implementing these policies have begun to be published,[2] a sense of the overall landscape of policy implementation has only begun to emerge.

As more campuses adopt open access policies, sharing implementation methods and models is increasingly critical. As Shannon Kipphut-Smith notes in her summary of Rice University's implementation experience, libraries faced with the need to set up brand-new procedures find themselves in a "nuanced" environment without a roadmap. Their library, like others implementing policies, "had never before conducted activities similar to the implementation of the OA policy," so they found that "practically every activity has been experimental."[3]

Here, in an attempt to build that needed roadmap, we provide a snapshot of the open access policy implementation landscape by evaluating data from a survey of Coalition of Open Access Policy Institutions (COAPI) and characterizing each library's OA policy implementation models for its campus. We reflect on implications for services associated with campus

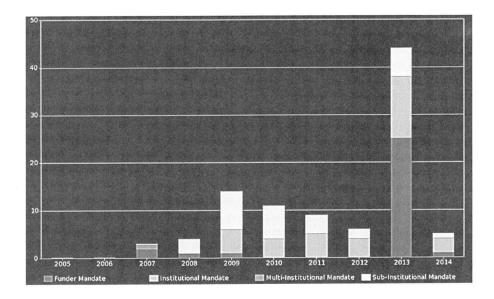

Figure 6.1. Open access policies in the United States as of July 2015. *(From ROARMAP, Registry of Open Access Repositories Mandatory Archiving Policies, at http://roarmap.eprints.org/.)*

institutional repositories (IRs) in meeting implementation needs, identifying relevant IR services that have emerged in relation to, and in support of, each of the implementation models.

OPEN ACCESS IMPLEMENTATION MODELS

The Coalition of Open Access Policy Institutions (COAPI) surveyed its members in early 2014 about the scope of their policies and implementation details. COAPI generously made the resulting survey data available for this chapter. Our analysis of the survey data confirmed anecdotal impressions that open access policy implementations on campuses in the United States tend to follow one or more of four models we have identified: systematic recruitment; targeted or opportunistic outreach; use of a faculty profile tool; and harvesting from other sites. We define each of these models below and provide examples from the campuses that responded to our follow-up inquiry to the COAPI survey, asking for feedback about our categorization of implementation models.[4]

1. Systematic Recruitment by Liaisons or Other Staff

The systematic recruitment approach involves the library, or a related department, gathering or obtaining metadata on faculty publications, and then using it to perform systematic outreach, usually through subject liaisons, to request and acquire publications from all campus departments.

Columbia, Harvard, Florida State, Lafayette, Massachusetts Institute of Technology (MIT), University of Rhode Island (URI), and Wellesley are characteristic examples of this approach. Princeton is building planned workflows based on the expectation that this will be a major implementation approach as well. Duke reported this as a secondary approach; Emory's plans track this model; and Kipphut-Smith refers in her article to some outreach efforts of this kind at Rice.

Relevant IR Services

An IR-based service that several campuses, including Harvard and MIT, are using to support this kind of systematic recruiting is the provision of author usage statistics. Download data for the author's papers is sent to authors, often when requesting additional manuscripts. This is seen as a tool that can incentivize deposits. Along with aggregated download from individuals, groups, or departments, or the number of visitors to the IR, the data can be automatically collected and shared to encourage authors to participate by depositing papers in the IR. MIT's service[5] allows authors to log in to see their own article download statistics; aggregated download data for MIT's departments, labs, and centers are available through a public view. At Harvard, download statistics are automatically e-mailed to authors on a monthly basis and used to create a visualization showing the dissemination of the open access works available through the repository (see Figure 6.2).

A heat map shows downloads of all the works deposited in the Harvard repository, Digital Access to Scholarship at Harvard (DASH). Libraries have received anecdotal feedback from authors that this kind of world map, whether for all works in the repository or for a single author or work (see Figure 6.3), encourages authors to contribute articles, because it demonstrates the need for access as well as the breadth of access possible with OA. For authors, the heat map brings the OA policy to life.

Figure 6.2. Harvard repository (DASH) download heat map at https://osc.hul .harvard.edu/dash/mydash?v=geomap&gi=alldash&t=1&p=alltime

2. Targeted and Opportunistic Outreach

In this approach, specific departments or faculty are targeted with requests for papers; the approach is not broadly systematic, but tends to focus on departments that are perceived as more receptive. Nine campuses reported using this model, including Caltech, Columbia, Connecticut College, Duke, Emory, Florida State, Oberlin, University of Kansas, and Washington University, with the latter two campuses using this as their primary model. At Emory, this model has included, in the past, CV reviews for faculty with associated deposits. Florida State has found this model most successful when drawing on personal connections and when targeting research centers or institutes, rather than departments.

The main reasons cited for adopting this model were reported to be a lack of staff sufficient to implement a more systematic approach, or having used this as a secondary approach where a particular opportunity emerged (as with Caltech).

A specific subset of this model, using news reports to target outreach, is being successfully used at Caltech, Columbia, Duke, Lafayette, and MIT;

Figure 6.3. Harvard repository (DASH) download heat map for an individual article.

Florida State is beginning to build this kind of connection. Both Duke and MIT use this approach where, in partnership with the campus news office, the news office notifies the library about research-related stories, and the library follows up by requesting the manuscript from the author so that the article can be made openly accessible via a link from the news story to the repository. Columbia has a similar workflow in partnership with their Public Affairs Office.

At Caltech, the Library and Media Relations departments have been collaborating since May 2014 on incorporating IR links in press releases. George Porter reports: "Although it took years to establish a solid connection, the effort has been paying off for all parties and seems to be institutionalized at this point."[6] Several sites have had the same experience—that it can take time and persistence to build these partnerships, but that they are highly productive once established.

Relevant IR Services

Targeted outreach is particularly well suited to social media–based marketing efforts like this kind of connection with campus news services. Such a connection allows for an unusually compelling kind of outreach to authors, connecting with them when their work is being highlighted in the news—a time when they are particularly likely to want to share the relevant work widely.

At MIT and Duke, the campus news service links from their story to the paper available in the repository as a way of making the work openly accessible for all readers of the news story. MIT and Duke find authors quite receptive to providing their papers when their research is being discussed in the news. In the first four months of a pilot program, MIT acquired well over 40 papers for the IR that had not otherwise been available for the IR, or deposited.

Harvard has supported this mutually beneficial relationship with the campus news services by creating an automated feed from their IR, offering it to Communications and other departments. This helps raise awareness of research coming from the institution; and campus news services value having a permanent link to the OA article, which the repository can provide, in addition to the link to the published version.

Social media approaches are not limited to news stories. Harvard is also generating Twitter feeds from the IR with links to recently deposited articles, as a quick and simple way to raise awareness about the research and to encourage authors to contribute articles. Similarly, Caltech and University of Washington offer RSS or Atom feeds to share deposit information.

Several institutions, including Connecticut College, Harvard, MIT, University of Rhode Island, and Washington University have "Top 10" lists for the most downloaded articles from their repository, or a list of recent submissions on the IR landing page. At URI, they also send a "congratulations" e-mail to all faculty each month, highlighting the top three most downloaded open access policy articles in the last month. Andree Rathemacher reports: "This seems to have gotten some positive attention and no one has complained about spam."[7]

Another social media approach being used by several campuses (including MIT and Harvard) is collecting comments from readers of papers in the repository. The idea, at least for U.S.-based implementations, seems to have originated with Sean Thomas, the repository services program manager at MIT, who, inspired by a similar approach at MIT's OpenCourseWare, suggested a simple method to enable campuses to learn how and why people

Readers Share Their Stories: Comments on Open Access Articles

Since July, 2012, we have been soliciting stories from individuals who download papers from the Open Access Articles Collection in DSpace@MIT, which contains articles made available under the MIT Faculty Open Access Policy. Every story matters, and we encourage you to share yours with us.

Here is a sampling of the stories we have received:

"I am an independent researcher from a third world country not affiliated to any university or a company. Thus I neither have access to paid journals nor I can afford them. MIT's Open Access is something I love and rely upon...Thank you again for thinking about the unfortunates and keeping the information free and open." –*Independent researcher, Nepal*

"I am extremely grateful to the MIT faculty for allowing individuals like me to get access to such valuable resources." –*unemployed engineer, preparing for interviews, US*

"My wife was diagnosed with [lung cancer]. As her husband and caregiver, I try to do everything I can to make her journey easier, and everything I can to create a full recovery for her. Part of that is arming myself with EVERY bit of knowledge I can gather about her cancer. Your resources allow a non-medical, non-academic, like myself access to this invaluable and leading edge data. I cannot THANK YOU enough." – *Reader, US*

"Thanks a lot, :D. I live in India and its really disheartening when a site asks for money to display their research work. This initiative will .... accelerate research in the emerging nations. Thanking you –" – *Student, India*

Figure 6.4. MIT Libraries' Web page of reader comments on open access articles.

are using articles in their repositories under OA policies. Each paper includes a cover sheet with metadata about the paper and a "Share your Open Access story" link, which allows readers to describe how the access affects or benefits them.[8]

MIT consistently receives messages of thanks and compelling stories about access needs through this Web form[9] (see Figure 6.4). One typical response was from a researcher in Nepal:

> I am an independent researcher from a third world country not affiliated to any university or a company. Thus I neither have access to paid journals nor I can afford them. MIT's Open Access is something I love and rely upon. . . . Thank you again for thinking about the unfortunates and keeping the information free and open.

Another campus implementing this idea receives between 50 and 70 stories every month—from real people, reading and benefiting from open access articles.

Stories can be shared on Web pages, on the IR landing page, through videos,[10] and with the author of the original article, particularly if campuses are careful to protect confidentiality and ask for permission to share names and comments. This is a unique benefit of OA materials distributed from a repository; it's not always possible for authors to receive such personal feedback about the impact of their work. Whether as part of targeted or systematic outreach, sharing such stories can offer a strong incentive for authors to deposit papers, and provides an ongoing and very real demonstration of the value of making the papers open access.

With a small amount of review and editing, these stories can become an automated feedback loop for authors on how their OA articles have impacted readers. The stories can also be used in marketing campaigns. For example, Harvard used these stories for Open Access Week 2013 publicity and posters (see Figure 6.5).

3. Use of Faculty Profile Tool

In this approach, faculty outreach is mediated at least in part by a researcher profiling or bibliography tool, through which faculty are responsible for reviewing and/or adding metadata for—and uploading—their papers. Use of such a tool (e.g., Symplectic Elements) allows for unmediated deposit, with faculty managing their metadata and uploading papers. In all cases, these tools are being used internally only, not for public-facing profiles (though some campuses, such as Duke, feed data from their internal profiling tool into a public-facing profiling service, VIVO.) Most campuses that use a profiling tool reported using a commercial system, but Florida State has been leveraging a homegrown system on their campus, which contains CV information.

Implementing an open access policy by using other campus reporting or profiling tools offers clear efficiencies and the potential for avoiding redundancies in data collection. For this reason, campuses do generally seek a means of connecting open access policy implementation with any campus systems that track and report on faculty publications. Neil McElroy of Lafayette could be speaking for many campuses when he comments that

Figure 6.5. Harvard OA Week poster featuring reader comments from "Share Your Story" link.

"it's possible we can find a workflow whereby the faculty's reporting of their publications to the Provost's Office is done by depositing eligible publications in the digital repository."[11]

Some campuses are already moving in that direction; for example, Kansas has been working with their university's Digital Measures application. Duke is the only campus currently reporting this approach as the primary implementation method (though they make use of all methods described here). Duke looks to more fully using the functionality of their Symplectic Elements system: "The Elements tool that we are using harvests metadata, and for sources that it can identify as being open access, provides one-click functionality to retrieve the item and deposit it in our local repository." They hope to begin "retrieving and depositing publications systematically through this process."[12]

Other campuses are also using profiling tools: Caltech (as a secondary strategy), Emory, Oberlin, the University of California (UC), and the University of Kansas, which focused originally on targeted outreach but which recently began using a campus profiling system as part of their implementation as well. At Emory, they are just now transitioning to the use of Symplectic Elements, which has been implemented in the School of Medicine and will be rolled out to other schools on campus. The University of California has just begun implementing their policy using this method. They will be sending out e-mail alerts asking faculty to confirm harvested metadata and to upload the full text of their articles.

Relevant IR Services

Institutions can use article-level metadata from their institutional repository to populate other campus systems, such as a faculty activity report or faculty profile tool. Faculty in the Harvard Faculty of Arts and Sciences, for example, are required to complete a Faculty Activity Report each year through a reporting tool. Harvard hopes to prepopulate that tool with data from the Harvard repository, which would prevent the faculty, or faculty assistants, from having to rekey information into the annual report, providing significant efficiencies. At Emory, articles from their repository OpenEmory were used, as Lisa Macklin reports, "as a way to pre-populate faculty profiles in Elements because we had already verified the citations and authorship of the articles in the repository."[13] UC has plans to "integrate our Elements system with the [public-facing] faculty profile projects throughout the UC campuses,"[14] and they are working on that now. Duke has also built connections between the profiling tool and the IR, and they find this mechanism is more meaningful for authors than the concept of an "IR": "Having the OA repository links directly in the faculty profiles is something we're pretty proud of, as it makes it easier for authors to see the connection between uploading their work and having it be associated directly with them, rather than with an institutional repository, which is kind of an abstract idea to most people who aren't librarians." As Duke's Paolo Mangiafico stresses, with authors and researchers seeking from places such as Google,

Google Scholar, an organization's Web site, or a researcher's profile, the IR becomes "the ultimate destination, but not the starting point."[15]

These integrations of IR data with other campus tools create efficiencies and reduce redundancy when managing and sharing publication data on campus, and help lead readers to the information in the IR without expecting the IR to be a known source that is sought in and of itself.

4. Harvesting

Harvesting involves automatically, semiautomatically, or manually copying manuscripts or published versions from repositories or publisher sites. Eleven campuses report using this method, though only one, Caltech, indicates it is their primary implementation model. Some campuses such as Columbia and MIT have implemented automated deposit into their repository for some articles, including, for example, SWORD deposits of BioMed Central articles;[16] other campuses are collecting papers from resources such as Creative Commons–licensed journals, PubMedCentral (where permissible), or other repositories that allow copying. UC harvests some articles through Symplectic Elements, though primarily this service grabs only metadata.

Emory's and Harvard's approaches to harvesting focus on the open access subset of PubMedCentral. Emory has a script that uses an API provided by the National Library of Medicine that "brings back metadata or the article (if [the] article is published with a CC license) for articles authored by someone at Emory."[17] These are reviewed and then deposited if the articles are CC licensed.

Relevant IR Services

Automated deposit is a labor-saving repository service that supports a harvesting approach for implementation. Campuses like Columbia and MIT that are taking advantage of this option benefit from automatically supplied metadata and reduced steps in handling article deposits. Deposits are also more timely: identification of relevant articles for a given repository is generally handled by the publisher and is very current.

Many campuses, including MIT, are watching the evolution of the Sponsoring Consortium for Open Access Publishing in Particle Physics (SCOAP³) repository service that will allow harvesting articles automatically for deposit into the campus repository, and have plans to use this service. As part of the SCOAP³ commitment to making high-energy physics articles openly accessible, the European Organization for Nuclear Research, known as CERN, has established a repository to house the articles included in the program. CERN promised that SCOAP³ library partners will "have the option to automatically populate their institution's digital repository with the SCOAP³ peer-reviewed articles."[18] As of July 2014, it was announced that the SCOAP³ repository was "open for the community to harvest content through OAI-PMH feeds."[19]

DISCUSSION: FACTORS INFLUENCING
CHOICE OF IMPLEMENTATION MODEL

In general, the campus context is influential in determining which implementation models are adopted. For example, campuses where a faculty profile tool has been implemented have a means of collecting papers under their open access policies not available to other campuses. While rolling out such tools may involve coordination with the library, as is the case with Kansas, where the library participated in early discussions, for the most part being able to leverage a profiling tool as a means of engaging faculty is determined by the presence of an existing broader campus initiative (as at Duke and Emory).

The main reasons cited for adopting the targeted and opportunistic approach are a lack of staff to take a more systematic approach, or having adopted this as a secondary approach where a particular opportunity emerged (as with Caltech). Connecticut College and Kansas report using this model while building toward a more systematic approach, particularly as more staff become available. Other campuses, such as Columbia, follow this targeted model when a policy doesn't apply to all authors on campus, using more focused outreach for departments where a policy is still in development. Columbia notes that this approach can help build a base of support for a possible future policy, in that it can demonstrate that "the work required from them is minimal while the benefits of their content within the IR are clear."[20]

At Emory, they began with a focus on harvesting and targeted outreach, but they are transitioning to the use of a profiling tool. As Lisa Macklin reports, "Our main reason for making the change mid-stream is the opportunity tying into the faculty profiling tool will provide. When we held our Open Access Conversations with faculty as part of the process of adopting an OA policy, we consistently heard from faculty that they wanted deposit into the repository to be a part of the work they are already doing. By connecting the repository with the faculty profiling system, we have the opportunity for faculty to deposit content in the repository while reporting their annual activities." This shift is extremely important, for it integrates the repository and open access policy implementation into workflows that the faculty are already engaged in. As Lisa Macklin concludes, "Taking advantage of this opportunity to make the repository "simply a part of what faculty [already] have to do is where we all need to head if we can." [21]

Campuses that have "permission-based" policies (like all those reported on here, with the exception of Florida State) also differ in the degree to which review of publisher policies informs their deposit strategy. One campus, for example, notes that they avoid depositing under the university's license through the policy "where the publisher prohibits it and the author failed (or didn't try) to secure permission by means of an author addendum prior to publication." Other campuses review publisher policies only where the license to the institution does not apply to the article (e.g., if there is no faculty author on the paper).

Many of these decisions emerge from the campus culture and resources, such as faculty preferences, administrative choices about services and tools that will be offered, risk tolerance, and staff or software development resources. While this chapter identifies various methods campuses could take to implement a policy, libraries need to operate within these specific institutional realities when making implementation decisions.

These models in some sense describe a set of progressive steps in a maturing implementation environment. For example, Kansas reported that they began with a targeted outreach, and then moved on to a faculty profiling tool when the provost's office implemented such a system, having brought the libraries in on the conversation early on; and they have now begun to build the resources and work processes necessary to adopt a harvesting approach.

Whatever methods a campus uses, the repository offers the possibility of increasing efficiency through data sharing, whether for campus systems that track publications, or for social media outlets that raise awareness about the research carried out on campus. Implementing an open access policy thus provides new paths for leveraging the IR infrastructure, providing needed and relevant services on campus. At the same time IR services assist in bringing the open access policy to life and enhancing policy implementation by providing usage data, reader stories, and other services that demonstrate the policy's impact and inspire authors to contribute papers.

CONCLUSION

Campus open access policies have become more common in the six years since the Harvard Faculty of Arts and Sciences passed the first license-style policy in the United States, with growth surging in 2013. Thus, many libraries are now grappling with how best to implement their faculty's wish to share their work as openly as possible, and to identify best practices in implementing the specific terms of their campus's policy. A recent guide to good practices[22] is an essential tool for libraries evaluating specifically how to create and implement a new policy; this current survey of campus policies provides a complementary view of the existing implementation environment. We have identified and described four main implementation models, offering a glimpse of an emerging—and still evolving—landscape for open access policy implementation in the United States.

The COAPI survey and our follow-up inquiries have confirmed that most campuses are using more than one of these methods, at times maturing from less systematic and more manual processes toward models that are more systematic (e.g., using a researcher profiling system to target all papers) or more automated (e.g., using the SWORD protocol or assistance from vended services like Symplectic Elements) to perform repository deposits. Other campuses have shifted strategies based on the availability of additional staff for outreach, or access to new tools, such as the adoption of campus publication reporting systems.

A common thread among all of the campuses is the desire to meet author needs by building repository-related services around the deposited papers. These include integration with researcher profiling/bibliography tools and campus publication reporting systems; development of repository-based usage statistics tools and reports of reader impacts; and using repository links and information to partner with news and communication services on campus. No matter what implementation method a campus uses, we see from the examples provided here that campuses with open access policies are using repository-related services to improve efficiencies in relation to their own campus policies, but also for funder or other administrative requirements, to support the social media presence, and to share data efficiently between systems.

Automatic harvesting and deposit are beginning to take hold and expand on some campuses. To make SWORD deposits more widely available and scalable, however, we will need to see advancement and success from projects like the SCOAP[3] repository services and the JISC Open Access Repository Junction,[23] which would establish an intermediary or "broker" to direct articles deposited by publishers or other repositories to the appropriate repositories. This kind of project makes it possible, in theory, for publishers to set up just one delivery mechanism—to the broker—rather than having to establish and maintain connections to every campus repository, which is unlikely to be sustainable. Such projects show the way toward a sustainable environment for sharing publications and supplementary material through campus repositories and more seamlessly complying with grant requirements.

With respect to grant requirements, the implementation of the 2013 White House directive on public access to data and publications[24] will no doubt further shift the landscape we snapshot here. At the time of this writing, only one agency, the Department of Energy (DOE), has provided details of their implementation plan. The DOE's Public Access Plan[25] requires the final accepted manuscript to be deposited in an open access repository, and campus institutional repositories are well positioned to fulfill researcher obligations under this plan. Because the DOE is such a significant funder of U.S. research, this requirement is likely to create a new incentive for many authors to deposit their manuscripts in their local IR, particularly if the library is also able to support the DOE's metadata, accessibility, and interoperability requirements.

It remains to be seen whether campus open access policies will continue to grow in number once campuses begin to grapple with implementing the U.S. government funder policies under this directive. Meanwhile, integrating our campus policy implementations with research funder requirements will be a key area of focus on our campuses, potentially initiating new implementation models and inspiring new repository services.

ACKNOWLEDGMENTS

We gratefully acknowledge the following individuals and their institutions for providing information directly to us about their open access implementations, in addition to their COAPI survey responses. This chapter would not have been possible without their generous participation. Any errors are completely our own.

- Andrew Wesolek, Coalition of Open Access Policy Institutions (COAPI)
- Alan Boyd, Associate Director of Libraries, Oberlin College
- Jane Callahan, Archivist, Wellesley College
- Ada Emmett, Scholarly Communications Librarian, The University of Kansas
- Ray English, Director of Libraries, Oberlin College
- Rebecca Kennison, Director, Center for Digital Research and Scholarship, Columbia University
- Anne Langley, Head Librarian, Science and Technology Libraries, Princeton University
- Ruth Lewis, Scholarly Communications Coordinator & Science (Biology, Math, History of Science) Librarian, Washington University in St. Louis
- Yuan Li, Scholarly Communications Librarian, Princeton University (who also provided information on Syracuse University)
- Lisa Macklin, Director, Scholarly Communications Office, Robert W. Woodruff Library, Emory University
- Paolo Mangiafico, Coordinator of Scholarly Communications Technology, Duke University Libraries Office of Copyright & Scholarly Communication, Duke University
- Neil McElroy, Dean of Libraries, Lafayette College
- Catherine Mitchell, Director of Publishing Services, University of California, California Digital Library
- Benjamin Panciera, Ruth Rusch Sheppe '40 Director of Special Collections, Connecticut College
- George Porter, Interim Head, Research and Information Services, Sherman Fairchild Library, California Institute of Technology (Caltech)
- Andree Rathemacher, Professor/Head, Acquisitions, University Libraries, University of Rhode Island
- Micah Vandegrift, Scholarly Communication Librarian, Florida State University

- Jen Waller, Scholarly Communication Liaison, King Library, Miami University (policy for librarians only)

NOTES

1. This total is for campuses, not department- or school-level policies on a single campus.
2. See for example the discussion of the Rollins implementation in Miller, J. (2011). Open access and liberal arts colleges: Looking beyond research institutions. *College & Research Library News, 72*(1), retrieved from http://crln.acrl .org/content/72/1/16; and Kipphut-Smith, S. (2014, Summer). Engaging in a campus-wide conversation about open access. *Texas Library Journal, 90*(2), 70–71, which describes some of the barriers to effective policy implementation at Rice's Fondren Library; and the authors' prior overview: Duranceau, E. F., & Kriegsman, S. (2013). Implementing open access policies using institutional repositories. *The Institutional Repository: Benefits and Challenges*. Chicago: ALCTS, 81–105, retrieved from http://www.ala.org/alcts/sites/ala.org.alcts /files/content/resources/papers/ir_ch05_.pdf
3. Kipphut-Smith, S. (2014, Summer). Engaging in a campus-wide conversation about open access. *Texas Library Journal, 90*(2), 70.
4. We sent inquiries to 18 campuses with a proposed characterization of their implementation model(s) based on the COAPI survey results. Our goal was to confirm our proposed scheme of implementation models and be sure we reflected each campus's approach accurately. The campuses' confirmed responses form the basis for the models and data discussed here. We excluded campuses whose policies were still in development or where the policy applied only to library staff.
5. MIT's service is accessible at oastats.mit.edu.
6. George Porter, Interim Head, Research and Information Services, Sherman Fairchild Library, California Institute of Technology (Caltech), personal communication, October 17, 2014.
7. Andree Rathemacher, Professor/Head, Acquisitions, University Libraries, University of Rhode Island, personal communication, October 20, 2014.
8. See http://libraries.mit.edu/forms/dspace-oa-articles.html.
9. See http://libraries.mit.edu/scholarly/comments-on-open-access-articles/.
10. See example of comments incorporated in a video from Harvard: https://www

.youtube.com/watch?v=7Ah86t49DI4&list=PL2SOU6wwxBosuycszlpa2ltzb WqmYk2pg&index=1

11. Neil McElroy, Dean of Libraries, Lafayette College, personal communication, August 7, 2014.

12. Paolo Mangiafico, Director of Digital Information Strategy, Duke University, personal communication, August 7, 2014.

13. Lisa Macklin, Director, Scholarly Communications Office, Emory, personal communication, October 23, 2014.

14. Catherine Mitchell, Director of Publishing Services, University of California, California Digital Library, personal communication, October 17, 2014.

15. Paolo Mangiafico, Director of Digital Information Strategy, Duke University, personal communication, August 7, 2014.

16. BioMed Central has been offering SWORD deposit at no extra cost to members (see http://www.biomedcentral.com/libraries/aad). For a description of this process, see Duranceau and Rodgers: *Automated IR deposit via the SWORD protocol: An MIT/BioMed Central experiment* at http://uksg.metapress.com /content/l437x1631052407r/?p=f61c630cf6f54ae4bd16513a2cd180f4&pi=11. SWORD stands for Simple Web-service Offering Repository Deposit.

17. Lisa Macklin, Director, Scholarly Communications Office, Emory, personal communication, October 23, 2014.

18. See http://scoap3.org/faq.

19. E-mail announcement to SCOAP3USA contacts list: "The SCOAP3 repository: OAI-PMH feed now available," July 18, 2014. And see http://scoap3.org/news /the-scoap3-repository-oai-pmh-feed-now-available.html

20. Rebecca Kennison, Director, Center for Digital Research and Scholarship, Columbia University, personal communication, August 8, 2014.

21. Lisa Macklin, Director, Scholarly Communications Office, Emory, personal communication, October 23, 2014.

22. See *Good Practices for University Open-Access Policies,* http://cyber.law .harvard.edu/hoap/Good_practices_for_university_open-access_policies.

23. See http://www.jisc.ac.uk/whatwedo/programmes/inf11/oarj.aspx.

24. Memorandum from the OSTP: http://www.whitehouse.gov/sites/default /files/microsites/ostp/ostp_public_access_memo_2013.pdf

25. http://www.energy.gov/sites/prod/files/2014/08/f18/DOE_Public_Access %20Plan_FINAL.pdf

APPENDIX
Open Access Implementation Models
Survey Results Matrix

	Systematic Recruitment by Liaisons or Other Staff	Targeted and Opportunistic Outreach	Use of Faculty Profile Tool	Harvesting
Totals	10	9	6	11
Caltech		x		x
Columbia University	x	x		x
Connecticut College		x		
Duke University	x	x	x	x
Emory University	x	x	x	x
Florida State University	x	x	x	
Harvard University	x			x
Lafayette College	x			
MIT	x			x
Oberlin College		x	x	
Princeton University	x			x
University of California			x	x
University of Kansas		x	x	x
University of Rhode Island	x			
Washington University		x		x
Wellesley College	x			x

7 | Electronic Theses and Dissertations: Preparing Graduate Students for Their Futures

Gail McMillan

The convergence of electronic theses and dissertations (ETDs)[1] and institutional repositories (IRs) has raised some concerns. Among them is the appropriateness of requiring that works in the repository be publicly accessible. This should not be an issue at the many universities that include dissemination of knowledge in their mission statement.[2] For example:

> Texas A&M University is dedicated to the discovery, development, communication, and application of knowledge. (Texas A&M University, 2015)

> The University of Virginia . . . serves the Commonwealth of Virginia, the nation, and the world by . . . advancing, preserving, and disseminating knowledge. (University of Virginia, 2015)

> The discovery and dissemination of new knowledge are central to [Virginia Tech's] mission. (Virginia Polytechnic Institute and State University, 2014)

IRs enable institutions to fulfill their knowledge dissemination goals by providing public access to the institutions' "knowledge products" such as ETDs. In "The Value Proposition in Institutional Repositories" Blythe and Chachra describe the role of libraries as IR managers that "capture, retain, and leverage the value in the knowledge products of institutions and their members" (Blythe & Chachra, 2005, p. 77). Of course, all higher education institutions have a responsibility to their communities to have clear and accessible policies and to balance the intellectual property rights of their knowledge-product authors with the mission of the institution and the goals of its IR. Members of the university community are also responsible for informing themselves about their institution's policies.

GRADUATE STUDENTS' RESPONSIBILITIES

When students enroll in graduate programs it is incumbent upon the students to understand the goals and requirements of their programs, which are extensions of the goals of their universities. Graduate students should understand from the beginning whether they will be required to produce a thesis or a dissertation in partial fulfillment of a degree. They should understand that these works are part of the knowledge disseminated by their universities and they should understand the dissemination policy. Graduate students expect their theses and dissertations to go to the library and they similarly expect them to be available to library users. Students today are well aware that libraries are so much more than a building on campus with shelves of books and journals, that libraries are remotely accessed information resources available to and used by their institutions' constituents and sometimes the general public.

Graduate students have chosen their institutions based on a variety of factors, and public-access policies for ETDs should be one of those factors. This will be a lesson well learned by those who will seek funding since they will need to know which federal agencies and private funders require that articles based on funded research be available to the public in open access repositories. Some funding agencies allow delayed open access, just as most institutions allow access to ETDs to be temporarily restricted to the home institution or embargoed (i.e., withheld) from all access according to the "2013 NDLTD Survey of ETD Practices" (McMillan, Halbert, & Stark, 2013). At 39% of the survey respondents' institutions all ETDs are publicly available, 2% reported that none are, and 54% of the 171 institutions responding reported that they "temporarily limit some or all ETDs to university-only access." There was an interesting drop to 108 survey responses to the question, "Does your institution have embargoed ETDs?" Ninety-one percent embargo some ETDs, 8% have no embargoed ETDs, and 1% embargo all of their ETDs.[3]

Libraries were at the forefront of ETD initiatives even before they took the lead in the open access movement. In both cases libraries advocated a universal public good. While libraries have traditionally focused on meeting readers' needs, 21st-century libraries are increasingly involved in the entire life cycle of information, including publishing where they are not usually constrained by profit or even cost-recovery motives.

GOALS OF THESES AND DISSERTATIONS

The thesis or dissertation requirements at American universities and colleges are designed to meet a variety of goals. According to the Council of Graduate Schools (Lang, 2002, p. 690; substantially unchanged from *The Role and Nature of the Doctoral Dissertation* [CGS, 1991, p. 3]), the thesis or dissertation

- Reveals the student's ability to analyze, interpret, and synthesize information
- Demonstrates the student's knowledge of the literature relating to the project or at least acknowledges prior scholarship on which it is built
- Describes the methods and procedures used
- Presents results sequentially and logically
- Displays the student's ability to discuss fully and coherently the meaning of the results

In 2009 the CGS acknowledged that "The bound doctoral dissertation or Master's thesis are now things of the past. . . . In the future, graduate education must grapple with encouraging new outputs such as three-dimensional models, video footage, and non-linear research projects. It is likely that in the future these and other innovative forms of the presentation of research will come to dominate graduate education. Digital imaging and new publication formats will likely raise new ethical questions and make some old ethical challenges such as image manipulation and plagiarism more prevalent. At the same time libraries and future researchers will continue to require ready access to such materials" (CGS, 2009, p. 14).

The Carnegie Initiative on the Doctorate described the purpose of graduate education as preparing stewards of the disciplines—people "who will creatively generate new knowledge, critically conserve valuable and useful ideas, and responsibly transform those understandings through writing, teaching, and application" (Walker, Golde, Jones, Bueschel, & Hutchings, 2008, p. 161). Covey defined a steward as someone who works beyond one's own career, "transforming knowledge through creative application and effective communication to different audiences in a different media" (Covey, 2013, p. 544). Restricting ETD access is an example of poor stewardship. "What is at play here is a profound cultural and cognitive tension between the safe and familiar closure of print literacy and the wild and unknown openness of digital literacy" (Covey, 2013, pp. 544–545). Among the ETD stakeholders are representatives of the tensions that this chapter briefly examines.

ETDs are stewarded by organizations as well as individuals. A notable organization is the Networked Digital Library of Theses and Dissertations (NDLTD), with a board of directors that is made up of many international ETD stakeholders. The NDLTD "support[s] electronic publishing and open access to scholarship in order to enhance the sharing of knowledge worldwide" (http://www.ndltd.org/). In the mid-1990s the NDLTD assumed the role of ETD advocacy and support, among other activities creating an annual conference for all stakeholders to share their successes and challenges.

In May 2002 the NDLTD formalized its mission during a strategic planning meeting, which presented a balance among the ETD stakeholders' goals. Specific objectives were the following:

- Improve graduate education by allowing students to produce electronic documents, use digital libraries, and understand issues in publishing
- Increase the availability of student research for scholars and preserve it electronically
- Lower the cost of submitting and handling theses and dissertations
- Empower students to convey a richer message through the use of multimedia and hypermedia technologies
- Empower universities to unlock their information resources
- Advance digital library technology

In 2004 the NDLTD began two award programs, one recognizing graduate students with the Innovative ETD Awards, and one recognizing leaders of ETD initiatives. The purpose of the Innovative Awards program is to "acknowledge the importance of technological innovation, to promote the open exchange of scientific and cultural research information as well as to facilitate the potential for change in scholarly communications" (NDLTD, 2013). Brief descriptions of NDLTD award winners and their successes following graduate school tell the very positive effects and benefits of publicly accessible ETDs.

Shirley Stewart Burns wrote and made accessible "Bringing Down the Mountains: The Impact of Mountaintop Removal on Southern West Virginia Communities" for her dissertation at West Virginia University in 2005 (http://hdl.handle.net/10450/4047). It was later published as *Bringing Down the Mountains,* a bestseller for the WVU Press (http://wvutoday .wvu.edu/n/2008/03/26/6644). Burns went on to serve as historical consultant for the documentary film *Coal Country.*

Pete Souza wrote and made accessible "A Photojournalist on Assignment" for his master's thesis at Kansas State University in 2006 (http:// hdl.handle.net/2097/254). He went on to become an assistant professor at Ohio University and then the official White House photographer for President Barack Obama.

Heather Forest wrote and made accessible "Inside Story: An Arts-based Exploration of the Creative Process of the Storyteller as Leader" for her dissertation at Antioch University in 2007 (http://aura.antioch.edu /etds/9/). She is the founder and executive director of Story Arts Inc. in Huntington, New York.

As if drawing on these future examples in her 2002 article, "Electronic Dissertations: Preparing Students for Our Past or Their Futures?" Susan Lang, professor of English at Texas Tech University, pointed out that ETDs have the potential to extend the work of the academy more deeply into the public sphere (Lang, 2002, p. 686). Jude Edminster and Joe Moxley (English faculty at Bowling Green and the University of South Florida, respectively) similarly wrote, "If we are to realize the potential that ETDs have to further equitable distribution of the information wealth many cultures in the West take for granted, then perhaps graduate students' more studied consideration of the ethical limits of authorship rights is warranted" (Edminster & Moxley, 2002, p. 100).

But today we hear entreaties from the American Historical Association (AHA) and others to embargo ETDs, countering Lang and Edminster and Moxley with warnings of dire consequences if ETDs are publicly available. As the Council of Graduate Schools put it in *Graduate Education in 2020,* "the continuing struggle [is] to articulate the vision of graduate education as a public benefit, not simply as a private good" (CGS, 2009, p. 8).

International NDLTD Innovative Award winners like Franci Cronje exemplify this philosophy. She wrote and made publicly accessible "Problems Presented by New Media in South African Public Art Collections" for her master of arts in fine art thesis at the University of Witwatersrand in Johannesburg, South Africa in 2002 (http://hdl.handle.net/10539/10092). She went on to get her PhD at the Centre for Film and Media Studies at the University of Cape Town before becoming the head of academics at Vega School of Brand Leadership in Cape Town, South Africa.

ETDs provide their authors with a preview of participating in, and contributing to, the scholarship of the academic community. Libraries are the intersection between authors and readers/researchers, hosting the works of the authors and making them available to readers. ETDs provide us with pedagogical opportunities on many fronts. Among these opportunities is instruction about copyright issues. Librarians instruct both groups about their rights and responsibilities.

OWNERSHIP

Lawyer and librarian Kenneth Crews is well known for his wise council and instructional sessions on copyright. He has written about educational and library exceptions in copyright law for the World Intellectual Property Organization, and he was tapped by ProQuest to prepare a guidance document for ETD authors. "The recurring point of this overview is the importance of making well-informed decisions" (Crews, 2013, p. 5):

> *You are most likely the copyright owner.* Copyright ownership vests initially with the person who created the new work. If you wrote the dissertation, you own the copyright. However, it is possible that you may have entered into a funding or employment arrangement that would place copyright ownership with someone else. Review your agreements carefully.

These agreements include those between graduate students and their institutions. Like knowledge product dissemination, copyright ownership is another institutional policy that all ETD authors should inform themselves about. Like many universities, Virginia Tech's policy is easily found from a search for "intellectual policy" or "copyright policy" from the university's home page. VT Policy 13000 refers to the "traditional results of academic scholarship," which include theses and dissertations:

> Intellectual properties in the first (traditional) group are considered to make their full contribution to the university's benefit by their creation and by continued use by the university in teaching, further development, and enhancement of the university's academic stature; the presumption of ownership is to the author(s). Thus, unless there is explicit evidence that the work was specifically commissioned by the university, the IP rights remain with the author(s) and the university rights are limited to free (no cost) use in teaching, research, extension, etc. in perpetuity.

Another sample copyright policy that clearly articulates ownership can be found at Texas Tech University (TTU, 2014, p. 7):

> TTUS does not claim ownership to pedagogical, scholarly, or artistic works, regardless of their form of expression. Such works include . . . those of students created in the course of their education, such as dissertations.

In spite of these policies, according to some legal interpretations, universities are not necessarily required to get agreements from ETD authors regarding the accessibility of their works. LeRoy S. Rooker, director of the Department of Education's Family Policy Compliance Office, specifically addressed student works when he wrote that

> Undergraduate and graduate "theses" often differ in nature from typical student research papers and other education records,

such as written examinations, in that they are published or otherwise made available as research sources for the academic community through the institution's library. It has been and remains our understanding that in these circumstances an educational institution would ordinarily have obtained the student's permission to make his or her work available publicly before doing so, perhaps in connection with notifying the student of specific course or program requirements.

Consequently, an institution need not obtain a student's signed and dated specific written consent to disclose or publish a thesis in the library or elsewhere at the institution. Neither the statute, the legislative history, nor the FERPA regulations require institutions to depart from established practices regarding the placement or disclosure of student theses so long as students have been advised in advance that a particular undergraduate or graduate thesis will be made publicly available as part of the curriculum requirements. (ALAWON, 1993)

"We do not change our policies simply because our educational delivery methods have changed" was the admonition by Richard Rainsberger, FERPA expert, when speaking at the 2001 ECRURE conference, Preservation and Access for Electronic College and University Records (Rainsberger, 2001, slide 7).

Prior to ETDs universities did not ask authors for permission for the library to store and provide access to their works. But the authors were required to submit copies for the library to preserve and make available. With the advent of ETDs universities began asking their authors to formally give permission for preservation and access through the library's IR. What had been standard practice for more than 100 years became codified.

At the beginning of its ETD initiative Virginia Tech adopted what has become a typical agreement between ETD authors and their institutions:

> I hereby grant to Virginia Tech and its agents the non-exclusive license to archive and make accessible, under the conditions specified, my thesis, dissertation, or project report in whole or in part in all forms of media, now or hereafter known. I retain all other ownership rights to the copyright of the thesis,

dissertation, or project report. I also retain the right to use in future works (such as articles or books) all or part of this thesis, dissertation, or project report. (Virginia Polytechnic Institute and State University, 2012)

Hawkins, Kimball, and Ives pointed to the "unequal relationship of power between universities and students" (Hawkins et al., 2013, p. 33) when they derided ETD requirements. Other faculty, however, see the university as willingly challenging the "hierarchical dynamic" by requiring ETDs. Char Miller at Pomona College described it as granting "privilege and power to student [ETD] authors. . . . Open Access empowers all scholars, not just those with a Ph.D. appended to their last names" (Miller, 2013, p. 5).

A huge part of dealing with ETD issues is a graduate education that clearly informs students about their copyrights. But graduate students must also understand what options they will have to chose from about providing access to their capstone projects. Choices about access should be based on real data and not perceptions and fears based on hearsay or isolated incidents. These data have been gathered and reported since 1998 (Eaton, Fox, & McMillan, 1998, 2000),[4] and as recently as 2011 (Ramírez, Dalton, McMillan, Read, & Seamans, 2013; Ramírez et al., 2014). Well into the second decade of ETD requirements at many institutions the AHA recommended the already common practice: universities should have flexible policies that will allow PhD candidates to decide whether or not to embargo their dissertations (AHA, 2013). But its six-year embargo recommendation controverts the data that are readily available.

"The Role of Electronic Theses and Dissertations in Graduate Education" appeared in the January 1998 issue of the *Communicator,* the Council of Graduate Schools' newsletter. The authors, Eaton, Fox, and McMillan from Virginia Tech, outlined the benefits and challenges, concluding:

> Hopefully this editorial will help graduate deans and others understand the potential and real benefits of this [ETD] project, and to realize that, contrary to what some have claimed, it is not a threat to the employment of graduate students in academic positions, not a threat to faculty promotion and tenure, and not a threat to the publishers who through the peer review process

improve derivative manuscripts that are based upon the rich mine of information contained in ETDs. (Eaton et al., 1998, p. 4)

DATA

Eaton and colleagues followed up in the November 2000 *Communicator* with the results of a survey of the first cohort of graduate students whose ETDs had been available on the Web for more than a year (n = 329). Of the 166 ETD authors who returned the survey, 29% responded "yes" when asked if they had "published derivative works (journal articles, books chapters)" from their ETDs. When asked if they "encounter[ed] resistance from any publishers to accepting your manuscript for publication because it was 'online,' 100% said, 'No'" (Eaton et al., 2000, p. 1).

Another survey question was about satisfaction with being contacted as a result of having a Web-accessible ETD:

If you were contacted, how satisfied were you with the contact:
    a.   Helped you advance your research interest?
    b.   Helped you to locate a job?
    c.   Helped you expand your network of research colleagues?

The results were as follows:

	Satisfied or Somewhat Satisfied	*Unsatisfied or Somewhat Unsatisfied*
Advanced research	68%	32%
Locate job	40%	60%
Expand network	82%	18%

Additional studies done in 1998–2001 by Joan Dalton and Nan Seamans showed that journal editors would consider manuscripts derived from ETDs. Ramírez and colleagues updated the Dalton and Seamans studies in 2011–2012, subsequently reporting findings in *College and Research Libraries*. In their 2014 article, "Do Open Access Electronic Theses and Dissertations Diminish Publishing Opportunities in the Sciences?" they

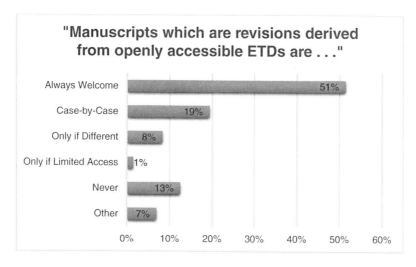

Figure 7.1. Survey responses from science journal editors.

provided data to mitigate the fears concerning the negative effect online discoverability of ETDs might have on future opportunities to publish those findings. Science journal policies regarding open access ETDs revealed that more than half of the journal editors (51.4%) responding to the 2012 survey by Ramírez and colleagues reported that manuscripts derived from openly accessible ETDs are *welcome* for submission and an additional 29% would accept revised ETDs under various conditions (see Figure 7.1). The previous (2011) survey by Ramírez and colleagues of university press directors and humanities and social science journal editors had consistent results.

As Ramírez and colleagues pointed out in the online comments following publication of "Do Open Access Electronic Theses and Dissertations Diminish Publishing Opportunities in the Social Sciences and Humanities? Findings from a 2011 Survey of Academic Publishers," the data clearly indicate that 72% of these journal editors and university press directors would either welcome or consider on a case-by-case basis manuscripts derived from ETDs. Only 4.5% of respondents indicated they were unwilling to consider manuscripts derived from publicly accessible ETDs (Ramírez et al., 2013; see Figure 7.2).

Though university press directors' responses vary from those of the social sciences and humanities journal editors, no more than 7% would never consider a manuscript based on an accessible ETD. This points to the need

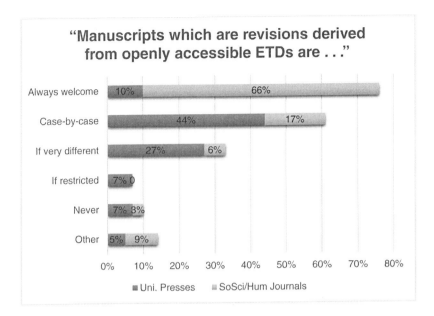

Figure 7.2. Survey responses from social sciences/arts/humanities journal editors and university press directors.

for graduate students to consider publishers' policies prior to completing their ETDs so that the graduate students can make fact-based decisions about ETD accessibility choices rather than relying on urban legends to inform last-minute decisions about the level of access their ETDs should have. Comments from the university press directors and journal editors were overwhelmingly positive that manuscripts based on ETDs should be submitted to them for consideration (Ramírez et al., 2013, pp. 375–376). Following is a sampling of survey respondents' comments.

> Whether in hard or e-copy, we expect the dissertation to be completely revised before we will consider a manuscript. We do not consider the dissertation to be the equivalent of a book. It is a student work; a book is a professional work. (Press director)

> A PDF of an unpublished work is still an unpublished work. It simply can't work to have a scientific model where work-in-progress is disqualified for publication if it's been posted on a web server. (Journal editor)

Some manuscripts, even if published electronically as dissertations, are appealing regardless of their electronic availability because the audience for them in print form is substantial enough that it does not matter. There is a substantial market for certain works of Civil War history, for instance, that is quite broad. The lay readership for Civil War history, for instance, wants to have the book and would not likely know or have access to the text in dissertation (electronic) form. Even if they knew, they would likely still want the book. (Press director)

I base my judgments on value added, as it were; i.e. whether there is sufficient original material to warrant space in the space limited environment of my journal. (Journal editor)

During the 2011 survey, science journal editors commented (Ramírez et al., 2014, p. 817):

Work which has not been published in archival peer reviewed journals is considered appropriate for submission, even if it is accessible elsewhere.

Our journal has essentially ignored any potential conflict arising from publication of ETDs, because the situation is really not different from the days of hard copy thesis holdings by University libraries. They . . . are simply more easily available now. . . . Thesis without peer review in an open access format will never be considered "double publishing."

A peer-reviewed publication that comes out of a dissertation or thesis should not only be encouraged but is crucially important for the scholar's development and the advancement of scientific knowledge.

There were many commonalities among the social sciences, humanities, and sciences survey respondents. For example, for an ETD to be published, they all require that ETDs be revised to appeal to a different audience and to meet the quality standards of the publisher, among other considerations.

The data show that manuscripts derived from ETDs would not be rejected outright, but would be welcomed, considered on their own merit, or considered provided they have met other criteria, giving a clear indication that not only was the open access digital availability of the source not the only issue, it also was not the overriding issue. Quality of content and potential market for the work, quite rightly, remain the overriding considerations of publishers (Ramírez et al., 2013)

These data should override the hearsay and urban legend. These data should replace unsubstantiated statements like those the AHA made when it neglected to support the claim that "an increasing number of university presses are reluctant to offer a publishing contract to newly minted PhDs whose dissertations have been freely available via online sources" (AHA, 2013). The AHA failed to address another source of ETDs, the commercial vendor ProQuest, previously known as UMI.

SEARCH ENGINES, UNION CATALOGS, AND PROQUEST

A tradition many universities continue is based on the days when *Dissertation Abstracts* was the most comprehensive source of information about completed dissertations. Today there are several sources, not only of dissertations but also theses metadata. These include the NDLTD as well as WorldCat[5] and the Open Access Theses and Dissertations portal (http://oatd.org),[6] among others. Graduate students are often unaware of these harvesters that don't require forms, signatures, or payment to make ETD metadata publicly available.

Some graduate students see ProQuest as providing an additional opportunity for recognition and a potential source of royalty income. Some students mistakenly believe that ProQuest plays a validating role for their works. Others see it as a solely commercial enterprise that they should not be required to support even once by giving ProQuest their ETDs to sell, never mind twice by also paying ProQuest to gate their ETDs behind a paywall. Some are confused by the ProQuest option for the graduate students to pay an additional fee to remove the paywall for readers' access to their ETDs in ProQuest databases when most of their universities simultaneously provide payment-free public access.

Every few years the topic of the ProQuest requirement resurfaces on the listserv devoted to all topics related to ETDs, ETD-L, beginning November 27, 2007, and most recently February 23, 2011, when ETD-L distributed the query, "Has anyone stopped sending ETDs to ProQuest?" On January 8, 2013, ETD-L hosted Gail Clement's announcement that her blog, "FUSE: Free US ETDs," addressed "U.S. Institutions Respecting Student Choice in Disseminating Their ETDs" (Clement, 2013). It listed 17 well-respected universities that went against tradition and made submission to ProQuest an option for their graduate students. Among others, her blog pointed to "Stanford Dissertations Moving from ProQuest to Google: An Interview with Mimi Calter" by Mary Minow (at http://fairuse.stanford.edu/2009/11/20 /stanford-dissertations-google/). Calter expressed a not atypical sentiment among those who have moved to optional ProQuest participation by graduate students.

> Minow: I understand that this move away from ProQuest means that Stanford student work will no longer be included in Dissertation Abstracts unless the student makes an affirmative effort to submit to ProQuest. What are the implications for the broader research world of such a step?

> Calter: It is a concern, but our sense is that the wide availability and visibility of the dissertations through the Stanford catalog and Google will more than compensate for the lack of a listing in Dissertation Abstracts.

In addition to Stanford the 16 universities that discontinued the traditional ProQuest requirement are Boise State University, Brown University, Florida International University, George Tech, Louisiana State, MIT, Miami, University of Central Florida, University of Georgia, University of Michigan, University of North Florida, University of Tennessee Knoxville, University of Texas Austin, Worcester Polytechnic, Johns Hopkins, and Carnegie Mellon (Clement, 2013). ETD-L contributors suggested additional universities, including the University of Pittsburgh, University of Kentucky, University of Memphis, Auburn University, University of Oregon, California Polytechnic State University San Luis Obispo, and in Canada, Laval

University and the University of British Columbia (http://listserv.vt.edu/cgi-bin/wa?Ao=ETD-L).

Other institutions have less transparent policies in response to student complaints about the ProQuest requirement. While many institutions require that all doctoral candidates, upon approval of their ETDs, submit the ProQuest form, not all institutions follow up to ensure that the forms have been properly completed and signed or that the ProQuest fee has been paid. These staff are listening to their constituents, graduate students, and adhering to the letter of their institution's requirement. They are not doing this in secret, but it is the road they have chosen to follow when their institution is not willing to examine their tradition of requiring students to engage in a commercial relationship with a party outside the academy in order to graduate.

CONCLUSION

Various stakeholder communities have developed around ETDs. There are the graduate student ETD authors, their faculty advisors, graduate schools that oversee the degree processes, libraries as curators of knowledge products, readers and researchers, organizations such as the NDLTD and ProQuest, and ETD search engines. This chapter has briefly considered the relationship each community has with ETDs. This chapter also provides some of the data gathered in the last 15 years about publicly available ETDs.

If the data currently available are not sufficient, then let us gather more and share it openly, not embargo it behind gated repositories or journal paywalls. Let's eschew using statements like a "fair number of publishers" and the faculty member's adage, "at least one former graduate student," when we do not have the data or actual examples. Let's use the data from journal editors and university press directors to encourage graduate students to make their ETDs publicly accessible through their institutional repositories. Let's encourage graduate students to research which publishers they should consider submitting their ETD-based manuscripts to rather than letting them make spur-of-the-moment decisions to limit or embargo access. The NDLTD Innovative ETD Award winners, among others, demonstrate the success of publicly accessible ETDs.

As information professionals we need to curb our enthusiasm for open information access and emphasize what graduate students need to know to thrive once their works are publicly available in the IR. We do not hide any of the facts; we are open about ETD and IR access options. We do not favor default embargoing information and knowledge products such as ETDs. We favor open by default so as not to make hiding information too easy, but we are not coercive. Graduate students must inform themselves about the requirements for their degrees, including whether their ETDs will be publicly accessible by default and whether they must pay to have them placed behind a paywall. Limiting access on the basis of financial contracts is not an ethical way to promote the academy's knowledge products.

In "The Academic Ethics of Open Access to Research and Scholarship," Willinsky and Alperin (2013, p. 33) note:

> What we cannot do is ignore the ethical dimensions of this issue. We must come to a shared understanding of what our obligations are in undertaking this research and scholarship. . . . Our hope is that . . . we might move forward "in search of the ethical university," so that the ways and means by which we distribute what we have learned, as a matter of public trust and public good, might become more public and widely available. It seems like the right thing to do.

NOTES

The title of this chapter is borrowed from Lang (2002, p. 680).

1. Here we use the American definition of master's theses and doctoral dissertations. In this chapter ETDs refers to born-digital theses and dissertations.

2. Hawkins, Kimball, and Ives, English faculty at Texas Tech and Texas A&M, seem to miss the point about "the library's and university's core mission and values" when they complain about the "enthusiasm for OA [open access]" (Hawkins, Kimball, & Ives, 2013, p. 34).

3. Unpublished data associated with McMillan et al. (2013; https://vtechworks .lib.vt.edu/handle/10919/50978) presentation prepared for the 16th International Symposium on Electronic Theses and Dissertations, Hong Kong.

4. See also Dalton, J. (2000, March). ETDs: A survey of editors and publishers. In *Proceedings of the 3rd International Symposium on Electronic Theses and Dissertations ETDs*. Retrieved from http://docs.ndltd.org:8081/dspace/han dle/2340/169; Seamans, N. (2003). ETDs as prior publication: What the editors say. *Library Hi Tech, 21*(1), 56–61.; and Dalton, J., & Seamans, N. (2004).

ETDs: Two surveys of editors and publishers. In E. A. Fox, S. Feizabadi, & J. M. Moxley (Eds.), *Electronic theses and dissertations: A sourcebook for educators, students, and librarians*. Books in Library and Information Science Series (ed. 1). New York, NY: Marcel Dekker.

5. "WorldCat consistently had twice as many citations for which ProQuest had no records. WorldCat provides an important means of locating electronic theses and dissertations" (Procious, 2014, p. 144).

6. As of September 23, 2015, OATD indexes 2,918,516 theses and dissertations (https://oatd.org/).

REFERENCES

ALAWON. (1993, September 8). Department of Education clarifies access to theses. *ALA Washington Office Newsline*. Retrieved from http://serials.infomotions .com/alawon/alawon-v2n37.txt

American Historical Association. (2013, July 23). American Historical Association statement on policies regarding the embargoing of completed history PhD dissertations. *AHA Today*. Retrieved from http://blog.historians.org/2013/07 /american-historical-association-statement-on-policies-regarding-the -embargoing-of-completed-history-phd-dissertations/

Blythe, E., & Chachra, V. (2005, September/October). The value proposition in institutional repositories. *Educause Review, 76–77*.

Clement, G. (2013, January). U.S. institutions respecting student choice in disseminating their ETDs. *FUSE: Free US ETDs*. Retrieved from https://sites.tdl.org /fuse/?page_id=372.

Council of Graduate Schools. (1991). *The role and nature of the doctoral dissertation: A policy statement*. Washington, DC: Council of Graduate Schools.

Council of Graduate Schools. (2009). *Graduate education in 2020*. Washington, DC: Council of Graduate Schools.

Covey, D. T. (2013). Opening the dissertation: Overcoming cultural calcification and agoraphobia. *tripleC, 11*(2), 543–557. Retrieved from http://www.triple-c.at /index.php/tripleC/article/view/522

Crews, K. (2013). Copyright and your dissertation or thesis: Ownership, fair use, and your rights and responsibilities. ProQuest. Retrieved from http://www .proquest.com/documents/copyright_dissthesis_ownership.html

Eaton, J., Fox, E. A., & McMillan, G. (1998). The role of electronic theses and dissertations in graduate education. *Communicator: Council of Graduate Schools, 31*(1), 1, 3–4. Retrieved from http://hdl.handle.net/10919/50963

Eaton, J., Fox, E. A., & McMillan, G. (2000). Results of a survey of Virginia Tech graduates whose digital theses and dissertations are accessible worldwide. *Communicator: Council of Graduate Schools, 33*(9), 1, 7–8. Retrieved from http://hdl.handle.net/10919/50963

Edminster, J., & Moxley, J. (2002). Graduate education and the evolving genre of electronic theses and dissertations. *Computers and Composition, 19*, 89–104. Retrieved from http://www.editlib.org/p/92688/

ETD-L Archives. Retrieved from http://listserv.vt.edu/cgi-bin/wa?A0=ETD-L

Hawkins, A. R., Kimball, M. A., & Ives, M. (2013). Closing the deal: Coercion, ethics, and the enthusiasms for open access ETDs. *Journal of Academic Librarianship, 39*(1), 32–60. http://dx.doi.org/10.1016/j.acalib.2012.12.003

Lang, S. (2002). Electronic dissertations: Preparing students for our past or their futures? *College English, 64*, 680–695. Retrieved from http://www.ncte.org/library/NCTEFiles/Resources/Journals/CE/0646-july02/CE0646Electronic.pdf

McMillan, G., Halbert, M., & Stark, S. (2013). *2013 NDLTD survey of ETD practices.* 16th International Symposium on Electronic Theses and Dissertations, Hong Kong. Retrieved from https://vtechworks.lib.vt.edu/handle/10919/50978

Miller, C. (2013, July 25). Riding the wave: Open access, digital publishing, and the undergraduate thesis. Retrieved from http://scholarship.claremont.edu/pomona_fac_pub/377/

NDLTD. (2002). *Networked Digital Library of Theses and Dissertations strategic plan: Draft report of the Strategic Planning Committee.* Retrieved from http://scholar.lib.vt.edu/staff/gailmac/Files4Berlin/NDLTD/NDLTDStrategicPlan.doc

NDLTD. (2013). *NDLTD ETD award winners 2004–2009: Case studies in success.* Retrieved from https://sites.google.com/a/ndltd.org/ndltd/events/news/ndltdetdawardwinners2004-2009casestudiesinsuccess

Procious, A. W. (2014). WorldCat, the other ETD database: An exploratory study. *The Reference Librarian, 55*(2), 144–150. http://dx.doi.org/10.1080/02763877.2014.880276

Rainsberger, R. (2001, October 12). *FERPA in the digital age: What you need to know.* ECURE: Preservation and Access for Electronic College and University

Records. Mesa, AZ. Retrieved from http://www.asu.edu/ecure/2001/ppt /rainsberger.ppt

Ramírez, M., Dalton, J. T., McMillan, G., Read, M., & Seamans, N. H. (2013). Do open access electronic theses and dissertations diminish publishing opportunities in the social sciences and humanities? Findings from a 2011 survey of academic publishers. *College & Research Libraries, 74,* 368–380. http:// dx.doi.org/10.5860/crl-356

Ramírez, M., McMillan, G., Dalton, J. T., Hanlon, A., Smith, H. S., & Kern, C. (2014). Do open access electronic theses and dissertations diminish publishing opportunities in the sciences?" *College and Research Libraries, 75,* 808–821. http://dx.doi.org/10.5860/crl.75.6.808

Texas A&M University. (2015). Mission statement. Retrieved from http://www .tamu.edu/statements/mission.html

Texas Tech University. (2014). *Operating policy and procedure OP 74.04: Intellectual property rights.* Retrieved from depts.ttu.edu/opmanual/OP74.04.pdf

University of Virginia. (2015). Code of ethics and mission statement. Retrieved from http://www.virginia.edu/statementofpurpose/

Virginia Polytechnic Institute and State University. (2012). Graduate school thesis and dissertation approval form. Retrieved from http://graduateschool.vt .edu/academics/forms

Virginia Polytechnic Institute and State University. (2013, June 3). *Policy and procedures: No. 13000: Policy on intellectual property,* rev. 4. Retrieved from http://www.policies.vt.edu/13000.pdf

Virginia Polytechnic Institute and State University. (2014). Office of the president/ mission and vision statements. Retrieved from http://www.president.vt.edu /mission_vision/mission.html

Walker, G. E., Golde, C. M., Jones, L., Bueschel, A. C., & Hutchings, P. (2008). *The formation of scholars: Rethinking doctoral education for the 21st century.* San Francisco, CA: Jossey-Bass.

Willinsky, J., & Alperin, J. P. (2013). The academic ethics of open access to research and scholarship. In S. Davis-Kahl & M. K. Hensley (Eds.), *Common ground at the nexus of information literacy and scholarly communication* (pp. 25–33). Chicago, IL: Association of College and Research Libraries.

8 | Systematically Populating an IR With ETDs: Launching a Retrospective Digitization Project and Collecting Current ETDs

Meghan Banach Bergin and Charlotte Roh

The University of Massachusetts Amherst Libraries established their institutional repository (IR), ScholarWorks@UMass Amherst, in 2006, and we began by systematically populating it with electronic theses and dissertations (ETDs). We currently have a little over 4,500 dissertations and theses in our IR, and they are some of the most highly used content in our repository. Through a partnership with the Graduate School, we collect and disseminate all of our current master's theses and doctoral dissertations through ScholarWorks. We recently launched an ambitious project to scan all 24,000 of our print dissertations and theses and upload them to our IR.

In this chapter we will outline the details of our retrospective digitization project as well as our policies and procedures for collecting current ETD submissions. We will also discuss our recent decision to stop requiring our graduate students to submit their dissertations to ProQuest and the reasons we decided to make this change. At a glance this timeline shows the development of our ETD program:

1997: Began accepting electronic submissions of doctoral dissertations through the ProQuest online ETD submission system.

2006: Began a Digital Commons repository, called ScholarWorks@UMass Amherst, to showcase the research and scholarly output of our students, faculty, and researchers.

2007: Started collecting electronic submissions of master's theses for the first time. Students submit their theses via an online deposit to ScholarWorks.

2009: UMass Amherst Graduate Council institutes a new policy allowing students to choose open access, campus access, and embargoes for their theses and dissertations.

2010: Library decides to go completely e-only for dissertations and theses; print copies are no longer accepted.

2013: Began retrospective digitization project for our print theses and dissertations.

2014: Revised access options for current ETD submissions. We eliminated the permanent campus-only restriction option and replaced it with a temporary campus-only restriction for one year or five years, after which it becomes open access (except for the MFA theses).

2014: Stopped submitting dissertations to ProQuest through their online ETD submission system. All dissertation submissions are now deposited directly into our IR and submission to ProQuest is optional.

BACKGROUND

At the University of Massachusetts Amherst we started our Digital Commons institutional repository, called ScholarWorks@UMass Amherst, to showcase the research and scholarly output of our students, faculty, and researchers. At that time Digital Commons was sold and supported by ProQuest, and one of the selling points of the Digital Commons platform was that it would come prepopulated with a metadata feed linking to all of our digital dissertations in ProQuest's Dissertations and Theses database. This way we did not have to start with a completely "empty box." We knew that for the IR to be successful and to attract our faculty to deposit their research, it had to contain high-quality scholarly content. One of the easiest types of content to collect was our dissertations and theses, since graduate students were already accustomed to submitting their print theses and dissertations to the library. So in 2007, shortly after implementing our IR, we approached the Graduate School about having students submit their master's theses to the IR. The doctoral dissertations were already being submitted electronically to ProQuest for inclusion in their Dissertations and Theses database, but the master's theses were still being submitted on paper, bound, and added to the libraries' print collection. The Graduate School wanted to move to electronic submission for master's theses, and the IR proved to be just the right solution at just the right time. With the metadata feed linking to our dissertations at ProQuest and the current master's theses being submitted to our IR, we began to think about digitizing all of our older print dissertations and theses in order to build a comprehensive collection.

RETROSPECTIVE DIGITIZATION

It was a long and winding road to launching our retrospective thesis and dissertation digitization (RTD) project. The project had been under consideration since the establishment of our institutional repository. Though we were unable to dedicate time and resources to the RTD project, we did not forget about it. By digitizing our print collection of theses and dissertations and disseminating them through ScholarWorks, we knew they would receive much more use than they do in print format, since print versions are only available to those outside of our university through an ILL request. There were approximately 12,000 print theses and 15,500 print dissertations in our libraries' stacks. Looking back at our circulation statistics, we found that most of them had not circulated since 2006. Only about 3,000 out of 15,500 dissertation titles had circulated since 2006, and the highest circulation amount for any title was 14. Only 1,500 out of 12,000 thesis titles had circulated since 2006, and the highest circulation amount for any thesis was 21. Primarily to make our print theses and dissertations more accessible and increase their chances of being used, we wanted to start digitizing them as soon as we had the resources available to undertake such a large and complex project.

After several years of focusing on scanning books through our scanning contract with the Internet Archive, we had digitized most of the out-of-copyright unique books in our collection and were thinking about what materials to digitize next. An obvious body of unique material was our print dissertations and theses collections. In December 2011, our associate director for Library Services convened a working group to draft a project proposal for our Senior Management Group (SMG) to consider. The working group included the associate director for Library Services, the head of the Information Resources Management (IRM) Department, the Bibliographic Access and Metadata coordinator, the Materials Management Unit coordinator, our Copyright and Information Policy librarian, and our director of Library Development and Communication. The proposal outlined some of the major benefits of the project, which included showcasing our university's research, making the theses and dissertations openly accessible to a worldwide audience of users, providing access for the graduate students who authored the works, and preserving fragile paper copies. We proposed that the project use an "opt-out" model to digitize these materials. We would make reasonable efforts to contact the authors and let them know about the project to digitize their thesis or dissertation. If the author or copyright holder didn't object, we would make the work openly available through our institutional repository, ScholarWorks@UMass Amherst. If they opted out, their dissertation or thesis would still be digitized but the digital copy would be restricted to campus-only access and ILL lending. We also proposed withdrawing the circulating copies of UMass print dissertations and theses after they are digitized. However, we would be careful to make sure that there was an archival print copy available at the Five College Libraries Depository first. If there was no print copy at the depository, the circulating copy would be transferred to that facility instead of being discarded.

PROJECT IMPLEMENTATION AND WORKFLOW

The retrospective digitization project proposal was approved by the Senior Management Group and a team was formed. The team was headed by the assistant to the associate director for Library Services as project manager and representatives from the IRM Department, Library Development and Communication, and the Scholarly Communication Office. The plan was to first digitize all of the pre-1923 dissertation and theses titles that were in the public domain, and then to start digitizing the W. E. B. Du Bois Department of Afro-American Studies dissertations in the fall of 2013. This department seemed appropriate as the main building of the UMass Amherst Libraries is the W. E. B. Du Bois Library, and there is a strong connection between the libraries and the Afro-American Studies Department. From there we would go department by department to digitize all of the theses and dissertations. In 2015, we are digitizing all of the theses and dissertations from the Astronomy, Chinese, History, Psychology, and Polymer Science Departments, which will total about 2,400 titles. At this rate, we estimate that it will take about 10 years to complete the project.

Initially it took quite a bit of planning and preparation to get the project up and running. Our database analyst/programmer pulled a list of all of our dissertations and theses and created an Excel spreadsheet with columns for author, title, year of publication, call number, department, and other information from the bibliographic records in our Aleph library catalog. We then added a number of other columns to the spreadsheet to aid us in tracking and organizing the project. These included fields such as scanning status, permissions response, link requests, and author contact information, among others. We call this spreadsheet the Master List.

We also drafted detailed workflow documentation for the project. Our director of Library Development and Communication worked with the university's Alumni Office to obtain contact information for our graduate alumni and worked on drafting a letter to use when contacting authors about the project. The letter informs the authors that UMass Amherst Libraries are undertaking a project to digitize all of our print theses and dissertations and that our goal is to preserve the documents and provide public access to them. We convey to them that we intend to include their thesis or dissertation in the project. We include a form with the letter and tell the authors that if they wish to receive a link to their dissertation after it has been digitized and made available through ScholarWorks@UMass Amherst, they should return the form to us along with their current contact information. We also let them know that if they do not want their dissertation made available for public access, they should select "Opt-Out" on the form. If they do not return the form with the opt-out option checked off, we will digitize the dissertation and make it publicly available through the ScholarWorks IR. We are also placing a list of authors and dissertation titles on our libraries' Web site that we hope allows authors to contact us to either opt-out or request updates. Staff in the Scholarly Communication Office collect the responses from the paper forms and track the information in the Master List. Our library director also writes a letter to the department head to inform him or her about the project each time a new department's theses and dissertations are scheduled to be digitized.

So far the response to the project has been very encouraging. As we notify alumni of the project, we have been asking them to consider a gift to the library in support of the digitization effort, and we're happy to see our graduate alumni giving back. To date we have sent 1,517 letters to our alumni and we have only received 52 opt-out requests. We received another 456 replies from alumni offering their support of the project and requesting a link to their dissertation. So far only 3% of our authors have chosen to opt out of having their work digitized and made openly available online, and already we have had many positive communications and interactions with our graduate alumni.

One of the most interesting of these exchanges happened when our Book Repair coordinator found several handwritten notes and seven one-dollar bills tucked inside a bound psychology thesis from the 1970s by the author, Rod Kessler, class of '78. Kessler explained that when he returned to campus with his son, a sports reporter, for athletic events or for Undergraduate Research conferences, he would leave a note and another dollar in the pages of his thesis, each time upping the ante for a potential finder and reader. After graduating from UMass, Kessler eventually went on to become an English professor at Salem State, teaching writing, coordinating the Creating Writing program, managing the campus literary magazine, and serving as head of the magazine before retiring last year. Our director of Development invited Professor Kessler to visit the library, and he accepted the invitation. While at UMass, Professor Kessler expressed his approval of the project, saying, "People spend a lot of time and energy to write these things, and then many of them are never read. I'm glad to have the work out there." Another author wrote to us saying, "I wrote my dissertation in 1980. I bought one of those IBM typing balls to give to various typists who typed my dissertation. I wanted to be sure that every page looked like it was typed on the same typewriter. I had a few graphs to describe my data. I went to the art supply store and bought some press-on letters and some very thin black tape for the axes and data line. I was very proud of the finished result. Little did I know that one day I would be writing via e-mail to UMass about something called 'digitizing' and that I would get a link to my dissertation. Things have changed a lot in 35 years." While contacting each author has been a lot of work, it has been encouraging to hear the positive responses from people who are glad their work is available to both them and the public.

After the letters were sent out to the authors, the basic workflow of the project was divided into prescanning work and postscanning work. The print copies of the dissertations to be digitized are pulled from the stacks by the Materials Management unit in the Information Resources Management (IRM) Department. Our project includes a detailed prescanning quality control check to inventory the material, inspect its condition, make repairs, dis-bind if appropriate, note if a copyright symbol is present, and page the archive copy to be sent for scanning if the circulating copy is in poor condition. An Excel spreadsheet that lists all of the titles being sent out for scanning is generated and sent to the Internet Archive. (The Internet Archive calls this spreadsheet a picklist.) Materials are checked out for scanning in the library catalog so we know where they are and so they do not show as available to patrons. The materials are then packed and shipped to the Internet Archive to be scanned.

After the dissertations are scanned by the Internet Archive, the returned shipment is unpacked and the preservation specialist inventories the items and updates the titles in the Master File with the date of digitization. The circulating print copies are then withdrawn from the library catalog and discarded. The completed picklist is sent to our Bibliographic Access and Metadata Unit so that the digital versions of the theses and dissertations can be cataloged and uploaded to our institutional repository. The digital versions of the theses and dissertations are cataloged with an automated cataloging process. We use the completed picklist to identify the Aleph bib numbers of the catalog records for the print versions and then derive new catalog records for the digital versions from the print version records. Those MARC records are then transformed to the bepress XML schema, and the PDFs and their associated metadata are batch uploaded to ScholarWorks. Once the dissertations and theses files have been uploaded, a list of their ScholarWorks URLs is generated and those URLs are inserted into the MARC records with another automated process.

MOVING AWAY FROM PROQUEST

In 2014, we ceased making it a requirement for graduate students to submit their dissertations to ProQuest and instead made it a requirement that they be submitted to our IR. When we initially started working with ProQuest, it was a clear solution because it was the only solution available not only for us but for most academic libraries. ProQuest was, quite frankly, the only game in town, and it was in the common interest for everyone to use the same system so that ETDs would be discoverable in that same database. However, as IRs came into use and as more and more people were using Google and other search engines to find ETDs, it became unnecessary to have them disseminated by ProQuest. In fact, the statistics show that our dissertations are receiving much more use in our IR than they are in the ProQuest database. In 2011, we contacted ProQuest to ask how much use our dissertations received on ProQuest's website, and ProQuest reported that they were only downloaded seven times on average. This is compared to 360 downloads on average for a dissertation in ScholarWorks.

Another reason we made this change had to do with the fact that the ProQuest and UMass systems did not "talk" to each other, so there was no way to automatically get the dissertation files into our IR. ProQuest would FTP our dissertation files to us and then student library workers had to manually upload them to the IR. This took a lot of time and cost quite a bit in terms of student salaries. Graduate students would also ask ProQuest to embargo things without permission from the Graduate School, which governed policy regarding embargoes. In several instances students embargoed items with ProQuest so that UMass actually did not have access to the dissertations! Through some work, we set up ScholarWorks so that it was capable of handling our ETD submissions with our particular embargoes and access restrictions. We also found that the search engine optimization was much better through the bepress Digital Commons system that ran ScholarWorks, so that search results to a particular title through Google led directly to the ScholarWorks version, which was open and accessible, rather than the entry in the ProQuest database, which was limited to paid subscribers.

Another issue that led to our departure from ProQuest was that our graduates began to find their theses and dissertations for sale on Amazon.com and Barnes & Noble. Legally, ProQuest was within their rights, since students had agreed to third-party sales. However, this check box was not fully explained and was assumed to be for the sake of third-party sales in the form of library databases, not as published books and articles. Students were dismayed to find their work for sale, and there was a real fear that publishers would not contract a book that was already on the market. On the one hand, it behooves all of us to be more careful when reading the fine print. On the other hand, since tenure and promotion is directly tied to publication with established venues, it was difficult to understand why ProQuest did not more thoughtfully consider the impact of its sales program. In November 2014, ProQuest announced that it would no longer sell theses and dissertations through third-party retailers like Amazon.com, and that it would remove all items currently for sale. This announcement came two years too late, as UMass Amherst, like many libraries, felt that trust had been broken and had already moved away from ProQuest as an ETD solution.

COPYRIGHT AND POLICY

Many of our policies for theses and dissertations were created with the Graduate School. Graduating students retain the copyright to their work, and they can make their work accessible by choosing:

- Complete open access through ScholarWorks (and ProQuest, if they so desire)
- One-year or five-year campus-only access, which moves to open access after the one year or five years is up
- Six-month or one-year embargo, which is a complete restriction to both campus and noncampus users (can be extended)

The embargo can be extended for any number of reasons, whether because a patent is pending, because of issues of research subject privacy, and even for national security. One exception to note is the Master of Fine Arts program here at UMass, which has the option of a permanent campus-only restriction, due to the unique circumstances of the students who are concerned about future publication and sales of their original work.

Students who previously had restrictions will still have those restrictions honored as applicable. For example, James Foley, a journalist who perished in Syria, graduated from UMass Amherst and had chosen to make his thesis available through campus access only. This is a request we continue to honor here at UMass Amherst.

We sometimes receive requests from alumni or recently graduated students asking if they can go back and edit or delete parts of their dissertation or thesis. In situations like this we let the author know that unfortunately we can't make edits to their dissertation or thesis. We explain to them that the libraries are the custodian of the dissertations, but the Graduate School is the approving authority and that requests to alter the works have to go through the Graduate School.

As previously discussed, we work hard to contact all our authors and respect their wishes. However, like many repositories, we find that sometimes that communication is not returned or the rights holder cannot be found. Our policy is to digitize and make public the work and include a responsible take-down policy if the creator contacts us (unless, of course, the work is in the public domain). This policy was formulated with our copyright lawyer/librarian and is based on the legal rights that go along with an implied license. By submitting their work to the library, the authors have given UMass Amherst license to disseminate their work through the library circulating system. Previously this was done in print, but as so many resources have moved online, it is implied that the library has license to disseminate the works through electronic discovery and access.

Every year there are some students who ask if they should register the copyright for their work. It is an additional fee to register a copyright, and typically we advise students that, unless they plan to benefit commercially from their work, registration does not provide additional rights. In fact, making one's work available publicly through the IR does the work of establishing copyright, since there is a record of creation.

CONCLUSION

Our retrospective digitization project is a large, costly, and labor-intensive project, but by spreading the scanning costs and labor out over a 10-year period, rather than trying to digitize everything all at once, we are able to manage it. Since this is still a fairly new project for us, we are continually working to refine and improve our processes. This project requires a great deal of tracking and organization between many different staff members in various departments in the libraries as well as coordination with the authors of the dissertations and theses. We would like to develop better tools and more efficient methods for keeping track of things like permissions, correspondence with authors, whether a title has been digitized or not, if it has been cataloged, and if it has been uploaded to ScholarWorks.

However, there is no denying that there have been huge benefits to students, faculty, and alumni by having work available through ScholarWorks. The usage numbers are dramatic. As previously mentioned, prior to digitization, only 3,000 out of 15,500 print dissertations were checked out. The most highly used print dissertation was checked out 14 times. Only

1,500 out of 12,000 print theses were checked out, and the most highly used print theses had been checked out 21 times. Since digitization, we can see that every single electronic thesis has been downloaded at least once on ScholarWorks. Even if this is just by the author, it is good that the author has easier access to his or her own dissertation or thesis. The average number of full-text downloads for an electronic thesis is 994, and the most highly used thesis on ScholarWorks has been downloaded 231,000 times. As the numbers show, having ETDs available through the IR has been an excellent way to showcase the work of UMass Amherst graduate students and provide worldwide access to their unique and important research.

Part 3

RECRUITING AND CREATING CONTENT

Once the repository platform has been selected, and the practitioners have made the policy-setting decisions, the next stage is populating the repository with content. As the notion of institutional repositories has expanded, so have the numerous types of content and the strategies and initiatives employed to add them. From the recognized versions of previously published scholarship and multiple forms of gray literature, to the emerging array of repository-based publishing outputs, there are many forms repository content can take, as well as the means to acquire them. The authors in Part 3 examine the different mindsets, rationales, strategies, and initiatives that work best with the various types of potential repository materials that could be deposited, as well as the development of emerging and diverse library publishing programs focused on the creation of new content.

Davis-Kahl begins by discussing the traditional model for content within an institutional repository, previously published scholarship in the form of green open access, specifically on both the engagement and resistance by faculty to self-archiving their scholarship in the repository. Davis-Kahl tries to answer the questions surrounding the themes and patterns to discussing green archiving with faculty, the differences between the disciplines, and what may be the future for self-archiving practices and the general adoption of open access. Davis-Kahl argues that librarians cannot depend on a one-size-fits-all approach toward faculty when conducting their repository outreach and engagement. While faculty perceptions will not be changed in the short term, librarians must make the long-term commitment to raise awareness of the IR, increasing faculty knowledge of their author rights, and to understand and respond to the individual priorities and concerns of the faculty. This way, librarians will possess a better understanding of individual behaviors of their faculty, and also the social constructs within which they operate that may form their individual behaviors.

While Davis-Kahl mentions the strategies for addressing green archiving principles with faculty, Scherer elaborates by presenting the need for a diverse marketing and outreach programs, as well as repository-based services, resources, and opportunities that are focused toward content creators and users. Scherer focuses on what is needed to make an IR more appealing, and what incentives are necessary to increase acceptance and deposits. He further argues that one has to identify the key internal and external stakeholders so that one can better understand the information, capabilities, and services that will create the incentives for participation and deposit. Beyond developing a marketing plan, repositories will need a developed infrastructure of related services, which may include copyright, deposit assistance, metrics and measurement services, and content development.

While green open access has been the standard strategy for content for institutional repositories, there has been an emerging trend in developing publications and other forms of scholarly communication content through library publishing programs. Although there are those who believe the function of a repository should be separate from active publishing, Sacchi and Newton draw together the connections and shared components of both. Sacchi and Newton present the correlations between institutional repositories and scholarly publishing programs for journal-like publications and, as these two programs begin to shift and share additional components, make clear that there are several conclusions that can be drawn about the appropriateness of these two programs merging. Sacchi and Newton's argument is closely built on their own case study of Columbia's Center for Digital Research and Scholarship (CDRS). With more institutions adopting integrated models and cross-institutional relationships being further developed to foster publishing expertise, Sacchi and Newton argue that the current barriers to introducing significant change into the scholarly communication ecosystem become less problematic.

Beyond merging parallel programs and initiatives as a means to introduce significant change, there are other useful benefits of combining institutional repository and library publishing initiatives. As a mechanism for teaching and learning, these interwoven initiatives provide an excellent opportunity for librarians to provide hands-on instructional experiences and learning opportunities to students. Mitchell and Schiff offer an outline for moving beyond the traditional role of a repository to one that becomes the platform for transformative publishing practices and educational opportunities. Mitchell and Schiff explore the role of the repository as both a pedagogical prompt and a necessary piece of the training of future scholarly journal editors. While working with close collaborators at both their home and affiliated institutions allows a starting point for a pedagogical experience as Schiff and Mitchell discuss, it also presents an opportunity for librarians to better understand the variations of the needs and values among the academic disciplines they work with. By attending to the specific disciplinary-based needs, the library publishing program can provide a more dynamic set of benefits and solutions for the entire community it serves.

In Part 3 we see that there are many traditional and emerging mechanisms and programs to build repository collections. We also see how marketing to the creators of the content can be used as a means to further educate constituents on open access and other scholarly communication topics and practices. Each chapter begins with a conversation about past practices and lessons learned from previous scholars and practices. We then see how those past practices and lessons formed the models and initiatives created to address the multiple avenues practitioners may take to populate the repository, while also offering strategies to educate constituents on the value of the content deposited to or created through the repository and possible publishing programs.

9 | Faculty Self-Archiving

Stephanie Davis-Kahl

This chapter explores faculty practices of both engagement in and resistance to self-archiving journal articles in institutional repositories. The view is intentionally broad; examples from different types of institutions across the globe are included, as well as from a variety of disciplines. Though this chapter focuses on what has been reported in the peer-reviewed literature, some highly relevant conference papers and reports are included. This chapter seeks to help us understand and strategize around nonarchiving by faculty, addressing the following questions:

1. What are the major themes and patterns seen in the literature discussing faculty practices of green archiving?
2. What are the differences between disciplines in terms of embracing open access and self-archiving?
3. What are the future directions for examining faculty and self-archiving practices and adoption of open access in general?

Librarians have been working to highlight and showcase faculty research through a variety of means: faculty publication databases (Armstrong & Stringfellow, 2012; Schwartz & Stoffel, 2007; Tabaei, Schaffer, McMurray, & Simon, 2013; Vieira et al., 2014), annual scholarship celebrations, collections of faculty monographs, and so on, so the repository is a natural step forward in providing enhanced access to faculty work for both university communities and the public. Green archiving of faculty articles in institutional repositories has been a standard practice to engage faculty in open access (OA) issues, building on the grassroots efforts that Johnson alluded to in an article published in *D-Lib:* "Institutional repositories build on a growing grassroots faculty practice of posting research online, most often on personal web sites, but also on departmental sites or in disciplinary repositories" (Johnson, 2002). Raym Crow, in a position paper published by the Scholarly Publishing and Academic Resources Coalition, stated that IRs:

- Provide a critical component in reforming the system of scholarly communication—a component that expands access to research, reasserts control over scholarship by the academy, increases competition and reduces the monopoly power of journals, and brings economic relief and heightened relevance to the institutions and libraries that support them; and,
- Have the potential to serve as tangible indicators of a university's quality and to demonstrate the scientific, social and economic relevance of its research activities, thus increasing the institution's visibility, status, and public value. (Crow, 2002)

Clifford Lynch offers a broad perspective on the institutional repository (IR) as a "set of services" and fully acknowledges, "[A]n effective institutional repository of necessity represents a collaboration among librarians, information technologists, archives and records managers, and university administrators and policymakers" (Lynch, 2003). Green OA efforts are active across a variety of institutions and disciplines, using both hosted and open source platforms, with varied levels of faculty involvement and success. Outreach to faculty has long been a cornerstone of efforts to shift and transform the scholarly communication environment, with IR efforts often at the forefront as an option for green OA.

Green archiving, or self-archiving, provides an avenue for faculty to share their work pre– or post–peer review, even when copyright has been transferred to a publisher. Libraries have often built repository services around mediated green archiving as a way to increase participation in the repository, and every year, more universities and colleges enact faculty-driven mandates or policies for open access, with green archiving as a central tenet. Librarians have also broadened the scope of content recruitment beyond the journal article in the hopes that more faculty will become interested and invested in the institutional repository. Collections of educational resources, working papers, gray literature, images, and data are increasingly common in repositories. Federal funding agencies are a vital partner in green archiving as well. The National Institutes of Health (NIH) Public Access Policy requires authors to deposit their NIH-funded work in PubMed Central, and several other agencies at both the federal level will follow in order to meet the new Office of Science and Technology Policy (OSTP) requirements released by the White House in February 2013 (Holdren, 2013). In September 2014, California became the first state to require researchers to provide public access to research funded by the state's Department of Health (2014), and the Illinois legislature passed the Open Access to Research Articles Act (2013), which requires each state university to convene a task force to decide on a course of action for research published by faculty. Major private funders are also requiring open access to the products of research they support, including the Bill and Melinda Gates Foundation and the Howard Hughes Medical Institute. More may follow as open access continues to gain support.

MAJOR THEMES

Comparing the early entries into the literature on IRs and OA with current literature shows the tensions between expectations and reality as well as how far librarians and advocates have worked to engage faculty and to shift perceptions of IRs and OA within constraints (discussed in the following sections). In addition, it is useful to understand that a confluence of concerns persists today when discussing green archiving, and librarians must be ready to respond during discussions with faculty. The articles discussed provide useful background and context for planning outreach to individual faculty and departments and for long-term strategy around self-archiving or for IR implementation in general.

In their seminal paper published in 2005, "Understanding Faculty to Improve Content Recruitment for Institutional Repositories," Nancy Fried Foster and Susan Gibbons examined faculty research habits and behaviors in order to better understand their reticence to utilize IRs. Foster and Gibbons's work also identified a list of individual faculty needs through faculty interviews, a number of which can be fulfilled with the institutional repository. Surfacing these individual needs encouraged changes in the way library liaisons engaged with faculty, moving to an approach tailored to the individual faculty member and his or her research. Davis and Connolly, in 2007, also interviewed faculty to study the low deposit rate into Cornell's repository and learned that generally, the faculty they spoke with had concerns related to copyright, concerns over plagiarism, and concerns that without proper vetting via the peer-review process, any research posted on an IR would be perceived as lower quality, thus negatively impacting a researcher's reputation (Davis & Connolly, 2007). "Learning curve" was also a common response, as was lack of functionality of the IR software (Davis & Connolly, 2007). Xia, also in 2007, echoes some of these themes, but also notes that in departments and institutions where deposits are mediated, deposit rates are higher (Xia, 2007). Both Covey (2011) and Salo (2008, 2013) paint a bleak picture of institutional repository efforts in general, for many of the same reasons as listed above, even though in Covey's study of faculty, participants acknowledged the value of linking self-archiving with annual reporting processes, and also acknowledged the usefulness of features in the repository software.

Kim's 2010 article provides a useful study of factors and variables that have an impact on faculty self-archiving, identifying "support for the spirit of OA" as a main driver, but other factors have a mitigating effect. Kim found differences in self-archiving culture not only between humanities, social sciences, and sciences faculty, but also *within* these disciplines, and that the culture of the discipline does have an effect on self-archiving practice. Copyright, technical skill and age, and time and effort were found to be factors in limiting self-archiving practices. A follow-up study published in 2011 examined other factors that encouraged or hindered participation in the IR, this time focusing on faculty across 17 doctorate-granting institutions. This second study found that copyright concerns, accessibility, altruism, and trust were the significant continuous factors, while tenure was also identified as a major influence on participation in the IR.

Tenure was also examined more closely in a study of English faculty (Casey, 2012). After analyzing faculty deposits in the repository and finding that more than a third came from the English Department, a librarian on the institutional repository implementation team created a study to investigate why, since typically English faculty are not active contributors to repositories. One focus group was made up of tenured faculty, while the other was made up of tenure-track and adjunct faculty at a large university in the Midwest. This research offers a new perspective in the discussions of faculty engagement in the IR by broadening the scope of work to the entire spectrum of faculty work: research and scholarship, teaching, and service. The faculty who participated in the study indicated a willingness to deposit a number of different items related to all three areas, even though both groups acknowledged it may "be difficult to judge the reliability of unpublished material" (Casey, 2012). Both groups also acknowledged issues with sharing teaching materials, referencing "themes of ownership, currency of an item that is updated regularly, and the amount of time and effort it takes to develop many of these items" (Casey, 2012). This study also found that despite a relatively high rate of faculty deposits into the IR, there was still a "lack of understanding about open access publication and IRs in general," with knowledge about both generally uneven in each group. The author did report that the participants appreciated the focus groups for dispelling the misconceptions around open access and IRs.

It is curious that open access is still an area of confusion and myth for many faculty members, given the progress since the 2002 Budapest Open Access Initiative, the increasingly advocacy activity by SPARC, and related legislation in California and Illinois. It is clear that despite major steps forward (e.g., funder mandates; federal policy and federal legislative efforts; vocal, high-profile champions; and even a mention on the Colbert Report), open access is still seen as an outlier. If open access isn't valued by the faculty member because of erroneous definitions or a lack of understanding (let alone awareness), then self-archiving isn't even a possibility. There are several studies that explore faculty attitudes toward open access, which has a direct impact on faculty self-archiving practices. Waller, Revelle, and Shrimplin, in a paper presented at the 2013 meeting of the Association of College and Research Libraries, used Q methodology to better understand faculty attitudes toward open access and identified three main "opinion groups"—Traditionalists, Pragmatists, and Evangelists. By identifying these groups and their support or concerns about open access, Waller and her colleagues can diversify outreach and engagement strategies for each group. The authors said that while they expected to find faculty on either end of the continuum, they were pleased to find the middle group—the Pragmatists—who support OA in general, but have concerns that are "identifiable and addressable" (Waller, Revelle, & Shrimplin, 2013). Kocken and Wical, librarians at University of Wisconsin–Eau Claire, studied their faculty to assess awareness of open access and found that "many faculty members do not have a sophisticated understanding of open access, let alone the level of awareness we hypothesized" (Kocken &Wical, 2013). In 2007, Park and Qin explored perceptions of faculty attitudes toward publishing in and use of open access journals using grounded theory methodology. Their findings reflected several other studies, and also highlighted that publishing choices are becoming more varied thanks to the options afforded by OA initiatives. They also found that attitudes and behaviors are often based not only on the individual researcher's preferences, but also on the community's perceptions: "They assess journal reputation based on social norms established within the field" (Park & Qin, 2007). Further, they found connections through axial coding between several factors, presented in the brief summary below:

- Perception of topical relevance is positively affected by journal reputation.
- Journal reputation is positively affected by career benefit.
- Career benefit is negatively affected by cost.
- Open access journal reputation is positively affected by content quality and vice versa.
- Availability is positively affected by ease of use, but is negatively affected by perception of content quality. (Park & Qin, 2007)

These connections illustrate the complexity of why it has been and continues to be difficult to convince some faculty in some disciplines to change their behaviors and attitudes regarding OA. Finally, Rodriguez addresses generational differences, another anecdotal rationale for nonparticipation in open access, and finds that the results "suggest that faculty authors are not prejudged by their age or tenure status as to their perception of or experience with OA, because these indicators do not appear to be strong predictors" (Rodriguez, 2014).

DISCIPLINARY DIFFERENCES: SCIENCES, SOCIAL SCIENCES, AND HUMANITIES

Attitudes Toward Open Access

Another long-accepted truism in scholarly communication circles is that faculty in the sciences are more likely to accept open access, while faculty in the social sciences and humanities have been slower to engage with open access habits and behaviors. The sciences are funded more robustly than either the social sciences or the humanities at the federal level, which allows more flexibility in paying author processing fees for open access; however, all three groups have had challenges to funding levels in the past. ArXiv.org is often cited as an example of a core preprint archive, and the highly visible examples of open access journals (PLOS ONE, BioMedCentral) are in the sciences. The Office of Science and Technology Policy, announced in 2013, will have the greatest impact on agencies related to the sciences, as will the Fair Access to Science and Technology Research Act (FASTR), first introduced into Congress in 2013 (FASTR, 2013) and reintroduced in March 2015 (FASTR, 2015). The sciences also seem to be more active in the debates over sharing research data and discussions and implementation of altmetrics.

However, even though the humanities do not have an established archive like arXiv, the Social Science Research Network (SSRN), or Research Papers in Economics (RePEc), there are signals that humanists are grappling with questions of access and making inroads into open access. In 2012, the Modern Languages Association (MLA) announced that their journals would allow authors to retain copyright and to deposit the final versions of manuscripts online, on personal or departmental Web sites, institutional repositories, or subject repositories (MLA, 2012). In 2013, the American Historical Association (AHA) released the "Statement on Policies Regarding the Embargoing of Completed History PhD Dissertations," calling for a six-year embargo on dissertations, causing a flurry of debate in the field. A follow-up Q&A with Jacqueline Jones (2013), the vice president of the association's Professional Division, and a column by former AHA president William Cronon (2013) discuss the themes of control of intellectual property, the differences between the sciences and social sciences, and the importance of the monograph in the discipline, especially for tenure and promotion. Finally, the Open Library of the Humanities and Open Humanities Press are two initiatives that have great potential to invite more humanities faculty into discussions and action around open access.

It should be noted that the social sciences have two well-established and well-regarded online systems for early dissemination of research: the Social Science Research Network (SSRN), started in 1994, and Research Papers in Economics (RePEc), started in 1997. While both systems are potential competitors with IRs, librarians can use them to complement the IR and as an informational resource to identify faculty who could be future IR users, and to understand the value of disciplinary repositories compared to institutional repositories (Lyons & Booth, 2011). Even with these long-standing subject repository models, the social sciences have also had their own disciplinary debates regarding open access and the sustainability of scholarly publishing. The Executive Board of the American Anthropological Association (AAA), in early 2012, released a letter stating that "while we . . . share the mutual objective of enhancing the public understanding of scientific enterprise and support the wide dissemination of materials that can reach those in the public who would benefit from such knowledge (consistent with our associations' mission), broad public access to such information currently exists, and no federal intervention is currently necessary" (AAA, 2012a). They later ameliorated their stance with a statement reading in part, "the AAA opposes any Congressional legislation which, if it were enacted, imposes a blanket prohibition against open access publishing policies by all federal agencies" (AAA, 2012b).

Attitudes Toward Self-Archiving

Xia questioned attribution of nonparticipation in IRs to "disciplinary culture theory" (Xia, 2007, 2008), pointing instead to factors such as mandates and policies, and mediated deposits as major factors in developing institutional repository content. In his 2007 study comparing faculty in disciplines with established disciplinary repositories (physics and economics) with faculty in disciplines without disciplinary repositories (chemistry and sociology), he found that in the two institutions with the highest number of deposits, library liaisons or administrative assistants were responsible for 97.7% of those deposits and even at institutions with a mandate or policy, mediated deposits still made up more than half of total deposits. Xia's studies also establish "operational aspects" as key to an institutional repository's success, such as ease of use and presentation of content. In 2012, Xia and colleagues examined self-archiving mandates and policies and concluded that "it is too early in the development of OA repositories to theorize a policy effect, especially given the fact that the change in deposit rate of repository content varies among different types of mandate policies" (Xia et al., 2012). He also seems to shift his position on the impact of disciplinary culture on self-archiving, stating "participation largely depends on the existing publishing traditions within a given institution or discipline" (Xia et al., 2012).

In the library literature focused on faculty self-archiving, there are several interesting threads. In a survey of 279 business faculty, Hahn and Wyatt (2014) found that 69% of respondents did not know if their institutions had an IR and were unconvinced of the value of depositing their works. Respondents also critiqued IRs in general for being time consuming and difficult to use, and a few cited copyright concerns as well. Mischo and Schlembach (2011) had similar conclusions in their study of engineering faculty attitudes toward open access, finding that there is low awareness and low rates of participation. Antelman, in 2006, found not only that social scientists in general engage in self-archiving at a significant rate, but also that publisher policies for self-archiving seem to have little effect on the rate of self-archiving. This led her to conclude, "Just as it is authors and not publishers who self-archive, it is discipline-based norms and practices that shape self-archiving behavior, not the terms of copyright transfer agreements" (Antelman, 2006). Atchinson and Bull (2015) studied citation rates of self-archived articles in political science and found that the authors in the sample have been quite active in self-archiving, and that this has led to a high rate of citation. One fascinating entry into this topic that could serve as a model for future research is Tomlin's study of OA and art history. He notes that one obstacle to greater adoption of self-archiving practices in art history is the lack of access to or lack of policy related to self-archiving: "since the greater mass of art historical journals are published not by large university presses but by smaller societies and associations across North America and Europe, their policies on self-archiving are not readily accessible or, even more troubling, are altogether non-existent" (Tomlin, 2009). Further, Tomlin points out that art history has not fully embraced electronic publishing for scholarship, and that the conversations to push OA forward, within art history specifically, will need to include society publishers, art associations, and museums in conversations about sharing art history research, especially to establish best practices for sharing images in the open access literature.

It stands to reason that different disciplinary practices and attitudes toward open access and publishing in general will have an impact on faculty approaches to self-archiving. Even within the same discipline, faculty may have opposing viewpoints and levels of comfort with the idea of self-archiving, or with the idea of using the *institutional* repository for their postprints. It is also worth mentioning that in order for open access outside of the sciences to be successful, it must reflect the priorities implicit in the social sciences and humanities. It follows, then, that it is vital that on the local level, librarians move away from a one-size-fits-all approach to outreach and engagement. We must employ the skills gained through reference interviews and information literacy instruction and combine those with effective methodologies to form a better understanding of how faculty work, how they share their work, and how they see future uses of their work in order to gain their perspectives on open access and self-archiving. It is well established that the misconceptions and myths about OA, specifically regarding self-archiving, are persistent and many. Librarians must become well versed and conversant in matters of open access, copyright, and pro and con arguments, so they can provide a balanced, nuanced perspective to help guide faculty. Librarians must also understand the scholarly habits, practices, behaviors, and priorities for the faculty and their discipline. Understanding the faculty perspective is crucial, and effective advocacy must take a variety of viewpoints into account to be relevant and trusted. In their study, Park and Qin noted:

> There are two main social constructs driving open scholarly publishing. One is the noble idea of disseminating and sharing knowledge freely, both within learned communities and with the public; the other is the demand for faster, wider, and more effective dissemination of research products, including not only papers but also the data sets and graphics generated in the research process. While technological advances made

open scholarly publishing possible, these social constructs will determine its success or failure. (Park & Qin, 2007)

Librarians stand at the intersection of the social and the technological, and they can act as navigators and translators for faculty who need guidance in both regards. We cannot change the status quo of scholarly publishing alone; we must work with the faculty over the long-term to raise awareness of our IRs, to increase their knowledge of their author rights, and to understand and respond to their priorities and concerns.

FUTURE DIRECTIONS

In summary, the following are still major concerns and obstacles to faculty practices of self-archiving:

- Awareness of the IR as a resource and tool
- Understanding of the advantages of self-archiving (sharing work, citation advantage)
- Misconceptions about open access
- Perceived quality of self-archived materials
- Concern regarding copyright
- Concern regarding plagiarism
- Concern regarding impact on promotion and tenure
- Disciplinary culture and practices
- Status (tenure, tenure-track, adjunct)
- Time (to deposit materials, check publisher policies, alert the library to new publications)
- Effort to learn a new system/interface
- Technical skills

Even though OA is increasingly accepted and utilized as a publication method, business model, and philosophy in some disciplines, both OA, and by extension institutional repositories, are still viewed by some as highly suspect. Framing self-archiving in IRs as a first step toward adopting OA behaviors, such as submitting articles to fully OA journals, could contribute to the overall acceptance and use of *open* in general, especially as faculty and other contributors see increased citation rates and download counts, and as faculty use institutional repository content found via search engines in their own work (either in their research or scholarship, teaching, or service work). It is clear that there are still layers of misunderstanding and lack of awareness, and that outreach and engagement on the part of librarians and faculty champions will be needed in the future to build repositories as a trusted system for sharing faculty work.

Future questions that could aid librarians and advocates in their work include exploring faculty use and perceived benefits of systems such as ResearchGate and Academia.edu in relation to the repository, and effective ways of outreach to and engagement with faculty within and across disciplines not only for awareness but also for action; and, as Molly Kleinman writes, "more work is needed to develop and apply conceptual frameworks to the subject of open access broadly, and to the particulars of faculty attitudes and behaviors with regard to sharing their scholarly work online" (Kleinman, 2011). Finally, as librarians explore faculty practices more deeply, we need to share with one another our best and worst practices so others can apply what we have learned on our individual campuses. As open access continues to grow, we must continue to understand both individual faculty attitudes and behaviors and the different attitudes and behaviors of the distinct communities of scholars that exist on our campuses. Understanding how both the individual and social constructs impact each other is a key element in engagement, debate, and change.

REFERENCES

American Anthropological Association. (2012a). Response to November 3, 2011 OSTP RFI, Public access to scholarly publications. Retrieved from http://www.whitehouse.gov/sites/default/files/microsites/ostp/scholarly-pubs-%28%23282%29%20davis.pdf

American Anthropological Association. (2012b). American Anthropological Association position on dissemination of research. Retrieved from http://www.aaanet.org/issues/policy-advocacy/American-Anthropological-Association-Position-on-Dissemination-of-Research.cfm

American Historical Association. (2013, July 22). American Historical Association statement on policies regarding the embargoing of completed history PhD dissertations. Retrieved from http://blog.historians.org/2013/07

/american-historical-association-statement-on-policies-regarding-the
-embargoing-of-completed-history-phd-dissertations/

Antelman, K. (2006). Self-archiving practice and the influence of publisher policies in the social sciences. *Learned Publishing, 19*(2), 85–95. http://dx.doi .org/10.1087/095315106776387011

Armstrong, M., & Stringfellow, J. (2012). Promoting faculty scholarship through the university author recognition bibliography at Boise State University. *New Review of Academic Librarianship, 18*(2), 165–175. http://dx.doi.org/10.108 0/13614533.2012.717901

Atchinson, A., & Bull, J. (2015). Will open access get me cited? An analysis of the efficacy of open access publishing in political science. *PS: Political Science & Politics, 48*(1), 129–137. http://dx.doi.org/10.1017/S1049096514001668

California Taxpayer Access to Publicly Funded Research Act, California Government Code, Chapter 789, Statutes of 2014. Retrieved from http://leginfo .legislature.ca.gov/faces/billNavClient.xhtml?bill_id=201320140AB609

Casey, A. M. (2012). Does tenure matter? Factors influencing faculty contributions to institutional repositories. *Journal of Librarianship & Scholarly Communication, 1*(1), 1–11. http://dx.doi.org/10.7710/2162-3309.1032

Covey, D. T. (2011). Recruiting content for the institutional repository: The barriers exceed the benefits. *JODI: Journal of Digital Information, 12*(3), 1–18. Retrieved from https://journals.tdl.org/jodi/index.php/jodi/article/view/2068

Cronon, W. (2013, July 26). Why put at risk the publishing options of our most vulnerable colleagues? Retrieved from http://blog.historians.org/2013/07 /why-put-at-risk-the-publishing-options-of-our-most-vulnerable-colleagues/

Crow, R. (2002). The case for institutional repositories: A SPARC position paper. *ARL: A Bimonthly Report on Research Library Issues & Actions,* (223), 1–4. Retrieved from http://www.sparc.arl.org/resources/papers-guides /the-case-for-institutional-repositories

Davis, P. M., & Connolly, M. J. L. (2007). Institutional repositories: Evaluating the reasons for non-use of Cornell University's installation of DSpace. *D-Lib Magazine, 13*(3). Retrieved from http://www.dlib.org/dlib/march07/davis/03da vis.html

Fair Access to Science and Technology Research Act of 2013, H.R. 708, 113th Cong. (2013). Retrieved from https://www.congress.gov/bill/113th-congress /house-bill/708

Fair Access to Science and Technology Research Act of 2015, H.R. 1477, 114th Cong. (2015). Retrieved from https://www.congress.gov/bill/114th-congress /house-bill/1477

Foster, N. F., & Gibbons, S. (2005). Understanding faculty to improve content recruitment for institutional repositories. *D-Lib Magazine, 11*(1). Retrieved from http://www.dlib.org/dlib/january05/foster/01foster.html

Hahn, S. E., & Wyatt, A. (2014). Business faculty's attitudes: Open access, disciplinary repositories, and institutional repositories. *Journal of Business & Finance Librarianship, 19*(2), 93. http://dx.doi.org/10.1080/08963568.2014.8 83875

Holdren, J. P. (2013, February 22). *Memorandum for the heads of executive departments and agencies* [Memorandum from the Executive Office of the President, Office of Science and Technology Policy]. Retrieved from https:// www.whitehouse.gov/sites/default/files/microsites/ostp/ostp_public _access_memo_2013.pdf

Illinois State Legislature, Open Access to Research Articles Act, Public Act 098-0295. (2013). Retrieved from http://www.ilga.gov/legislation/publicacts /fulltext.asp?Name=098-0295

Johnson, R. K. (2002). Institutional repositories: Partnering with faculty to enhance scholarly communication. *D-Lib Magazine, 8*(11). Retrieved from http://www.dlib.org/dlib/november02/johnson/11johnson.html

Jones, J. (2013, July 24). Q&A on the AHA's statement on embargoing of history dissertations. Retrieved from http://blog.historians.org/2013/07/qa-on-the -ahas-statement-on-embargoing-of-history-dissertations/

Kim, J. (2010). Faculty self-archiving: Motivations and barriers. *Journal of the American Society for Information Science & Technology, 61*(9), 1909. http:// dx.doi.org/10.1002/asi.21336

Kim, J. (2011). Motivations of faculty self-archiving in institutional repositories. *Journal of Academic Librarianship, 37*(3), 246–254. http://dx.doi .org/10.1016/j.acalib.2011.02.017

Kleinman, M. (2011). Faculty self-archiving attitudes and behavior at research universities: A literature review. Retrieved from http://mollykleinman.com/ wp-content/uploads/2012/02/Kleinman-self-archiving-literature-review -web.pdf

Kocken, G. J., & Wical, S. H. (2013). "I've never heard of it before": Awareness of open access at a small liberal arts university. *Behavioral & Social Sciences*

Librarian, 32(3), 140–154. http://dx.doi.org/10.1080/01639269.2013.817876

Lynch, C. A. (2003). Institutional repositories: Essential infrastructure for scholarship in the digital age. *ARL: A Bimonthly Report on Research Library Issues & Actions,* (226), 1–7. Retrieved from http://www.arl.org/storage/documents/publications/arl-br-226.pdf

Lyons, C., & Booth, H. A. (2011). An overview of open access in the fields of business and management. *Journal of Business & Finance Librarianship, 16*(2), 108–124. http://dx.doi.org/10.1080/08963568.2011.554786

Mischo, W. H., & Schlembach, M. C. (2011). Open access issues and engineering faculty attitudes and practices. *Journal of Library Administration, 51*(5–6), 432–454. http://dx.doi.org/10.1080/01930826.2011.589349

Modern Language Association. (2012, June 5). MLA journals adopt new open-access-friendly author agreements. Retrieved from http://www.mla.org/news_from_mla/news_topic&topic=596

Park, J-H., & Qin, J. (2007). Exploring the willingness of scholars to accept open access: A grounded theory approach. *Journal of Scholarly Publishing, 38*(2), 55–84. http://dx.doi.org/10.1353/scp.2007.0009

Rodriguez, J. E. (2014). Awareness and attitudes about open access publishing: A glance at generational differences. *Journal of Academic Librarianship, 40*(6), 604–610. http://dx.doi.org/10.1016/j.acalib.2014.07.013

Salo, D. (2008). Innkeeper at the roach motel. *Library Trends,* (2), 98–123. http://dx.doi.org/10.1353/lib.0.0031

Salo, D. (2013). How to scuttle a scholarly communication initiative. *Journal of Librarianship & Scholarly Communication, 1*(4), 1–14. http://dx.doi.org/10.7710/2162-3309.1075

Schwartz, V., & Stoffel, B. (2007). Building an online faculty publications database: An alternative to the institutional repository. *College & Undergraduate Libraries, 14*(3), 1–25. http://dx.doi.org/10.1300/J106v14n03=01

Tabaei, S., Schaffer, Y., McMurray, G., & Simon, B. (2013). Building a faculty publications database: A case study. *Public Services Quarterly, 9*(3), 196–209. http://dx.doi.org/10.1080/15228959.2013.816127

Tomlin, P. (2009). A matter of discipline: Open access, the humanities, and art history. *Canadian Journal of Higher Education, 39*(3), 49–69. Retrieved from http://ojs.library.ubc.ca/index.php/cjhe/article/view/476

Vieira, D., McGowan, R., McCrillis, A., Lamb, I., Larson, C., Bakker, T., & Spore, S. (2014). The faculty bibliography project at the NYU school of medicine.

Journal of Librarianship & Scholarly Communication, 2(3), 1–15. http://dx
.doi.org/10.7710/2162-3309.1161

Waller, J., Revelle, A., & Shrimplin, A. K. (2013). *Keep the change: Clusters of faculty opinion on open access* (ACRL 2013 Proceedings). Retrieved from http://
www.ala.org/acrl/sites/alaorg.acrl/files/content/conferences/confsandpre
confs/2013/papers/WallerRevelleShrimplin_Keep.pdf

Xia, J. (2007). Assessment of self-archiving in institutional repositories: Across disciplines. *Journal of Academic Librarianship, 33*(6), 647–654. http://dx.doi
.org/10.1016/j.acalib.2007.09.020

Xia, J. (2008). A comparison of subject and institutional repositories in self-archiving practices. *Journal of Academic Librarianship, 34*(6), 489–495. http://dx.doi
.org/10.1016/j.acalib.2008.09.016

Xia, J., Xia, J. F., Gilchrist, S. B., Smith, N., Kingery, J. A., Radecki, J. R., . . . Mahn, A. J. (2012). A review of open access self-archiving mandate policies. *portal: Libraries and the Academy,* (1), 85. http://dx.doi.org/10.1353/pla.2012.0000

10 | Incentivizing Them to Come: Strategies, Tools, and Opportunities for Marketing an Institutional Repository

David Scherer

With institutional repositories entering their second decade of existence there have been mixed reactions to their presence and acceptance. While usage data show that users are engaging with the repository, the same cannot be said about those who supply the repository's content. Early assumptions were that faculty would flock to use and contribute to repositories once the repository was established and functioning. But these assumptions never lived up to expectations. The notion of "If you build it, they will come" never happened for repositories (Foster & Gibbons, 2005; Russell & Day, 2010). What is needed to make the repository more appealing? What incentives are necessary to increase acceptance and deposits?

Even for institutions whose faculty began using the repository, the purpose for having it, and their direct benefits, were lost to them. Dorothea Salo describes this as a lack of necessary support provided by the libraries, and a failure of the repository to relate its value to faculty (Salo, 2008). The value proposition failed to continue once content was added to the repository in such a way that encouraged faculty to continue submitting their materials.

From the faculty's perspective, their publications went to the repository and did nothing. Salo elaborates, saying that the institutional repository became, in essence, a "roach motel" (Salo, 2008). Faculty scholarship was added to the repository where it went to "live and die." Faculty did not understand the purpose of the repository or experience the full range of benefits provided to them, their academic community, or the larger populace because these benefits weren't being disseminated in a manner that presented them as incentives.

These shortcomings are not just the results from certain repository platforms, strategies, or institutions, but are shortcomings that all repositories have faced at some point. No matter their background, libraries and repository managers simply could not sustain voluntary faculty engagement with the repository (Koopman & Kipnis, 2009).

An active multifaceted marketing strategy must be adopted for faculty to fully understand the internal and external value of repositories so that they may become active content contributors. Libraries must be able to relate the value of the repositories from multiple perspectives and to multiple invested parties. This may require the creation of new models for repository collection development, as well as the possible creation of new related repository service models provided by the repository itself, or in connection with related library partnerships and collaborations. Marketing a repository is not a one-time activity. Marketing a repository requires sustained engagement delivered on multiple occasions and avenues (Thiede, 2014). These campaigns should also be evaluated and assessed for future development.

This chapter is not intended to prescribe what types of materials the repository should collect, or what the structure or services of the repository should be, but rather is intended to be a chapter on why marketing a repository plays such a crucial role in its success. Developing a diverse, active, and constantly evolving repository marketing plan that emphasizes the numerous benefits and incentives requires an understanding of internal and external stakeholders, offerings, resources, and how they may be applied in effective marketing strategies and opportunities.

IDENTIFYING AND UNDERSTANDING STAKEHOLDERS

Prior to establishing a repository marketing plan, one must identify the key internal and external stakeholders. There are many common stakeholders for institutional repositories. By identifying these key repository stakeholders the repository can understand what information, capabilities, and services must be created to increase the incentives for participation. Repository stakeholders should be identified, and if possible consulted, when preparing the marketing plan (Russell & Day, 2010). The consequences of developing a marketing plan without thinking of those the plans are targeted to could be low levels of interaction and use. For the purposes of this discussion the major internal and external stakeholder groups for most institutional repositories have been identified.

Internal Stakeholder Groups

To effectively market a repository and its services to external stakeholders, the repository must first and foremost seek buy-in from internal stakeholders (Buehler, 2013). The repository cannot succeed under the outreach of one individual or one individual library unit. It will take collaboration among various internal library partners who will advertise the repository with those they interact with the most.

Liaison Librarians

As academic libraries move toward systems-based and campus-wide enterprises, the role of liaisons has also evolved. These evolving roles have turned liaisons into strategic repository partners (Buehler, 2013). Liaisons have the ability to serve as the repository's interpreter, relating the benefits of the repository to their constituency groups and serving as a champion and advocate. Liaisons can serve as the champions of the repository by delivering a more tailored message to groups that could not have otherwise had one in broader marketing campaigns.

For liaison librarians to become successful stakeholders they must understand the research culture of those they serve (Jantz & Wilson, 2008; Walters, 2007). By understanding where and how their faculty currently disseminate their research, liaisons will be able to address how the repository fits into those dissemination models. Liaisons have to see themselves as "change agents" who can express how the repository complements those current models or provides a better alternative. In this way, the liaison has to be comfortable serving as the "cultural intermediary" (Jantz & Wilson, 2008).

Most important, the repository must consider how it markets to liaisons as much as it considers marketing itself to other campus partners. If liaisons are not properly trained and educated about the repository, then they are unable to serve as change agents or cultural intermediaries. This is why training for those who will train others is so important (Bell, Foster, & Gibbons, 2005; Buehler, 2013). Whether it's through a direct point of contact, or through more formal libraries-wide trainings, the repository must first treat the liaisons like any other campus stakeholder requiring the repository's full attention and care.

External Stakeholder Groups

The repository must understand, beyond the overarching goal of providing global online access to the scholarship and research of its campus community, who the external stakeholders are that will be supplying said scholarship and research.

Faculty

While the general focus and makeup of the types of external stakeholders will be based on the type of institution the repository serves, for the most part, most repositories focus on their campus's faculty. Marketing directly to faculty can create the most challenges, but also produce the richest rewards. Faculty are fickle individuals. Although the higher philosophical notions of institutional repositories and open access may appeal to some, the major questions most faculty have when deciding whether or not to devote their time and energy will lie in what they will get in return. What can the repository provide? What benefits will faculty gain by adding their scholarship? Faculty should be made aware of what the repository does to make their content more discoverable (search engine optimization, indexing, metadata structuring) and how the content is being measured (usage statistics and altmetrics).

As many archivists may tell you, there are some faculty who do wonder about legacies. There may be some motivated by the repositories' capabilities for preservation and long-term management of their scholarship (Cullen & Chawner, 2011). While benefits and legacies may help to win over some faculty, the primary challenge in marketing to faculty is awareness and time. Davis and Connolly (2007) found in their study of Cornell University's repository that there were several reasons faculty do not participate in repositories. The primary reasons faculty did not participate included the following:

- Lack of awareness of the repository
- Redundancy with other models of dissemination

- Lack of knowledge and general confusion about copyright and author rights
- Fear of being plagiarized or having ideas scooped
- Preference to participate in disciplinary repository models over institutional-based repository models

Cullen and Chawner (2011) found in their study that the overwhelming majority of faculty surveyed weren't even aware of the existence of the institutional repository. From their study they identified that what faculty really wanted to do was conduct their research, share their findings, and discover the works of the colleagues in their field regardless of the medium. The repository will need to find ways to highlight its use in ways that will allow the faculty to do what they want by using the repository to do so. Faculty will need to have their perceptions altered so that they view the repository as the tool to achieve these goals, rather than a place their research goes to die.

STRATEGIES

When developing the overall marketing plan one should first decide the strategy. The strategy will become the marketing plan's raison d'être and determine its focus. The strategy is also crucial because it could potentially harm the repository if not carefully constructed. As Buehler (2013) points out, "What is said or thought about an institutional repository can determine a flourishing repository, or slow its intake, dependent on the library's messaging and action."

There are several ways to develop the strategy. In some cases, it may be more important to focus on the repository instead of its content. For example, one focus could be on how the repository aligns itself with the overall philosophy of open access. Another could be on the procedures and workflows that are utilized to make interacting with the repository as easy as possible. It may be more pertinent to focus on one or two aspects of the repository that are easiest to maintain and focus on.

When focusing on content, it may be pertinent to focus on what can be added quickly. This type of content is sometimes referred to as the "low-hanging fruit." In a recent study, Dubinsky (2014) noted that many repositories in recent years had experienced rapid growth by determining their low-hanging fruit and marketing directly to those particular stakeholders. No matter the approach, the strategy should be determined in advance and should concentrate on specific areas rather than those that are too broad or generalized.

The Repository

As previously stated, others have found their faculty were not aware of their repository's existence. Thus, focusing on awareness may be a good starting point. Fortier and Laws's (2014) main focus of their recent survey was on repository awareness (regardless if respondents had used the repository or not), the services the repository offered, and what faculty found were unfulfilled service needs. The results of their study found that the largest reason faculty were not participating was because they were unaware of the repository's existence and what purpose the repository was supposed to serve (Fortier & Laws, 2014).

Some have found that the lack of awareness has been due to the naming of the repository. When addressing the issue of a common language and terminology, some have noted that the usage of "institutional" isn't clear enough to relay the purpose of the repository (Jantz & Wilson, 2008). With many institutions having preestablished print repositories, many faculty simply may be confused about the differences between the print and digital repositories. To alleviate this, many institutions have removed the words "institutional repository" from their repository's name altogether. For example, at Purdue University the institutional repository is known as Purdue e-Pubs. (The name Purdue e-Pubs was chosen prior to the adoption of the EPUB format type.) At Clemson University, the newly formed repository is known as Tiger Prints. Both names highlight the close relationship to their home institutions (Purdue and the Clemson University mascot), while also relaying that the repository houses publications (e-Pubs and Prints).

Open Access Philosophy

The relationship of the open access philosophy and repositories can be addressed through both internal and external factors. Internally, with the rising costs of journals, libraries simply cannot afford to subscribe to every journal. Additionally, it also makes little sense to have to repay for the actual scholarship that was created on our own campuses through subscriptions to journals (Crow, 2002). Externally, the altruistic benefits of open access as a service for the greater good of science, scholarship, and knowledge plays a factor in motivating faculty who feel that their scholarship should be freely available. Jihyun Kim found in her study that faculty who most agreed with the altruistic motivation for self-archiving were more likely to have deposited to the repository (Kim, 2011). This implies that for some, it may be beneficial to point out what the repository does to ensure the widest array of discoverability and global accessibility.

Faculty Presence

As previously mentioned, one of the major reasons faculty are not participating in the repository is through a sheer lack of awareness. But another, equal reason is due to the time and effort required to self-submit materials (Fortier & Laws, 2014). This causes most participation to be done passively, creating large gaps of faculty participation in levels that are not reflective of the faculty's actual academic output.

Those faculty who have very little available in the repository may not be fully experiencing the benefits that the repository can provide. To entice faculty to participate, one could focus again on collections (e.g., gray literature such as technical reports or extension materials) that may be low-hanging fruit at their institutions (Bell et al., 2005; Dubinsky, 2014). In some cases, the gray literature may not have the same amount of copyright or versioning control issues that published scholarship may have. This allows faculty to "test-drive" the repository and see how the benefits they are receiving for their gray literature could be paralleled for their published works.

This also applies to the faculty's academic units. The best way for a repository to market its services to its academic community is to focus on its own academic unit—the libraries. This is especially useful if librarians hold faculty status at their institution and would be responsible for their own scholarship and research for promotion and tenure. By targeting the libraries as an academic unit, the libraries can market the repository to other units using itself as its primary example (Koopman & Kipnis, 2009).

SERVICES, RESOURCES, AND OPPORTUNITIES

In 2003 Clifford Lynch (as cited in Walters, 2007, p. 214) described institutional repositories as "a set of services that a university offers to the members of its community for the management and dissemination of digital materials created by the institution and its community." The repository is a service. For a repository to become successful it may need to develop an infrastructure of related supporting services.

These related supporting services and resources may or may not be built directly into the repository, but may be accessed through other related library services and support. They also may not be offered as traditional offerings, but could be offered as a function of the repository. Additionally, the affiliated librarians and staff of the repository should be seen as a part of these related services (Walters, 2007). Joan Giesecke describes this as "old wine in new bottles," where traditional library services are rebranded into functions of publishing that faculty may better understand than if they were offered in new "repository" models (Giesecke, 2011).

Repository Resources

Copyright Services

One of the major reasons noted earlier why individual faculty do not participate in repositories is their fear of copyright. Because of this fear, it logically makes sense that the repository (or related library services) would include some type of training or guidance on copyright and author rights. With copyright transfer agreements constantly changing, faculty will look to the libraries to better understand their rights and the agreements they sign with publishers. It's during those interactions that the libraries could inform faculty which agreements allow repository deposits. While the repository has to respect copyright, it should also provide mechanisms for faculty to understand their copyright, and should develop mechanisms so that faculty may request the necessary rights (either pre- or postpublication) to post a version of their work to the repository.

Deposit Services

While there are several models for faculty to deposit their works (Cullen & Chawner, 2011; Dubinsky, 2014; Giesecke, 2011), the one model that directly targets faculty's issues over time and energy is a repository-based mediated deposit. In this model, the repository serves as the author's proxy, and conducts the deposit on the faculty member's behalf. This model has expanded at some institutions where faculty also give the repository staff permission to seek the rights information on their works and allow the repository to deposit their works based on those findings (Dubinsky, 2014).

Institutions conducting deposits-by-proxy have reported that the leading motivation faculty had for depositing to the repository was due to someone from the repository asking for the work and depositing it on their behalf (Cullen & Chawner, 2011). For example, prior to May 2013, Purdue e-Pubs did not use a deposit-by-proxy model, which led to very little self-archiving by faculty. When deposit services were first offered in May 2013, faculty were more receptive to interacting with the repository, and they began adding their publications based on the libraries' reviews. To date, Purdue e-Pubs now offers faculty complete curriculum vitae reviews, which has tremendously increased the repository's previously published content (Scherer & Wilhelm-South, 2014).

Content Services

What the repository offers for collecting content will be based on several factors depending on the institution. Once content types have been identified, the repository can communicate its organization (faculty publications, theses/dissertations, etc.), as well as develop an institutional repository collection development policy. The central goal of any content policy will be how it affects the relevance of the repository (Crow, 2002). By developing a collection development policy, the repository can highlight to stakeholders the wide range of materials that the repository either accepts or does not. As content is identified these policies can be updated to reflect the collecting decisions for future materials.

Metrics and Impact Services

Many repository platforms now provide mechanisms to measure access and usage. Whether this usage is classified as access from Google Analytics reports, or through direct content downloads, repository usage can be tabulated quantitatively. These metrics provide impressive perspectives that the repository could share with individual authors and campus stakeholders. For instance, on the Digital Commons platform from bepress, authors are provided with automated monthly reports with COUNTER-compliant download statistics over the last 30 days and the lifetime of the material within the repository. These same reports can be aggregated so that schools, departments, and colleges can be informed about the availability and usage of items authored and produced by their faculty and students. This data can then be utilized in the creation of other tools and resources, which will be discussed later. Part 4 of this book provides more information about repository metrics and analytics.

Marketing Resources

Handouts

Although some may argue the effectiveness of physical marketing handouts, these materials allow information and messages to be conveyed when individual interaction isn't available. Handouts allow the repository to carry its message by either presenting additional information that could not be covered in traditional interactions, or passing on information that helps to solidify the messages that were conveyed during physical and digital interactions. Handouts can also take multiple forms and provide different messages. Some of the forms that could be used for repository handouts could be brochures, newsletters, postcards, bookmarks, magazine articles, and press releases (Ochoa, Taylor, & Sullivan, 2014).

Web Presence

Because of the wide range of topics and information that must be conveyed to authors and stakeholders, a secondary Web presence may be needed. Most repositories have one function with little to no educational component. During Open Access Week in 2013, the Purdue University Libraries launched a new Open Access Web site, Open Access @ Purdue (https://www.lib.purdue.edu/openaccess). This new Web site serves as a central location for key resources, timely information, and contact information for university expertise on the issues and topics related to open access.

More importantly, the site provides information and an easy workflow, which members of the Purdue community can use to make their work open access through Purdue e-Pubs with the mediated deposit service from the libraries. This Web site was based on the designs of other institutions with similar sites, such as the University of Kansas open access portal (https://openaccess.ku.edu/).

User/Author Narratives

Although repository usage and access data can provide a quantitative measurement of the repository, they cannot inform about the qualitative impact. Several universities have developed new systems that allow stakeholders to provide a level of feedback to the repository. This allows the repository to better understand its value.

First established in 2012, the Massachusetts Institute of Technology (MIT) repository, DSpace @ MIT, has been soliciting users of the content from the open access articles collections through a link that is embedded on the content's cover page. The link takes the user to a simple form that provides information back to the repository. The submitter then has the option to decide how MIT can use that information (e.g., share it publicly, make it anonymous, or for internal use only). Those stories that have been permitted to be made publicly available can be found through MIT's scholarly publishing portal (http://libraries.mit.edu/scholarly/comments-on-open-access-articles/).

This same activity has also been replicated at the University of Kansas. When asked why the libraries had done this, Ada Emmett, associate librarian for Scholarly Communication and head, Shulenburger Office of Scholarly Communication & Copyright, replied,

> These stories of how access to a particular work benefits a visitor supplements computer generated usage data we gather that includes downloads and locations of downloads. These anecdotal stories offer us additional insights into the reasons and meanings why our users want these items and are highly valuable. The user has to take the time to offer those thoughts and stories and we request permission to make those comments public in order to indicate to our authors and visitors that the intention—to share openly the rich and diverse collection of scholarship created at the University of Kansas—has potential personal and research benefits globally.

Opportunities

Once the services and resources have been established, there will be several opportunities that allow repository staff to interact with its stakeholders and market the repository. In the most recent Academic Research Libraries (ARL) SPEC Kit 341: Digital Collections Assessment and Outreach, Ochoa, Taylor, and Sullivan (2014) found that a majority of respondents (58%) used different outreach and promotion strategies through a mixture of events and opportunities.

Meetings and Events

The value of physical interaction with stakeholders through meetings and events is truly unmatched by any other marketing method. They allow the repository to directly tailor its message based on real-time interactions with stakeholders. These meetings and events can occur in multiple types and levels of formality, including but not limited to one-on-one personal meetings, department meetings, open houses, receptions, exhibits, presentations from outside speakers, and informal brown-bag presentations. By meeting with stakeholders in a multitude of venues, the repository's message can be carried to the widest possible audience (Ochoa et al., 2014). Stakeholders also agree that while the other avenues are important and useful, direct interactions through meetings and consultations provided the most personable approach and the most encouragement to participate (Dubinsky, 2014).

Awards and Recognition

Awards and repository-based recognition provide an excellent way to highlight the work with current repository stakeholders. They also can entice current stakeholders to become further involved with the repository and to become more active participants in submitting their materials. Two examples of how this can be applied would be during key repository milestones and through annual awards recognizing leading stakeholders on campus. In July 2012 (http://blogs.lib.purdue.edu/news/2012/07/16/purdue-e-pubs-reaches-milestone-2-5-millionth-download/) and October 2012 (http://www.purdue.edu/newsroom/releases/2012/Q4/purdue-e-pubs-reaches-milestone-with-3-million-downloads-from-across-globe.html) the Purdue e-Pubs repository celebrated surpassing 2.5 and 3 million downloads. To celebrate these milestones the repository highlighted the item that was downloaded to reach the milestone. On each occasion the repository asked the authors what the repository meant to them.

Since 2011 the Purdue University Libraries have recognized several campus units for their leadership in depositing publications and/or materials into Purdue e-Pubs, and for globally advancing the impact of Purdue scholarship and research (https://www.lib.purdue.edu/scholarlyComm). These events have taken place in the provost's office at the conclusion of Open Access Week. The award is presented by the provost to the awardee on behalf of the libraries. The live event is then followed by a press release that is published through the campus-wide news feed.

This recognition allows libraries the ability to give further recognition to campus partners, while further expressing to the awardees the libraries' gratitude for their participation. Having the press release sent out to all campus members allows campus colleagues to recognize the relationship the awardee has with the repository and to seek a similar relationship for the same incentives and benefits.

Social Media

As the presence of social media grows, its usage as a tool for libraries further extends to marketing the repository and its content. Social media (e.g., Twitter, Facebook, blogs, etc.) allows the repository to connect agnostically to stakeholders and users. While social media can be a cost-effective and low-impact marketing activity, it should not be seen as the marketing silver bullet. Social media may work well for reaching some stakeholders and users, but it will not reach as many as the more traditional marketing offerings avenues (handouts, meetings, etc.) potentially could reach, especially when reaching content suppliers (Ochoa et al., 2014).

CONCLUSION

Although repositories continue to emerge and become adopted, they still have not lived up to the expectations for growth and coverage. By developing well-designed, multifaceted marketing plans, libraries can highlight their capabilities, services, value, and impact, which hopefully will provide the necessary incentives to internal and external stakeholders.

As repositories seek to expand their coverage across their campuses, the need to market their services and impact to stakeholders and users will need to increase. As repositories develop their marketing plans and discover what has worked and not worked, there will need to be a way to disseminate both positive and negative outcomes so that the broader community can evolve and benefit. Marketing the repository can never be a single activity that is done on ad-hoc compartmentalized schedules. Repository marketing has to be an ever constant and persistent activity (Buehler, 2013). As more and more faculty adopt repository-based practices, the libraries will have to evolve their marketing plans so that stakeholders see the repository as more than a tool, but rather see the repository, and more broadly the libraries, as their partners advancing the access and discoverability of research and knowledge created on their campuses.

REFERENCES

Bell, S., Foster, N. F., & Gibbons, S. (2005). Reference librarians and the success of institutional repositories. *Reference Services Review, 33*(3), 283–290. http:// dx.doi.org/10.1108/00907320510611311

Buehler, M. (2013). *Demystifying the institutional repository for success.* Oxford, UK: Chandos.

Crow, R. (2002). The case for institutional repositories: A SPARC position paper. *ARL Bimonthly Report 223.* Retrieved from http://works.bepress.com /ir_research/7

Cullen, R., & Chawner, B. (2011). Institutional repositories, open access, and scholarly communication: A study of conflicting paradigms. *Journal of Academic Librarianship, 37*(6), 460–470. http://dx.doi.org/10.1016/j.acalib.2011.07.002

Davis, P. M., & Connolly, M. J. L. (2007). Institutional repositories: Evaluating the reasons for non-use of Cornell University's installation of D-Space. *D-Lib Magazine, 13*(4). Retrieved from http://www.dlib.org/dlib/march07/davis /03davis.html

Dubinsky, E. (2014). A current snapshot of institutional repositories: Growth rate, disciplinary content and faculty contributions. *Journal of Librarianship and Scholarly Communication, 2*(3), 1–22. http://dx.doi.org/10.7710/2162 -3309.1167

Fortier, R., & Laws, E. (2014). Marketing an established institutional repository: Marquette libraries' research stewardship survey. *Library Hi Tech News, 31*(6), 12–15. http://dx.doi.org/10.1108/LHTN-05-2014-0038

Foster, N. F., & Gibbons, S. (2005). Understanding faculty to improve content recruitment for institutional repositories. *D-Lib Magazine, 11*(1), 1–11. Retrieved from http://www.dlib.org/dlib/january05/foster/01foster.html

Giesecke, J. (2011). Institutional repositories: Keys to success. *Journal of Library Administration, 51*(5–6), 529–542. http://dx.doi.org/10.1080/01930826.2011.589340

Jantz, R. C., & Wilson, M. C. (2008). Institutional repositories: Faculty deposits, marketing and the reform of scholarly communication. *Journal of Academic Librarianship, 34*(3), 186–195. http://dx.doi.org/10.1016/j.acalib.2008.03.014

Kim, J. (2011). Motivations of faculty self-archiving in institutional repositories. *Journal of Academic Librarianship, 37*(3), 246–254. http://10.1016/j.acalib.2011.02.017

Koopman, A., & Kipnis, D. (2009). Feeding the fledgling repository: Starting an institutional repository at an academic health sciences library. *Medical Reference Services Quarterly, 28,* 111–122. http://dx.doi.org/10.1080/02763860902816628

Ochoa, M. N., Taylor, L. N., & Sullivan, M. V. (2014). SPEC Kit 341: Digital collection assessment and outreach (August 2014). *Association of Research Libraries.* Retrieved from http://publications.arl.org/Digital-Collections-Assessment-Outreach-SPEC-Kit-341/

Russell, R., & Day, M. (2010). Institutional repository interaction with research users: A review of current practice. *New Review of Academic Librarianship, 16*(1), 116–131. http://dx.doi.org/10.1080/13614533.2010.509996

Salo, D. (2008). Innkeeper at the roach motel. *Library Trends, 57*(2), 98–123. http://dx.doi.org/10.1353/lib.0.0031

Scherer, D., & Wilhelm-South, M. (2014). *Facilitating faculty participation: Providing the repository service model catalyst for faculty deposits with the Purdue e-Pubs repository* (Libraries Faculty and Staff Presentations, Paper 61). Retrieved from http://docs.lib.purdue.edu/lib_fspres/61/

Thiede, M. (2014). On open access evangelism. *Serials Librarian, 67,* 21–26. http://dx.doi.org/10.1080/0361526X.2014.915608

Walters, T. O. (2007). Reinventing the library—How repositories are causing librarians to rethink their professional roles. *Libraries and the Academy, 7*(2), 213–225. http://dx.doi.org/10.1353/pla.2007.0023

11 | Repository as Publishing Platform

Simone Sacchi and Mark Newton

Within academic libraries, programs around digital repositories and scholarly publishing have matured in tandem over the first part of the 21st century. Under the programmatic umbrella of *scholarly communication,* libraries have employed staff to work on common digital platforms to support institutional aims for partnering in the creation of and access to scholarly materials originating with authors, editors, and other content producers at their home institutions. Across the platforms that enable these programs and the library staff acting as agents to operate them, there are many correlations. In some instances, it is precisely the same staff members and the same platforms performing the core functions of both the repository and scholarly publishing programs. This chapter examines the functions and processes across both of these areas of programmatic emphases, making a more precise specification of this correlation. As repository- and library-based publishing programs are shown to share essential components, some conclusions about the appropriateness for integrating these programs, as well as for communicating the publishing role of the repository and the implication for libraries, are drawn out for discussion.

PRELIMINARY DEFINITIONS

The following discussion necessitates some definitional boundaries around *repository* and *publishing* for context.

Repository: By *repository,* we mean *institutional repository* (or IR), which is network-connected infrastructure that supports the discovery, access, and preservation of research materials produced by the faculty, staff, and students of individual institutions of higher education. Repositories, as discussed here, are library-administered programs, and local collection policies for content acquisition may vary. We distinguish here between *mediated repository* and *nonmediated repository*.

- **Mediated repository:** By *mediated repository* we mean a repository where the content submitted goes through a process of review and refinement in its description typically conducted by professional librarians and other library staff before acceptance.

- **Nonmediated repository:** By *nonmediated repository* we mean a repository where publication after submission in expedited after little or no human processing. *Nonmediated repositories* also typically enable the submitting user to make changes in the content of the repository, including changes in the files and related metadata description.

Publishing: By *publishing* here we restrict the context to *online scholarly publishing* (or e-publishing), the process of selecting, reviewing, refining, compiling, and making available the results of research and scholarship (such as articles into a peer-reviewed online journal).

Publication: By *publication,* however, we discuss the abstraction of communicating the results of science and scholarship, which may be accomplished through repositories and journals, among others.

Stewardship: By *stewardship* we intend *digital stewardship*, the series of managed activities to ensure access to digital content into the future and through changes in technology.

INTEGRATING REPOSITORY AND PUBLISHING PROGRAMS: A RATIONALE

There are many available examples of integration of digital repository and publishing programs in academic libraries. At the staffing level, it is often the role of a single person, small cluster, or FTE fraction to accommodate the functions of both programs, as is evident in the latest job advertisements seeking library professionals to staff scholarly communication programs (Bonn, 2014).

It is also true that platform investments commonly accommodate both *publishing* and *repository* functions. A recent survey of the respondents to a call for information on publishing activity in academic libraries suggests exactly this: 41% of respondents report using Digital Commons (a hosted hybrid journal publishing/repository solution). An additional 29% of respondents support publishing activity through the DSpace repository platform,[1] and yet another 15% do so on the Fedora Commons repository platform (Lippincott, 2014). Such crossover is hardly surprising, given the publication role repositories fulfill for institutions and the limited resources that libraries can allocate to development and areas of growth.

Despite the prevalent use of repository software among library publishers, the intentional separation of repository and publishing programs is also apparent at the platform level. The majority of respondents (mirroring results from a series of surveys over the past decade)[3] use the open source Open Journal Systems[2] to provide local editors with a manuscript solicitation, review, and publication toolkit. Even from an infrastructure perspective, sharing the same *platform* does not necessarily mean *service* integration: content in university-published journals is not always available in the repository, and similar processes (such as submission, review, archival, and dissemination) may be implemented separately.

Notwithstanding this apparent integration, repository and journal publishing programs may be administered separately, each with its own agenda, goals, and means. Library publishing programs indicate the intent of academic libraries to participate in the creation of new knowledge,[4] while repositories may be understood as vehicles for the distribution of scholarly communication and not, as Clifford Lynch notes in his landmark paper, as a "call for a new scholarly publishing role for universities" (Lynch, 2003). Reticence to formally, publicly affiliate repository and publishing programs may still be observed. Surveys of publishing activity in libraries routinely ask respondents to segregate repository and publishing activity in an apparent attempt to capture discrete pockets of activity. Open access advocates may find the publishing function of repositories to be an unwelcome conflation as well, diverting scarce resources and diluting the core message to potential content depositors.

Preliminary Observations

A call for an integrated approach between repositories and university-published journals is not new within the scholarly communication community. Soon after the publication of the Open Archives Initiatives[5] Protocol for Metadata Harvesting (OAI–PMH), advocates for a change in scholarly communication envisioned a global adoption of the OAI Protocol such that "overlay journals"[6]—that is, journals implemented and managed as service providers over content in a repository—could take advantage of a distributed network of interoperable repositories sharing their content. Their ambition, however, has yet to fully materialize.

The authors' proposal for an integrated model here is somewhat similar in approach, at least functionally, but it is applied in the context of repository and library publishing programs within an institution. This perspective is driven by an analysis of their internal situation at Columbia University where repository and publishing programs coexist at the Center for Digital Research and Scholarship (CDRS).[7] Whether repository and publishing programs are already established enterprises within an institution or just at a preliminary analysis stage, library administrators of such programs might benefit from the analysis presented here and the emerging assessment framework.

The Columbia University Case Study

The Center for Digital Research and Scholarship (CDRS) at Columbia University Libraries (CUL)[8] is engaged in both a mature repository program, with its Academic Commons[9] research repository, and a thriving journal publishing program, with more than 20 publishing partners across the university. Although the collective efforts of the center have always been driven by mutually fruitful conversations between the staff responsible for both repository and journals publishing, the two programs have been developed in parallel since the center's inception in 2007.

> **Repository Program:** Academic Commons runs on a Fedora Commons–based infrastructure (hereafter: *Fedora*[10]). The Fedora repository instance is shared with other digital collection projects within the CUL system. The Academic Commons collection, however, is independently indexed and presented online through a faceted-browse search-and-discovery front-end. Custom applications (e.g., self-deposit interface, cataloging tool) have been developed to manage mediated ingest and quality control over the object metadata descriptions.
>
> **Library Publishing Program:** Journal publishing at CDRS is achieved in a variety of context-dependent ways. Partner projects vary by platform (e.g., Open Journal Systems and WordPress), by type of content

published (full articles, abstracts only, supplementary content affiliated with the journal brand), and by build approach (collaborative development or CDRS-managed). The approach to partnership development (and a loose adherence to prescribed project tiers) therefore coheres the program above all else. Much of the team's recent work has focused on the development of custom journal publication templates to expedite production and improve the prospects for scaling to accommodate additional partners (Newton, Cunningham, & Morris, 2013; Perry, Borchert, Deliyannides, Kosavic, & Kennison, 2011).

To this point, integration between the two programs has been managed through specific terms that permit repository contribution of journal content as specified in the Master Service Agreements outlining the primary responsibilities of the partners (i.e., the editors). Center staff working on the repository and journals communicate the specific parameters using issue-tracking software, and additions of CDRS-published journal content to the repository are committed manually by repository staff.

A significantly tighter platform integration between the programs, however, has been proposed. Advantages could then be realized at several levels (from the practical and administrative to the programmatic and strategic):

- Reducing the overall number of platforms managed within the center, thus improving prospects for allocating limited development staff to work within a more aligned and sustainable codebase, thus scaling up the number of partner projects to meet demand
- Taking advantage of the preservation functionality of the repository infrastructure and avoiding content duplication
- Multichannel dissemination, facilitating discovery, reach, and impact of the submitted content from different interfaces
- Repurposing of content and metadata from a unique authoritative source, improving consistent dissemination and interoperability capabilities
- Coordinating outreach opportunities: leveraging both the repository and publishing program user bases for coordinated messaging and outreach

Integration, however, presents new challenges. From a technical perspective, platform-level integration means purposeful segue from well-worn tools and approaches to ones less familiar. Also, WordPress and Open Journal Systems employ one set of technologies and languages, while the applications developed to manage content within Fedora use another, making the transition or alignment less straightforward. Further, integration reveals swaths of policy questions to be resolved:

- All content published in Academic Commons is *necessarily* freely accessible, but not all of CDRS' partners produce open access journals. This is not a problem today as CDRS does not facilitate limited or gated access to journal articles through its partnerships. Still, the policies of the repository will constrain the range of possibilities for individual editorial policies in the matters of persistence, access, and reuse. It is unclear whether program integration would necessitate a series of policy reconciliation discussions.
- The matter of persistent identifier assignment is already complex. Persistent DOIs are created for published repository content, regardless of whether the files themselves are exact copies for which the original publisher also created an identifier. Identifiers are also prepared for a number of CDRS partner journals. Reigning in the multiplicity of identifiers at play as well as the locations and contents of their resolution will be necessary to further align the programs.
- It is presumed further that program integration will apply first to prospective partnerships and published content. How then to retrospectively reconcile the bodies of published content? To date, content published through CDRS partnerships has duplicative access points, retrievable both on the original publishing platform and the repository.

All of these concerns can, of course, be managed practically. Despite caveats and complications, the authors believe the benefits of deliberate program integration exceed them.

FUNCTIONS AND PROCESSES IN SCHOLARLY COMMUNICATION: AN ANALYSIS OF INTEGRATION STRATEGIES

The approach presented here is based on mapping the elemental functions in scholarly communication against processes in repository and library publishing programs to identify and assess integration strategies. The emerging framework—presented in the next section—is based on the analysis of the Columbia case study, but may be generalizable to other institutional contexts as an analytical device for assessing the feasibility and appropriateness of similar integration efforts.

A Functional Perspective on Scholarly Communication

Roosendaal and Geurts in an influential paper (Roosendaal & Geurts, 1997) presented an analysis of scholarly communication in terms of core functions—*Registration, Certification, Awareness,* and *Archiving*—that can be summarized as follows.[11]

> **Registration** allows claims of precedence for a scholarly finding.
> **Certification** establishes the validity of a registered scholarly claim.
> **Awareness** allows actors in the scholarly system to remain.
> **Archiving** preserves the scholarly record over time.

A 2002 position paper prepared for SPARC by Raym Crow (Crow, 2002) compares, with respect to these functions, the traditional academic journal system model of scholarly communication to a new online disaggregated model. The analysis demonstrates how the elemental scholarly communication functions, many of which are already performed (if not organized) by members of academic institutions, can be directly and effectively enabled and sustained within the institutions themselves. This visionary approach relied on the aforementioned distributed global network of interoperable repositories sharing their content via the OAI-PMH. While institutional repositories have constantly grown both in numbers and in content, the conditions—in terms of collective effort and shift in the academic culture and practice—required to realize such an interoperable infrastructure never really obtained.

The functions of scholarly communication are therefore covered in an environment where the traditional journal publishing system coexists with institutional repositories (see Figure 11.1).

Intuitively, the *Registration* and *Awareness* functions are fulfilled by both the traditional journal publishing system and institutional repositories: they both capture and record attribution and date of submission, and both provide means to the scientific community to access the submitted content

✔: enabled ○: incomplete	Registration	Awareness	Certification	Archiving
Traditional publishing system	✔	✔	✔	○
Repository system	✔	✔	○	✔

Figure 11.1. Scholarly communication functions enabled by the traditional publishing system and repository programs.

(once accepted in their final version). The other two functions—*Certification* and *Archiving*—when present, are typically expressed differently within the traditional publishing system and institutional repositories.

Repositories are not typically equipped to adequately fulfill the *Certification* function: the credibility granted by the "associative certification" applied by a recognized academic institution to content within its repository is insufficient to certify content quality. The peer-review process traditionally associated with journal publication, alternatively, persists as a widely acceptable means of certifying the quality of research within disciplinary communities, and publishing in established peer-reviewed journals is still a major component of the promotion and tenure system in academia.

Journal publishers operating in a traditional publishing environment used to rely on academic libraries for the *Archiving* function over print content. Although joint initiatives between participating libraries and traditional publishers have been developed to solve archiving and preservation issues over publisher-licensed digital content (e.g., LOCKSS,[12] CLOCKSS,[13] and Portico[14]), individual academic institutions retain an archiving interest over the entire range of scholarly outputs produced by their communities. Institutional repositories play an active role in this context, enabling the *Archiving* function within academic institutions by adopting platforms (e.g., Fedora) with which to manage digital content and support auditing functions such as those required by the ISO 16363/TDR Trusted Digital Repository.[15]

The SPARC paper imagines the outgrowth of repository programs to happen amidst a scholarly communication landscape where journal production is managed primarily by commercial and scholarly society stakeholders. Further, it does not explicitly address the presence of journal

Function	Process	Actor	Sponsor	Program
Registration	Submit to the repository	Authors	Academic Institution	*Repository Program*
	Submit to the journal	Repository team	Journal	*Library Publishing Program*
Certification	Associative certification	Institution	Academic Institution	*Repository Program*
	Peer review	Referees	Journal	*Library Publishing Program*
Awareness	Repository access / API	Repository Program	Academic Institution	*Repository Program*
	Journal access / API	Publishing Program	Journal	*Library Publishing Program*
Archiving	Perpetual access	Library	Academic institution	*Repository Program*

Figure 11.2. Functional affinity between repository- and library-based publishing programs.

publishing programs developed and administered within academic libraries—the same setting where repository programs frequently are established. If we apply the analysis criteria identified therein to library-based publishing programs, the convergence with the suggested repository-based disaggregated model becomes more apparent (see Figure 11.2).

Certain processes, such as *perpetual access,* completely converge, being components of the inherent mission of academic libraries. Other processes are apparently distinct. However, when abstracted from their contingent implementation they manifest shared essential characteristics. While the notion of *overlay journal* has yet to emerge as a competitive alternative to the established publishing system, a similar approach can be adopted locally at individual institutions by aligning and integrating library-based publishing and repository programs.

Processes in Repository and Publishing Programs Within Libraries

Repository programs and publishing programs within academic institutions can be understood in terms of processes that, combined, describe typical workflows within them.

Repository Programs

Consider the repository perspective first. We can describe the workflow of an institutional repository infrastructure according to the following macro-level managed processes. No assumption is made on how these processes are implemented at the technology level.

> **Submission:** The process by which new content is submitted to and received by a repository.
>
> **Review:** The process by which submitted content is assessed against eligibility criteria and accepted in the repository. Criteria include but are not limited to fitness to the collection policy and intent as well as quality assurance on the submitted item and the associated description. Such a process may be enabled entirely by policy (e.g., any item submitted by an eligible community member may pass *review*).
>
> **Distribution:** The process by which content accepted into a repository is made available online to the intended audience.
>
> **Curation:** The ongoing process of ensuring the persistent access and availability of content admitted into a repository, including but not limited to, routine audit, metadata remediation, infrastructure maintenance, and format migration.

Aspirationally (if not always functionally), repositories fulfill both a *Publication* and a *Stewardship* role within academic institutions (i.e., they are meant to provide persistent access to their content for the future). Therefore we included here a *Curation* process.

Library Publishing Programs

The workflow of individual journals within a library publishing program can be effectively described, appealing to similar, if not identical macro-level managed processes:

Submission: The process by which new content is submitted to and received by a journal.

Review: The process by which submitted content is assessed in scope, quality, and form, ending with a publishing decision over submitted content. Review is an iterative process that may account for a number of editor-, review-, and author-introduced revisions. Peer review is a component of *Review*. Production (the process of preparing content for publication, including but not limited to copyediting, formatting, typesetting, etc.) is as well.

Distribution: The process of publishing the content in a form intended as the final authoritative one for the journal.

Curation: The ongoing process of ensuring the persistent access and availability of the published content, including but not limited to routine audit, metadata remediation, infrastructure maintenance, and format migration.

The similarities with the repository processes presented above, in particular when considering mediated repositories, is not only in the common terminology adopted here; the essence of the described processes is very much the same if we abstract from the contingencies of how these processes are instantiated and the potentially different actors involved. Library publishing programs provide some level of *stewardship* over their content (part of which is involved in the iterative *Review* process), but not necessarily to the level expected by the mature digital stewardship program where content is curated for the long term. Nevertheless we include here the *Curation* process as well, with the expectation that mature library publishing programs would act to ensure the digital longevity of their published content.

The specifications for the high-level processes inherent in repository systems and journal publishing programs are similar enough to become indistinguishable at the program level. In both workflows, content to be published follows a process of submission, review, and preparation prior to publication. The functions inherent to each process step, the sufficiency criteria applied, and the agents conducting the assessment and performing the functions necessarily differ. For example, a fairly traditional journal publishing *Review* process involves a series of communications between editors and reviewers in the discussion of specific criteria applied to the

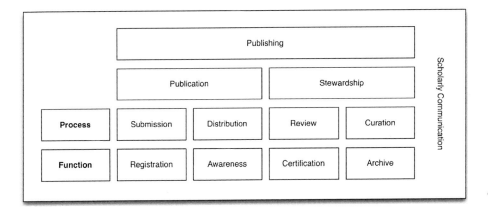

Figure 11.3. Assessment framework modeling functions and processes.

submission before arriving at a publication decision. In the repository, such an "academic quality" review might be covered by: (a) submission criteria that admit only postprints of accepted journal articles; (b) a collection policy that permits administrators to act as editors and curators over subsections of collected content; or (c) a single repository administrator acting upon ad hoc publication criteria.

AN EMERGING ASSESSMENT FRAMEWORK

The analysis presented so far allows us to derive an assessment framework defining the requirements to successfully fulfill the core functions of scholarly communication in terms of processes (see Figure 11.3). This framework applies an integrated perspective that considers both a repository program and a journal publishing program within a library.

The approach taken here models the activities that are required to enable the core functions of scholarly communication in terms of the aforementioned processes. The registration and awareness functions together describe the minimum requirements for communicating research and scholarship and correspond to *Publication* in the model. The core processes that instantiate *Publication* are *Submission* and *Distribution*. The *Publication* activity is, however, understood as a component of a broader *Publishing* enterprise, which also includes *Stewardship* of submitted content. *Stewardship* is instantiated by the processes of *Review* and *Curation* where content is iteratively assessed, refined, accepted for publication, but also where recurring auditing activities ensure its perpetual access and provide a long-term perspective on the issue of digital longevity, closing the circle of scholarly communication.

When considering a repository and publishing program, this framework can be applied at multiple levels for assessing the following:

1. The capabilities of an organization to satisfy the basic requirements for effective scholarly communication
2. The contextual feasibility and benefits of integrating a publishing program with a repository program
3. The modularity and extensibility of technical infrastructures

Applying this framework to existing or envisioned scenarios allows stakeholders to programmatically assess their programs in place. The previously presented case study at Columbia is provided as an example.

An Application Example

The Columbia University case study presented earlier in this chapter provides an example scenario where this framework can be applied to assess the integration feasibility of a mediated repository program such as Academic Commons and a mature publishing program such as the one carried on at CDRS.

Publication of content on both Academic Commons and in many of the journals that are managed within the CDRS Publishing Program involves the following managed processes: *Submission, Review,* and *Distribution.* Despite being implemented differently—in terms of both adopted technology and practical procedures—this convergence provides the common ground for evolving our *publishing* enterprise into a more integrated infrastructure.

When considered from this analytical perspective, the integration process can be decomposed into components that reflect the identified processes, each individual one addressed (potentially) at different stages. Academic Commons is also intended to provide long-term digital preservation capabilities, *de facto* implementing the *Curation* process. Right now some journals within the publishing program submit their content to Academic Commons, but this light integration leaves open a series of issues, including the replication of content between platforms, with the inevitable issue of version and variance management. A tighter integration would completely leverage the Fedora component of Academic Commons not only as a preservation infrastructure, but also as the infrastructure to provide access (though the individual journal front-ends) to the authoritative copy of each article.

The modular and layered infrastructure of Academic Commons is already suited to support not only multiple distribution channels, but also multiple submission channels, supporting a tighter, yet flexible integration of both the *Distribution* and the *Submission* processes via module extensions. The focus of this high-level assessment is to show how the framework can be leveraged to model real situations and break down an infrastructure into more manageable process-based components. The situation at CDRS can be described as a scenario with a *nonmediated repository* and a *publishing program*. Depending on the specific setting and contexts of an institution, other prototypical scenarios can be identified and analyzed according to the framework.

TOWARD AN INTEGRATED MODEL OF INSTITUTIONAL PUBLISHING

The proposed integrated model of institutional publishing suggests opportunities for libraries looking to advance both publication programs and persistent access and preservation repositories. For many existing programs, this is evident: either the selected repository platform promotes these possibilities out of the box (e.g., Digital Commons and DSpace), or the practical constraints around resourcing scholarly communication programs require the flexibility to apply staff and infrastructure to multiple service approaches.

But even for those institutions where journal publishing and digital repository programs have matured largely independently, such as at Columbia, the rationale for adjusting the program development roadmap toward purposeful integration becomes apparent. In the integrated view, the repository becomes the publishing platform, both in the outreach and communication and in the approach to platform development. Language matters, however, in outreach to authors and depositors about the availability of new library programs and services. Despite the alignment of function and process, program managers may prefer differentiation between the useful concepts "deposit" and "publish" to direct contributing authors to multiple service entry points, and still the benefits of observing the integrated model may persist.

Program integration may serve to enhance the scalability of services and to maximize the efforts of limited staff working with the publishing platform. This may be at odds at times with the spirit of experimentation and flexibility around the business model and customized application development approach to journal publishing in libraries. Does the integrated model of program development therefore pose a threat to the core value propositions and differentiating factors for journal editors participating in such programs?

Underlying all of this speculation, of course, rests the presumption that institutions will choose to continue resourcing a shift in scholarly publishing infrastructure in ways that bring capacity and expertise in-house, returning control of a once arcane and print-based process to authors and the universities that support their work. Integrated publishing programs within libraries lay the necessary groundwork for viable, complementary alternatives to traditional publishing and archiving scenarios. Covering most of the components of the scholarly communication workflow, repository programs have demonstrated that commitment to the requisite infrastructure; of particular note are the extensible platforms that have resulted from sustained, coordinated multi-institutional, volunteer, and consortial efforts. Through publishing programs in libraries, the remaining essential components come into view, aided again by formal, cross-institutional initiatives that foster publishing production expertise among library staff. The barriers to introducing manageable, cost-efficient options for publishing scholars through the proliferation of library-led repositories at the programmatic level are few and dwindling.

NOTES

1. See //http://www.dspace.org.
2. See http://openjournalsystems.com.
3. See review by Newton et al. https://authorea.com/users/6729/articles/7032/_show_article#article-paragraph-Literature__space__Review__dot__md
4. See http://acrl.ala.org/newroles/?page_id=263 for Barbara Fister's excellent overview as contributed to ACRL's New Roles for the Road Ahead (2015) on advancements in this area.

5. See http://www.openarchives.org.
6. The idea of "overlay journals" has been recently revamped within the humanities community. See https://www.openlibhums.org/2014/04/07/olh-overlay-jour nals/.
7. Center for Digital Research and Scholarship; see http://cdrs.columbia.edu.
8. See http://library.columbia.edu.
9. See http://academiccommons.columbia.edu/.
10. See http://fedorarepository.org/.
11. This summary is adapted from Van de Sompel and colleagues' "Rethinking Schol arly Communication," http://www.dlib.org/dlib/september04/vandesompel /09vandesompel.html
12. See http://www.lockss.org/.
13. See http://www.clockss.org/.
14. See http://www.portico.org/.
15. See http://www.iso.org/iso/catalogue_detail.htm?csnumber=56510.

REFERENCES

Bonn, M. (2014, March). Tooling up: Scholarly communication education and training. *College & Research Libraries News, 75*(3), 132–135.

Crow, R. (2002). *The case for institutional repositories: A SPARC position paper.*

Lippincott, S. K. (Ed.). (2014). *Library publishing directory 2015.* Library Publish ing Coalition.

Lynch, C. A. (2003). Institutional repositories: Essential infrastructure for schol arship in the digital age. *portal: Libraries and the Academy, 3*(2), 327–336.

Newton, M. P., Cunningham, E. T., & Morris, J. N. (2013). Emerging opportunities in library services: Planning for the future of scholarly publishing. In *Library publishing toolkit* (pp. 109–117). IDS Project Press.

Perry, A. M., Borchert, C. A., Deliyannides, T. S., Kosavic, A., & Kennison, R. (2011, September). Libraries as journal publishers. *Serials Review, 37*(3), 196–204.

Roosendaal, H. E., & Geurts, P. A. T. M. (1997). *Forces and functions in scientific communication: An analysis of their interplay.* Conference on Co-operative Research in Information Systems in Physics, September 1–3, 1997, Univer sity of Oldenburg, Germany (pp. 1–32). Retrieved from http://doc.utwente .nl/60395/

12 | Publishing Pedagogy: The Institutional Repository as Training Ground for a New Breed of Academic Journal Editors

Catherine Mitchell and Lisa Schiff

Institutional repositories are not just places to put stuff. While they often play an important role in establishing the archive of research associated with an institution (especially in the setting of open access policies), they also can provide a platform for transformative publishing practices and the educational opportunities embedded therein. The University of California's institutional repository (eScholarship) has, since its inception in 2002, provided open access publishing services for journals affiliated with faculty across all 10 University of California (UC) campuses. Spanning disciplines as diverse as emergency medicine, Italian studies, biogeography, and comparative psychology (to name a few), the eScholarship journals program has burgeoned as faculty have grown increasingly engaged in questions of access, editorial autonomy, and audience—and have thus sought to reclaim control of the journals they manage. Not surprisingly, this interest in new journal publishing models has similarly taken hold—often in advance of faculty initiatives—among UC's graduate and undergraduate students whose academic experience is increasingly steeped in an awareness of the political and financial implications of traditional scholarly publishing practices and the possibilities offered by new models.

For the past decade, eScholarship has provided publishing services for UC faculty and students interested in starting open access journals or transitioning extant journals from print to digital open access. The drivers for the establishment of these publications are often both professional and pragmatic. Particularly among graduate students, there is a great deal of interest in working at the helm of a scholarly journal as a means of developing both editorial skills and academic bona fides (Dunlap, 2006; Hopwood, 2010; Lemke, Lehr, & Calvoz, 2014; Thomson, Byrom, Robinson, & Russell, 2010). In the case of print journals, there is often an economic imperative to move to digital publication as plummeting subscription rates (Fischer & Steiner, 2013) threaten the viability of poorly resourced student publishing efforts. As the long-established model of academic publishing begins to unravel and reconstitute itself in any number of new forms, those involved in the process of publishing are becoming, by necessity, increasingly concerned with issues of legitimacy, value, and cost. Needless to say, it is crucial to encourage students to consider these complex and far-reaching issues as they embark on their own early contributions to this domain.

This chapter will explore the role of the institutional repository as both an explicit pedagogical prompt and a necessary piece of infrastructure for supporting the larger enterprise of student education, particularly the academic training of future scholarly journal editors. We will focus our discussion on the ways in which IR-supported student journals provide a forum for engaging students in important discussions about the thorny scholarly communication issues they are likely to encounter as they progress in their academic careers. Particularly as the scholarly publishing model shifts toward open access, students are likely to encounter complex and often spirited discussions within their disciplines about copyright and licenses, the quality/nature of peer review, submission guidelines and editorial standards, and journal sustainability. We will discuss eScholarship's practical potential as a space where students consider and negotiate these complex issues via a suite of tools and services associated with the journal publishing program, including the following:

- New journal proposal form and evaluation process
- Back-end system to support manuscript/peer review management
- Copyright and licensing educational sessions and policies
- Print-on-demand services

Following this discussion, we will shift to a Q&A session with Stacey Meeker, the director of a long-standing UCLA graduate student journal publishing program funded and managed by the UCLA Graduate Students

Association (GSA) Publications office. This program currently supports 29 journals, 20 of which are, to date, hosted by eScholarship, and stands as a high water mark for how consortial-level publishing tools developed by the California Digital Library (CDL) can work complementarily with the support and best practices advocacy provided by local campus staff and organizations to help student editors navigate the increasingly choppy waters of scholarly communication. Finally, in a reflexive turn, we will refocus the lens and discuss the ways in which the practices and concerns of UCLA's student journals have significantly informed the CDL development agenda and policies for eScholarship.

ESCHOLARSHIP JOURNAL PUBLISHING TOOLS

A few years ago, we realized that there was an opportunity to embed our eScholarship platform in conversations about serious and sustainable open access publishing via the tools and training we offered to new journals. This section surveys these tools and services, exploring their pedagogical nature and potential impact on students' understanding of some of the central issues in scholarly communication. Although these materials are now provided to all journals starting up in eScholarship, we pay particular attention to the student-run publications, where the conversations we are supporting are often new and professionally formative.

With these tools, we seek to engage students in at least some of the critical issues involved in producing a journal, but we also offer them the opportunity to experiment, within limits, with various choices and to observe the impact of those choices on their publications. Given the consortial nature of eScholarship as a repository and publishing platform for all 10 UC campuses, we seek to align these tools with campus-based journal support efforts and often collaborate with our campus colleagues in refining both.

New Journal Proposal Form

Any UC-affiliated researcher or student interested in starting a new journal (that is, a journal that has not yet published its first issue) in eScholarship is required to submit a completed journal proposal form (http://escholar ship.org/Proposal_for_New_eScholarship_Journal.docx). Motivated by a flood of new journal requests in the past few years and derived from journal planning documents developed by the Directory of Open Access Journals and the Open Society Institute (particularly OSI's "Model Business Plan"), this form enables us to engage early on with journals (often at the point of formation) and to delineate, through our questions, the planning and decision making we feel is necessary to launch and sustain a quality open access journal. Particularly for those students who lack a point person on campus who can help them explore the question of their journal's viability and acquaint them with the best practices of journal publication, the proposal form is a crucial exercise in journal planning. We first ask the students to address the following key issues of validity and relevance:

> **Credibility and quality:** Students name participants, from faculty sponsors to editorial board members, who are willing and able to provide scholarly guidance and do the work to ensure a high-quality publication. We also encourage the students to consider sponsors or editorial board members whose participation will be a signal of credibility to fellow scholars in the field.

> **Current work in the relevant domain(s):** Students are asked to specify which academic discipline(s) the journal will target and to distinguish their publication from at least three major titles in that field. These questions are designed to ensure that the students have carefully considered the purpose of their journal and its potential to provide a substantive contribution to the scholarly record.

> **Contributors:** Securing a sufficient number and quality of contributors is challenging and a key piece of ensuring the long-term sustainability of a publication. We ask the students to identify the pool from which they expect to receive article submissions, and if the pool is small, we encourage them to identify ways they might generate a broader interest in their journal as a publishing outlet.

> **Readership:** Students are asked to identify the audiences and the appropriate disciplinary indexes for their publication. These questions are closely tied to their ambitions for the journal as a contribution to their field: are they seeking simply to address other students on their campus, or do they imagine a broader reach for the journal?

The answers to the above questions serve both to "make the case" for the journal and to position its editorial staff to be explicit about the journal's unique contribution to a field of inquiry. The students' answers often serve as the basis for the public-facing material on the journal's eScholarship site, typically in the "Aims and Scope," "About Us," and "Editorial Board" sections. The point, then, of the proposal process is not just to convince a resource manager that the journal is ready to have repository resources committed to its creation but also to help the students best articulate the value of the publication they intend to create.

Beyond affirming the quality of their journal's scholarly contribution, student editors are asked to outline the policies and procedures they are implementing to ensure the longevity of their publication. While all journals necessarily face the challenge of sustainability, student journals are uniquely at risk because of two factors: rotating staffing and, in some instances, limited funding. We ask the students to consider the following:

Editorial board recruitment: Is there a pool of other students from which to select editorial board members? What is the nature of the selection process and which criteria are applied? Are there specific goals for the composition of the board?

Editorial board management: Are there policies in place to deal with the known attrition that results as students finish their degree programs and cycle out of the university? Are there well-established expectations with regard to term length for members of the editorial board? What mechanisms are in place to ensure knowledge transfer during times of editorial board member transition?

Identification of publishing services needs: Will the journal require copyediting or design resources? Is there an expectation that the journal will be available in print and digital versions? Is there a pool of willing and qualified peer reviewers?

Resource management: What are the sources of financing and/or volunteered labor? Are there sufficient resources to handle all of the tasks associated with maintaining the publication?

Marketing and outreach plans: Which audiences does the journal seek to reach? What mechanisms are in place to make the journal discoverable by those audiences? Are there discipline-specific indexes where the journal needs to be listed?

Back-End Peer Review and Manuscript Management System

eScholarship journals benefit from a back-end peer review and manuscript management system designed to help journal managers and editors coordinate the editorial and production activities necessary to bring a journal to publication. As journals transition to eScholarship, managers work with CDL staff to customize this platform to meet the specific needs of their publications, thereby shifting issues of journal management from the realm of the abstract (as expressed in the proposal form) to a concrete set of possible system modifications that will reflect the publishing choices and standards the students have articulated.

Peer-Review Processes and Management

Open access student journals can face a legitimacy problem within their disciplines, particularly in fields where open access publishing is still considered a less serious or less prestigious mode of publication. For many of these fields, establishing a carefully considered and clearly articulated peer-review methodology is a crucial step toward making the case for the gravitas of a journal enterprise and its publications. eScholarship journal editors, in determining how submissions will be selected for publication, typically choose a single- or double-blind peer-review process. Making this choice provides an opportunity to discuss and think through the strengths and weaknesses of the traditional review model and the challenges of devising alternative methods. The need to ensure that review processes occur consistently and reliably exposes students to the level of detailed decisions required to produce a quality journal, including both editorial guidelines for reviewers and the mechanics of how they will interact with the review system. Beyond articulating the specific editorial and content-specific expectations for articles under review (determined by the editorial board and unique to each journal), editors must establish the following:

- A mechanism for reviewers to access submissions (e.g., via log-in to the peer-review management system or as an e-mail attachment)
- Strategies for engaging reviewers who have not completed their reviews within a defined period
- Customized language to communicate with reviewers at different stages of the process

- Standards for rating reviewers based on their performance
- A means of establishing and maintaining a pool of strong and reliable reviewers within the journal's scholarly domain(s)

The term "peer reviewed" has historically functioned as shorthand for legitimate scholarly work. In recent years, however, the practice of peer review has become a lightning rod for controversy as the scholarly community engages in debates about its form, practice, and authenticity. Can review within specific and arcane fields of study ever truly be blind? Need review be blind in order to put an argument through its paces? What about postpublication peer review as a self-consciously transparent process of evaluation? Digging into the mechanics of managing a blind peer-review process challenges students to consider the truths and assumptions built into the traditional system of scholarly evaluation and the importance of academic legitimacy for the long-term success of a publication.

Editorial Production Workflow

Student editors grapple not only with the intellectual work of submission review and selection, but also with the task of establishing rational and efficient workflows for the editorial production of journal issues. Given that the production quality of a journal can indicate to readers—both explicitly and implicitly—the commensurate quality they may expect of its scholarship, the presentation of the journal and each individual piece therein carries great value. Journals with little or no budget must prioritize tasks, identify potential volunteers in editorial board members, and balance the desire for more complex publication formats (such as embedded multimedia) with the basic requirement of supporting adequate copyright, proofreading, and layout processes for the journal. Varying levels of funding necessarily determine the structure of the work to produce a publication, for instance, whether third parties can be used for services such as proofreading and layout.

Customizing the editorial production process offers students an authentic setting in which to explore the value and roles of traditional tasks such as copyediting and layout within a primarily online environment. Perhaps more importantly, this work provides both students and repository managers an opportunity to consider how scholarly publishing is conducted within a journal's community of practice and how best to reconcile that practice with the limitations of a journal publishing system that is genericized to work across many disciplines.

Copyright/Licensing Staff, Educational Sessions, and Policies

In the interest of promoting widespread dissemination of research articles, CDL staff recommend that eScholarship journals use a Creative Commons (CC) license to indicate the terms of reuse for the materials they publish. The choice of license comes up immediately for journal managers, during the initial setup of the publication, as they begin to work on developing the terms of their journal's author agreement. Although the text can be quite minimal (http://escholarship.org/sample_author_agreement_final.doc), we encourage journals to establish nonexclusive agreements with their submitting authors, thereby promoting broad use of the material (http://escholarship.org/help_copyright.html#agreements). Ultimately, the decision of whether or not to use CC licenses—and which one to use if choosing to do so—is up to the journals themselves. Although CC licensing can be a beneficial approach to increasing the visibility and reuse of these publications, some fields have legitimate constraints and accepted practices that limit reuse, most notably those humanities and social sciences publications that rely heavily on the integrity of the text and that are often encumbered by third-party content.

In light of the complexity of these matters, we maintain an FAQ on CC licensing (http://www.escholarship.org/help_cc_faq.html) and work with campus partners to host local information sessions on copyright and intellectual property issues for student editors. We also have an on-staff copyright specialist who is available to answer questions and help journal managers (student or otherwise) understand this complex terrain.

Print-on-Demand Service

eScholarship has an agreement with a print-on-demand (POD) vendor that allows journal editors to make their open access publications available for sale in print (see http://escholarship.org/publish_escholarship-plus_faq.html). A "Buy" link on the journal issue page in eScholarship takes the user to the vendor site where the purchase can be completed. We have found that, for some student journals, it is imperative to offer a print option as a means of legitimizing the journal in the eyes of a funder or faculty participant, particularly among law reviews. Aside from that specific use case, however, POD publication offers open access journals the opportunity to make their research available in multiple formats to address the needs of multiple user communities.

Built into that opportunity is the necessity for editors to work through some of the business issues associated with print publication, most particularly pricing and distribution. Do the journals hope to generate enough revenue to offset some of their production costs? If so, do they have a marketing plan in place to raise the visibility of their publication and generate sales? At what price point are they likely to make the case for their value? POD publishing options bring to the surface the economics of journal production and resource management. Few student open access journals have a robust financial profile, so any opportunity to inject revenue into their processes is an important step toward long-term stability. Particularly in cases where there is a known market for subscriptions to or print versions of open access publications, POD can offer a remarkable (and relatively risk-free) opportunity for students to explore trends in multiformat publishing and open access sustainability.

Q&A

As described above, the use of eScholarship's journal publishing platform necessarily draws student journal managers into some of the essential concerns in scholarly publishing today, from the value of peer review to the challenges of reuse licensing. We continually work to provide students with resources, guideposts, and structured opportunities to consult with staff experts as they wrestle with the complexities embedded in the process of producing a journal. At the same time, as a consortial service provider one step removed from the 10 physical campuses of UC, CDL has limited opportunities to interact directly with students and faculty. Though we have implemented a self-service help center (https://submit.escholarship.org/help/) to support eScholarship users, how-to videos and written documentation can never take the place of local expertise and support. While this consortial model creates distance between eScholarship staff and our journal editors, it also enables our campus partners, within the UC libraries and beyond, to leverage a centralized (and centrally resourced) platform as a means of extending their own local suite of services. Through this partnership, we have seen tremendous results when an investment is made to establish committed local resources to engage directly with students as they develop and manage their journals.

In the following Q&A section, we focus our lens on an especially robust example of the synergy between a centralized platform and local staffing to support student journals: the UCLA Graduate Students Association Publications program (http://www.gsa.asucla.ucla.edu/services/publications). The UCLA GSA supports nearly 30 journals spanning the humanities, literary and art productions (including both creative works and criticism), the social sciences, law, cinema and media, and interdisciplinary studies. As mentioned above, many, but not all, of these journals are published using eScholarship. Through a series of written exchanges and telephone conversations with Stacey Meeker, director of Publications at GSA, we explore the benefits of campus-level student journal support services, the use of the eScholarship journal publishing platform as the technical foundation for these services, and the major opportunities and challenges facing graduate student journal managers at this moment of transition within the realm of scholarly communication.

1. What do you consider to be your role in supporting the education of graduate students as journal managers/editors?

> As the director of Publications for the UCLA Graduate Students Association, I see our primary mission as that of advocating for the graduate and professional students who devote themselves to editing our journals. While assuring funding and providing support services for our journals, some of which are over 40 years old, our program serves the students who edit the journals, publish in them, and fund them with their fees. Because we work with most of the graduate and professional journals across campus, we are able to see and hopefully anticipate patterns of needs and concerns as they arise and communicate these concerns to eScholarship and our network of other partners. We provide assistance in technical aspects of publishing with which editors may be unfamiliar (e.g., metadata or tool choice), and we try to facilitate endeavors

requiring higher-level coordination (e.g., helping provide or advocate for additional administrative or technical services). In the rapidly changing world of scholarly communication in general and scholarly publishing in particular, we try to keep our editors up-to-date as efficiently as possible and provide them with information about feasible options available to them. One of our most crucial functions is to oversee journals' budget allocations, approve expenditures, and make sure that the journals whose legacies and futures are in our collective care can go on about the business of publishing.

2. What are the specific issues related to journal publishing that you have focused on with graduate students?

Our approach to open access has been an organic one that embraces the diversity of our journal community and its institutional complexities. Our overall goal could be described as facilitating opportunities for graduate students to gain experience in the nuts and bolts of scholarly communication as they generate, add value to, and disseminate high-quality content across a variety of disciplines and knowledge production structures. Rapid technological and institutional changes in scholarly communication have added to the traditional publication mix the necessity of reflecting on the nature of scholarly communication itself. We have done our best to encourage and enable this ongoing discussion.

Our editors have been obliged to give much thought to the implications of concrete choices involved in the implementation of an open access model of publication. The move to open access has encouraged a spirit of experimentation among editors considering today's publishing ecology. We talk about tools and how to use them, standards and the role they play, and the value that editors and publishers bring to their publications. Editors have debated these matters on campus, articulated their thoughts in introductions and forewords to their publications, and participated in conference panels on open access publishing in their individual disciplines. We have also discussed Creative Commons licenses at length, and editors have generally come to the conclusion that they prefer to offer authors a choice of license. Other landmarks on the open access landscape—the Directory of Open Access Journals, for example—have been topics of discussion and have become part of the working vocabulary of our community of editors.

3. What are the drivers for and challenges of transitioning student journals from print to digital?

Our experience has shown that when graduate and professional student editors are given the chance to weigh the pros and cons, they tend to move in the direction of open access. A major initial impetus for the move of some of our extant print journals to open access digital delivery and eScholarship was a digitization initiative undertaken by the UCLA Library and the Internet Archive in cooperation with GSA Publications. The result was not only the digital preservation and dissemination of five long-standing print journals' distinguished backlists through the Internet Archive but also a series of serious conversations about what moving future operations to an open access model hosted by eScholarship might mean for these journals: increased visibility and discoverability on a credible platform; a more structured working environment where peer review, file management, and communications could be centralized and yet accessed remotely by editors in different locations; freedom from cumbersome and labor-intensive print subscriptions that in most cases did not recover journal expenses; and a much lower up-front investment.

The move, however, was by no means a given. Some editors and authors as well as faculty were wary of digitizing the backlists, fearing a loss of prestige or even the eventual demise of the journals. This early experience with a set of well-respected journals was covered in our campus newspaper (Saraswat, 2010) and noticed by our graduate division, which published a feature showcasing the effort in the *Graduate*

Quarterly (Watkins, 2011). This campus endorsement, which included input from the library's scholarly communication team and from Information Studies professor Christine Borgman, a faculty expert on scholarly communication and open access, helped to further legitimize the move to free online delivery, which has become an accepted goal for most of our journals even if obstacles still block some paths.

Although the law journals were not prepared to join us at that point, I believe that the example of these first waves of journals helped to persuade other editors that remaining in a closed, print-first model is not desirable in the long term. However compelling the practical facts may be, though, the rapid adoption of an open access model by UCLA law journals—six in one year alone—shows the importance of the general embrace of the model by an institution's disciplinary culture and the need for acceptance of the model by a critical mass of faculty. In the case of the UCLA School of Law, two reference librarians are responsible for this. Vicki Steiner, recognized as UCLA's 2014 Librarian of the Year for her efforts to promote open access, and Cheryl Kelly Fischer assured a necessary level of disciplinary assent through ongoing efforts to engage faculty and students, ranging from individual conversations to general meetings. Their own publication on open access and legal scholarship (Fischer & Steiner, 2013) and their credibility with their colleagues were necessary factors in bringing about this rapid adoption. They have worked closely with GSA Publications to learn from our earlier experiences and to demonstrate the success of the model for journals on other parts of campus in terms relevant to legal scholarship.

[In terms of challenges,] graduate and professional journals face special difficulties related to workflows, record-keeping, and institutional memory because of the relatively short tenure of the editorial staffs and the varied levels and kinds of experiences that editors bring to the enterprise. Perhaps somewhat counterintuitively, these problems are often compounded in the era of free cloud computing. Records become tied to individual editors' accounts and vulnerable to accidental deletion or untethering from the institution, and documents can be difficult to track if continuity between teams isn't made a priority and codified as a process. These problems further compound the difficulty of providing the changing members of an editorial staff with a picture of an entire production workflow. The desire to have a well-structured, credible online working environment has been a consistent factor attracting our editors to open access publishing on eScholarship. Managing double-blind peer review is difficult. Maintaining centralized records of communication is difficult. Version control is difficult. . . . All editors, but graduate and professional student editors in particular, need the kind of infrastructure support that a well-developed and responsive IR can provide.

4. What are some of the most successful educational tools and processes you have developed to help student journal managers/editors navigate the scholarly communication environment in all its complexity?

Simply having an office and being accessible (both in person and remotely) as a go-to resource is an important foundation for helping editors navigate the scholarly communication environment. Editors need to feel comfortable about asking questions and talking through whatever issues they may be encountering. By conceiving of our program as an information hub grounded in student needs that complements and provides pathways to other resources, we have been able to encourage editors to stop by, communicate with each other, and stay connected to developments in scholarly communication on campus and elsewhere.

However standard their practices, each of our journals is unique, and editors must create their own collections of operational documents and tools, from aims and scope statements to style sheets. We try to provide journal editors with good models for those tools in workshops, and we work with them on an individual basis to assist in whatever ways possible to develop and refine those tools, which they can then share with their fellow editors. We have focused our efforts on matters such as workflows, wording of editorial letters, protocols for communicating with authors and reviewers, author agreements, file preparation guidelines, proofreading techniques, and even style and grammar, which we sometimes cover in conjunction with our Graduate Writing Center, which is also a GSA initiative.

Working closely with teams as they go through the steps of the editorial process helps them to acquire the specialized knowledge needed for effective copyediting, proofreading, and working with a complex remote information system. But most editors cannot be expected to learn, on their own, best practices concerning metadata or to keep abreast of developments in the areas of copyright, licensing, and fair use. In order to help our editors meet these specialized needs, we collaborate with the UCLA Library and the Law Library to host regular workshops. Our office serves at once as a filter and aggregator of useful information and a mechanism for leveraging campus resources and connections to help journals do their work without having to reinvent the wheel.

CONCLUSION

Although CDL has been in the business of publishing UC-affiliated journals in eScholarship for more than a decade, it is only in the last few years that we have begun to focus on the explicit pedagogical opportunities that are built into supporting a journal publishing platform. eScholarship staff take seriously our charge to provide consortial services that meet the real needs of our constituencies throughout the UC system. Rather than a vendor selling a product or a third-party provider satisfied with a "build it and they will come" approach, we work collaboratively with our campus partners to ensure that our systemwide services harmonize with local programs and initiatives. One such initiative, both at UC and within the larger higher education library community, focuses on the practical purposes and pedagogical potential inherent in maintaining local publishing programs that serve graduate and undergraduate students. Working at scale and set apart from a physical campus, we have constructed a suite of tools for establishing and managing journals that, by their nature, organically provide students with the structure and the space to reflect on significant issues in scholarly communication that are, more and more, shaping the published results of academic inquiry.

We have learned, however, through our close collaboration with UCLA staff at the Graduate Students Association, the library, and elsewhere, that our tools and services are only the starting point of a rich pedagogical experience for student editors. Committed local staff have the opportunity to understand more clearly the important variations in practice among academic disciplines and where those variations must be reflected in the tools we provide, in turn helping the eScholarship service to grow and adapt to the real needs and concerns of our user community. We have, as a result of this collaborative relationship with UCLA, grown to recognize the importance of supporting an array of reuse licenses, providing flexible publishing workflows, and establishing a robust practice of documentation in a setting in which student staffing is always in flux. Attending to the specific needs of this particularly engaged publishing program, while remembering our responsibility to maintain a service that is generalizable to the entire UC system, has enabled us to introduce a new level of refinement to the eScholarship platform. This kind of dynamic platform development benefits the entire population of eScholarship journal managers (across our 70+ journals), resulting in a stronger service that, simultaneously, supports the worldwide dissemination of new research and helps launch journal editors who are ready to take on the thorniest of publishing challenges.

REFERENCES

Dunlap, J. C. (2006). The effect of a problem-centered, enculturating experience on doctoral students' self-efficacy. *Interdisciplinary Journal of Problem-Based Learning, 1*(2). http://dx.doi.org/10.7771/1541-5015.1025

Fischer, C. K., & Steiner, V. (2013). Open access to legal scholarship. In E. Kroski (Ed.), *Law librarianship in the digital age*. Lanham, MD: Scarecrow Press.

Hopwood, N. (2010). Doctoral students as journal editors: Non-formal learning through academic work. *Higher Education Research & Development, 29*(3), 319–331. http://dx.doi.org/10.1080/07294360903532032

Lemke, M. A., Lehr, M. D., & Calvoz, R. R. (2014). To be of use: A narrative roadmap for creating an open-access, peer-reviewed, graduate student educational journal. *Texas Education Review*, *2*(1). Retrieved from https://journals.tdl .org/txedrev/index.php/txedrev/article/view/35

Saraswat, S. (2010, February 23). GSA's print academic journal *Carte Italiane* moves online. *Daily Bruin*. Retrieved from http://dailybruin.com/2010/02/23 /gsas-print-academic-journal-carte-italiane-moves-o/

Thomson, P., Byrom, T., Robinson, C., & Russell, L. (2010). Learning about journal publication: The pedagogies of editing a "special issue." In C. Aitchison, B. Kamler, & A. Lee (Eds.), *Publishing pedagogies for the doctorate and beyond* (pp. 137–155). London: Routledge.

Watkins, M. (2011, Spring). Publication revolution. *UCLA Graduate Quarterly*, 4–18. Retrieved from https://grad.ucla.edu/asis/library/gqspring11.pdf

Part 4

MEASURING SUCCESS

Getting a full and accurate picture of the use of repositories is essential not only as a means for evaluating the success of a given repository, but as a means for propelling the evolution of scholarly communication. As Bruns and Inefuku state in their chapter, "Purposeful Metrics": "In order for researchers, universities, and funding agencies to view institutional repositories as a central pillar of the OA movement, repository managers need to prove the value of their repositories." When done strategically and convincingly, using metrics to prove the value of repositories can result in a positive feedback response loop that can dramatically change the way that information is shared and knowledge is built: the more stakeholders can see that repositories are being used, the more they will be encouraged to use them. When contributors to a repository get reports on all of the avenues that led others to their work and the locations across the world where their work has been accessed, discussed, and cited, they are more inclined to contribute and to encourage their colleagues to do the same. When administrators can see that work from their home institution is being downloaded, cited, and tweeted, they are going to be more likely to provide funding and encourage expansion of service.

What might at first seem like a fairly straightforward endeavor, measuring the success of repositories involves an ever widening and nuanced spectrum of factors that can enhance and leverage raw upload and download counts. The chapters in Part 4 outline the various dimensions of measurement that have proven to be effective as well as new forms of measurements that are only beginning to take shape and resonate with various constituents. Bruns and Inefuku walk readers through the full range of metrics including various suites of performance indicators and even "empty" metrics that utilize a kind of proof by negation that can be used to spur contributions and use. When gathered honestly and systematically, this information can proactively shape the services and practices repositories can and should offer.

Because the concept is so new and the adoption of it has been so varied, the ways that social media have affected and influenced scholarly communication have only recently been studied and quantified. The practice of altmetrics—article-level metrics that can include social media—has begun to formalize and produce increasingly meaningful results that can be of use to scholars as well as administrators. In their chapter, "Social Media Metrics," Holmberg, Haustein, and Beucke build on more traditional measurement methods and lay out the various ways that social media can be mined for data that can be correlated to ever refined spheres of influence. These data can reveal the way that a given item may have been circulated as well as the ways that repositories are affecting scholarly communication on a global scale.

Peer review may seem out of place in Part 4, which is largely about measuring use, but the ways that repositories are ushering in a new, more open and broad-based peer-review system can greatly affect repository traffic and impact. Due to the popularity of arXiv and the way that contributors receive feedback more immediately from a large pool of peers, published journal articles that had preprints posted in arXiv have received significantly higher numbers of citations than those of a similar type that were not initially posted in the repository. "The arXiv preprints, when published, have already amassed an advantage that non-arXiv articles can never recoup" (Gentil-Beccot , Mele, & Brooks, 2009, p. 7). The repercussions of arXiv and other subject repositories are being felt by institutional repositories. Callicott discusses the ways that IRs are playing a role in the first significant shift in peer review that has taken place since the advent of the scholarly journal. By providing new ways to publish and share what was considered marginal scholarship, IRs are driving interest in gray literature, often to the point that distinctions between "gray" and "white" are muddied. By reconceiving and democratizing the traditional peer-review system, IRs are bringing important work to light and increasing the scope of scholarly discourse. Download counts and citations can serve as an ersatz peer review and demonstrate the value of an individual item as well as a new method of publication and discovery.

All of the measurements in the world are essentially ineffective and meaningless unless they are properly packaged, reported, and parsed for their appropriate audience. In the final chapter in Part 4, Buehler attempts to break down the measurements that are most important to the various constituents: scholars, deans, and administrators. Convincing administrators to champion an IR can have a ripple effect that involves not only IR-friendly policies but establishing a culture of open access and repository awareness. Making this connection with administrators and leaders and speaking the language of assessment and measures of success is essential for the continued growth and support of repositories.

REFERENCE

Gentil-Beccot, A., Mele, S., & Brooks, T. (2009). *Behaviours in high-energy physics: How a community stopped worrying about journals and learned to love repositories.* arXiv:0906.5418

13 | Purposeful Metrics: Matching Institutional Repository Metrics to Purpose and Audience

Todd Bruns and Harrison W. Inefuku

The last 10 years have seen gains in the acceptance of open access (OA) among scholars through the growing availability of OA journals (Laakso et al., 2011) and in the development of funder-based policies advocating or mandating open availability of funded research (Xia et al., 2012). Discipline repositories, starting with arXiv in 1993, have grown to a large number of repositories in more than 40 subject areas. Additionally, new avenues of OA have recently sprung up in the creation of "scholar commons" such as Academia.edu and ResearchGate.

Institutional repositories (IRs) are currently in the middle of their second decade of development, with the three most commonly used repository platforms launched in the early 2000s (EPrints in 2000, DSpace and Digital Commons in 2002). Despite being created to promote open access to research and scholarship, and growing in number and size over the past 10 years, institutional repositories continue to be seen primarily as the province of libraries (Thomas, 2007) rather than the new wave of scholarly communication that OA journals and discipline repositories are coming to be seen as.

In order for researchers, universities, and funding agencies to view institutional repositories as a central pillar of the OA movement, repository managers need to prove the value of their repositories. To prove their value, repository managers rely on metrics, some platform provided, some created in-house. Successful use of metrics relies on selecting metrics that are meaningful to repository stakeholders. In other words, metrics that are collected and reported need to support the interests and goals of their appropriate audiences.

Metrics are commonly thought of as quantitative—download counts to demonstrate access and visibility, leading to higher citation rates (Antelman, 2004; Eysenbach, 2006; Gargouri et al., 2010); upload counts to document institutional repository growth; and Web analytics to ascertain visitor demographics and behavior. All three primary repository platforms provide metrics tools for the purpose of assessing repository growth and access, supplemented by metrics provided by third parties (Web analytics, citation measures, and altmetrics, for example) and locally developed metrics. These metrics are valuable in communicating with stakeholders, although repository managers may not be taking full advantage of these tools. A recent survey on assessment for digital collections in Association of Research Library member libraries indicates that a significant majority of respondents used assessment to measure functionality and to guide development, while only half of respondents indicated that they used assessment for stakeholder buy-in (Ochoa, Taylor, & Sullivan, 2014).

This is not a chapter about institutional repository assessment. Rather, it is about the collection and reporting of repository metrics for a variety of purposes and audiences, including repository assessment. Metrics are a basic tool for proving the value of repositories. For library and university administration, institutional repositories need to demonstrate they are worth the financial and staff resources allocated to them. For academic and research units and faculty authors, repositories need to demonstrate they are worth the time needed to collect and submit publications. Effectively demonstrating the value of repositories through metrics requires an understanding of stakeholders and their objectives in using institutional repositories, and identifying and reporting metrics that show whether the repository is meeting those objectives.

IDENTIFYING METRICS: UNDERSTANDING AUDIENCE AND PURPOSE

Essential to the successful use of metrics is identifying an audience (repository stakeholders), recognizing a purpose (the stakeholders' interest in the repository), and tying it to a metric (what is being measured) that demonstrates how the repository is fulfilling that purpose (Inefuku, 2013). Commonly identified stakeholders in institutional repositories include the library, faculty members and other authors, academic departments and other campus units, university administration, the institution's governing boards, and accrediting agencies. These stakeholders form the audiences for repository metrics.

As noted by Poll and te Boekhorst (2007), "The perception of library quality will differ in the stakeholder groups. Users see library quality according to their experience with the services they use. They will not care for the efficiency of background processes, but for the effective delivery of services." Repository stakeholders will require metrics that are tailored to meet their needs. The type, granularity, and frequency of metrics reported is dependent on the audience, as each audience has differing interests in repositories:

University Administration
- Demonstrate scholarly output
- Increase visibility and impact
- Fulfill granting agency public access requirements
- Accreditation
- Comparison to peer institutions
- Membership in associations (e.g., Association of American Universities)

Campus Unit
- Demonstrate scholarly output
- Increase visibility and impact
- Fulfill granting agency public access requirements
- Accreditation
- Comparison to peer departments
- Recruitment of faculty and students

Faculty
- Demonstrate scholarly impact
- Increase visibility and impact
- Fulfill granting agency public access requirements
- Attain promotion and tenure, performance evaluations

Students

- Secure employment or further education
- Increase visibility and impact

Library and Repository

- Demonstrate impact of repository
- Assess growth and success of repository
- Improve services and discoverability

By providing useful and appropriate statistics to authors, departments, the university, and other stakeholders, the library demonstrates its value as a vital partner in research, scholarship, and scholarly communication. Reporting metrics can lead to new or continued usage of the repository's services. For internal purposes, gathering metrics provides a means of benchmarking success and growth, though some argue that the longitudinal aspects of growth should be studied to assess strength (steady upload amounts) *or* weakness (slow growth punctuated by bouts of large batch uploads), revealing the sustainability of repository growth (Carr & Brody, 2007).

Determining which metrics are appropriate for different audiences requires an understanding of the campus—its mission, its priorities, and its culture. This information can be gathered from the strategic plans of universities and campus units. The need for repository metrics may be driven by accreditation and external review cycles, grant reporting deadlines, and tenure and promotion calendars. These needs will also determine the schedule and frequency of metrics reporting.

The needs of common audiences will vary from university to university and each audience's needs are, to some extent, dependent on local contexts. Demonstrating the number of local and/or in-state visitors may be important for land grant universities, which have a mission to disseminate knowledge to the community, public universities that must be accountable to taxpayers, and universities interested in building strong town-gown relations. Smaller liberal arts universities may be more concerned with connections between institutional repositories and the classroom, or may place a greater emphasis on attracting student authors, while large research universities may focus their attention on increasing the visibility of grant-funded research. For research universities that are members of the Association of American Universities, repository metrics can be useful in demonstrating the impact institutional repositories have on increasing the visibility and usage of scholarship in support of membership criteria. Tying repository metrics to the missions of stakeholders will position institutional repositories as a key player in supporting their core functions. The following section describes commonly measured repository metrics that can be used to support the interests of a range of audiences. See this chapter's Appendix A for a crosswalk of commonly measured metrics, audiences, and purposes.

COMMONLY MEASURED REPOSITORY METRICS

Item Downloads

> **Audiences:** Accrediting agencies; governing board; university administration; campus units; authors; library; repository
>
> **Source:** Platform-generated

Item downloads is the most commonly used metric for institutional repositories, demonstrating usage of materials in repositories. This metric is used both to reinforce behavior (encouraging faculty/authors to continue to deposit new material) and to encourage behavior (bringing in new faculty/authors to the repository). The audience determines the level of granularity of this metric. Individual authors will need the item downloads for every item of theirs in the repository. For other audiences, this might be reported in aggregate, as an average, or in lists of top downloaded items.

Number of Items in Repository

> **Audiences:** Accrediting agencies; governing board; university administration; campus units; authors; library; repository
>
> **Source:** Platform-generated

For repositories that include metadata-only records, the number of items in the repository is an indicator of the scholarly output of a university. For these repositories, identifying the percentage of items in the repository that have full-text availability is useful in assessing the success of the library's engagement in scholarly communication and open access discussions on campus. Breaking the number of items in a repository into categories can also aid in measuring the research output of a university and tracking compliance with open access mandates of granting agencies.

Item Uploads

> **Audiences:** Accrediting agencies; governing board; university administration; campus units; authors; library; repository
> **Source:** Platform-generated

This metric measures how many items have been uploaded to a repository in a specific time period and can be tracked across time. Item uploads measures the growth of the repository. For repositories that are integrated into research information systems, tracking the number of uploads into a repository can measure the scholarly output of a university. This metric can be segmented by campus units, by type (peer-reviewed articles, theses), depending on the intended audience. Upload numbers are used mainly to demonstrate IR health and vitality, although as pointed out by Carr and Brody (2007), large batch uploads may be a sign of lack of sustainability. Uploads are often also referred to as "documents" or "content" or "items" in the repository, and this metric is often used to demonstrate not only sustained growth but also diversity of the content in an institutional repository. Many repository managers report uploads by content type or by collection. Upload metrics also seem to suggest explosive repository early growth averaging 366 documents per month, followed by slower sustained growth of 165 documents per month by the third year of the repository (Dubinsky, 2014).

Location of Visitors

> **Audiences:** University administration; campus units; authors
> **Source:** Web analytics (e.g., Google Analytics)

Tracking and reporting the location of repository visitors can be used to demonstrate several things, including the national/international reach of repositories and the percentage of visitors on college and university networks. Demonstrating the number of statewide or local visitors may be important for repositories of land grant universities or universities with strong town-gown relationships. Although many repository managers use Google Analytics to report visitor rates, locations, search terms, and sometimes search engines/traffic flow, these are rarely tied to specific downloaded items and instead are usually reported universally.

Participating Units

> **Audiences:** University administration; campus units; library; repository
> **Source:** In-house recordkeeping

If the repository is valued by university administration, then they may be interested in seeing who is utilizing the service. Repository managers can use this metric to assess the success of outreach and education efforts. Identifying which units have little to no participation is useful in targeting education and outreach activities.

Participating Faculty

> **Audiences:** University administration; campus units; authors; library; repository
> **Source:** In-house recordkeeping

Lists of faculty who have submitted their scholarship to institutional repositories are useful to university administrators and campus unit heads in determining uptake in faculty. Identifying gaps can allow repository managers to target influential faculty members and scholars on campus.

GATHERING METRICS

Platform Metrics: Downloads, Uploads, Location, Citations

Each of the three primary repository platforms provides download counts as a basic feature. EPrints reports download counts in a variety of graphic ways (graphs and pie charts), DSpace can display metrics at levels ranging from item to collection (if enabled by the repository administrator), and Digital Commons communicates download counts via e-mail reports to authors and repository managers, as well as an "Author Dashboard" that shows both download counts in graph form and Google Analytics–harvested locations and search terms used (Konkiel & Scherer, 2013).

As open source platforms, repositories and contractors working in DSpace or EPrints may develop more robust reporting infrastructures to supplement or replace the reporting features built into the platform.

In DSpace, download statistics may be displayed at the site, community, collection, or item level, if this feature is enabled by the repository administrator. Digital Commons provides a Readership Map that adorns the home, community, and collection pages of its repositories. This map lists the total number of downloads and items in the repository and places a pin on a world map identifying where each download has occurred since the page was loaded.

Third-Party Metrics: Web Analytics, Citation Measures, Altmetrics

Many repository managers supplement the reports generated by their repository platforms with metrics gained from third-party sources, including Google Analytics, Scopus, and altmetrics.

Web analytics (with the most popular system being Google Analytics) are used by repository managers to track repository visits, user demographics, user behavior, and usage of social media, and to improve search engine optimization. Tracking user behavior and measuring content discovery though search engines, social media, and referring Web sites is useful for repository managers looking to improve their systems and measure repository visibility.

DSpace and EPrints offer citation metrics if the hosting institution has a subscription to SciVerse Scopus API (Konkiel & Scherer, 2013). Each platform offers means of collecting or displaying altmetrics (alternative metrics, based on social media) as well. By integrating citation measures and altmetrics into their repositories, repository managers enable authors and readers to see the impact of scholarship in one location. This convenience may encourage authors to deposit their work in institutional repositories. "Publishers like PLoS and the subject specialist arXiv repository display article-level metrics along with the record describing the article. Institutional repositories . . . may do the same, but authors may be anxious to see visitor numbers aggregated and displayed in total each time, from all locations and versions of the article" (Kelly et al., 2012).

The Ranking Web of World Repositories (http://repositories.webometrics.info/en) is an initiative started by Cybermetrics Lab, a research group of the Consejo Superior de Investigaciones Científicas (CSIC) led by Isidro F. Aguillo. It is also a misnomer in that the research group states that the site is not actually a ranking (Ranking Web of Repositories, 2014), but rather aims to create quantitative standards for measuring the visibility and impact of scientific repositories and to promote OA (Ranking Web of Repositories, n.d.).

To list the repositories, the group compiles an index of four weighted criteria pulled from search engines (Aguillo, Ortega, Fernandez, & Utrilla, 2010): size (number of pages indexed by Google), visibility (the total number of external links pointing back to the repository, as determined by MajesticSEO and Ahrefs), rich files (the number of full-text items available), and a Google Scholar rating (number of pages in Scholar), which are used to determine the composite total ranking of the repository.

Although the ratings generated are an indicator of the visibility of repositories, the rich files ratings are based on the number of URLs accessed by Google ending in ".pdf." This leads to an undercounting of full-text items available in Digital Commons– and DSpace-based repositories, as these platforms include filename extensions in the URLs of full-text files. Additionally, search engines such as Bing provide different results than Google for this measurement.

In-House Metrics: Spreadsheets and Reports

Many repository managers create in-house–generated spreadsheets and monthly statistics that detail information that cannot be tracked easily or efficiently by repository software. These statistics may enumerate nonuploading work that has been accomplished (e.g., the number of items digitized) or tied to institutional structure (e.g., the number of faculty from a given department who have submitted publications to the repository). The style and range of in-house reports remains fluid and varies from institution to institution and repository manager to repository manager, although common in-house–generated metrics include campus institutional repository participation rates and benchmarking against previous years' metrics, peer institutions, or average repository growth.

Repository Networks

Federated repository systems that aggregate content from a range of repositories are useful in comparing repositories. In the United Kingdom, IRUS-UK (Institutional Repository Usage Statistics UK) provides COUNTER-compliant usage statistics from all participating repositories, providing opportunities for member institutions to benchmark their repositories against others.

The Digital Commons Network aggregates content from all Digital Commons–based repositories into a federated search platform. The network is organized by discipline and provides several tools for comparing repositories. Each discipline provides lists of "Most Popular Institutions" and "Most Popular Authors," which are updated monthly. There is also a pie chart that indicates what percentage of items available in each discipline are being contributed by which universities. There is currently neither automatic reporting of this metric, nor a means for requesting the metric for desired timeframes, so repository managers are obliged to manually gather these notices per month. Nevertheless, this can be a powerful metric for demonstrating faculty/author and institution impact.

REPORTING AND UTILIZING METRICS

Repository Assessment and Performance Indicators

Collecting and interpreting metrics is necessary for repository managers to assess the services they provide to their universities. For a young repository, generating quick metrics is essential (Gibbons, 2004): batch uploading electronic theses and dissertations as a first collection in a repository results in significant download count reports, which can then be used to market the repository to faculty by demonstrating real results even before most faculty are participating (Bruns, Knight-Davis, Corrigan, & Brantley, 2014).

Some, however, have argued that repository managers subsist on an overreliance on "bean counting" and lack of standardization (Cassella, 2010; McDonald & C. Thomas, 2008; G. Thomas, 2007), arguing for an establishment of performance indicators (PIs) that provide benchmarking as well as demonstrating contextual value and success, while still others (Royster, 2014) have advocated that institutional repository success is largely a product of being heavily invested as a faculty scholarship and publishing support service.

A key argument in favor of adapting performance indicators beyond metrics is that the value of an institutional repository is not only in producing upload and download numbers, but in effecting change in the scholarly communication environment (Mercer, Rosenblum, & Emmett, 2007). A number of scholars have advocated for assessment "beyond bean counting" in the establishment of PIs (Cassella, 2010; Thomas, 2007). As there is not yet an established standard of PIs, the advocated indicators vary. Appendix B in this chapter lists indicators that have been identified by different authors and standards.

The value of PIs is in providing context to metric statistics. Identifying the appropriate audience and connecting that audience to a metric, while providing the analysis as to what the metric means and why it matters, is essential to utilizing metrics to make repositories work. Institutional repositories have yet to mature as an embedded technology that is essential to the research enterprise of the institution. Making sense of metrics and demonstrating the success of the repository by using PIs assists with moving the repository into the center of the institution's research life.

Supporting Campus Unit and University Assessment

Institutional repositories are useful for universities and campus units seeking to summarize and highlight research activity. At Iowa State University, the associate department chair for research and the associate department chair for teaching for the Department of Agricultural and Biosystems Engineering were interested in illustrating departmental research activity at a faculty retreat. In order to do this, they requested download totals for each faculty member in the department, as well as average download counts for all departments in the College of Agriculture and Life Sciences and the College of Engineering. The repository manager provided these metrics to the associate chairs, who then manipulated the data so they were sorted by total downloads and average downloads, providing context to the download reports each faculty member could access individually.

Occasionally, the very existence of a repository leads to activities and creation of metrics data that can be used at the institutional level. At Eastern Illinois University (EIU), repository staff, inspired by the work of Margaret Heller (2013), ran a project where all library databases were surveyed to locate EIU faculty publications for the past five years. These data were compiled into a spreadsheet, run against the SHERPA/RoMEO copyright database, and used to find OA faculty publications that were not in the EIU IR, The Keep. This resulted in 19 new faculty members added to the repository.

An unanticipated use of this data came via a request from EIU's North Central Association Self-Study committee. Thanks to the repository study, there existed data on the publications of EIU faculty for the past five years, and the previously compiled spreadsheet was included in the institution's self-study documentation. These data would not have been readily available had the repository not existed. This fact was not lost on university administrators, proving the value of the repository to the institution.

Annual Reports

Annual reports are a common method used by repository managers to report their growth, highlight accomplishments, and promote their repositories to a general audience encompassing all of the repository's stakeholders. A sampling of repository annual reports is available through the Digital Commons Collaboratory, which features 11 annual reports. Although limited to Digital Commons repositories, these reports represent a variety of institution types, including two law schools, one Canadian institution, and by Carnegie Basic Classification, one Baccalaureate/Arts & Sciences college, four Masters/Large programs universities, one Research University/High Level of research, and three Research University/Very High Level of research universities.

Many of these annual reports meet both these purposes by reporting metrics and tying them to particular purpose(s) and/or audience(s). Frequently reported metrics include downloads and uploads by content type, lists of most frequently downloaded items, visitor location (including top countries), and average number of downloads/item. One report utilized downloads to demonstrate diversity of authorship in their repository. Two of the reports state vision/mission statements of the repository, while three specifically tie repository metrics to their institution's strategic goals or mission statement. The common usage of the Google Analytics maps and countries lists were used to demonstrate repository visibility and impact. In several cases metrics related to publishing were highlighted and clearly pitched in terms of marketing to potential new clients.

"Empty" Metrics

An example of metrics outside the box, one that has been utilized by both authors of this chapter, is the use of "empty" metrics, or the absence of participation or content. In the case of Iowa State University, the Digital Commons Network's discipline repositories were used to demonstrate to Agricultural and Biosystems Engineering faculty that they were absent because they hadn't been participating in the repository. Each discipline repository in the Digital Commons Network includes a pie chart that breaks down the proportion of OA full-text works contributed by Digital Commons repositories. Using this pie chart, the repository manager was able to tap into a regional and athletic rivalry, showing that more than half of agricultural engineering publications in the network were coming from the University of Nebraska–Lincoln (Inefuku, 2014). This inverse use of the metric resulted in an influx of faculty participation in the repository—within months, Iowa State was the largest contributor of agricultural engineering publications available in the network (Bankier, 2013).

A similar case of "empty" metrics was the creation of empty collections in the EIU institutional repository, The Keep, for the purpose of assessing potential value. A study of Google Analytics demonstrated that a placeholder page for the campus newspaper, without content, was receiving a lot of visitors. This demonstrated the value of that content, and digitizing the newspaper for inclusion in the repository became a priority.

Using Metrics to Argue for Funding

Another case of an outside-the-box metric is the use of a metric to demonstrate impact related to peer institutions and use those data to argue for funding. A useful tool for this purpose is the Digital Commons Network's monthly "Most Popular Authors" lists. At EIU, the regular appearance of Biological Science faculty on the "Most Popular Authors" lists was used in the university's initial pitch to the Illinois state legislature for funding for a new science building. The regular ranking of EIU faculty in a network of 260+ repositories across the world demonstrated the quality of research that, it was argued, validated the investment.

"Shout-Outs"

An undeniable thrill for authors participating in an institutional repository is discovering where their work is being downloaded. One of the benefits of the Digital Commons Readership Map is the visual element of seeing real-time downloads appear as pins being fastened to a map. This graphic element has been added to at least one journal as a selling point for journal visibility. Another use is e-mailing faculty/authors notices when their work has been downloaded to interesting areas: with the Readership Map one can zoom in on a location, so as an example, one of this chapter's authors was able to e-mail his faculty member that her paper had been "downloaded to someone in Central Park in New York." This kind of use of a metric adds a definite element of fun to faculty/author participation and is very likely to encourage positive word-of-mouth information about the repository.

CONCLUSION: THE REPOSITORY AT
THE HEART OF THE INSTITUTION

Academic libraries' increasing involvement in the scholarly communication process provides opportunities for libraries to insert themselves as invaluable partners in the research process. Institutional repositories provide two pivotal services to the institution: a digital embodiment of the scholarship, student work, activities, history, and value of the institution, and growing new open access publishing environments and services for scholars. In identifying purposeful metrics and reporting them to appropriate audiences, repository managers engage in an activity that is essential to making repositories work. The collection and reporting of metrics are valuable tools repository managers can exploit to sustain and encourage faculty participation in repositories.

As participation in institutional repositories increases across campus, the need to deliver meaningful metrics to stakeholders will increase. Royster (2014) argues that a service-oriented approach works to stoke high levels of voluntary deposit, and also works to highlight the unique contributions to scholarship of the institution and its scholars, thereby meeting one of the important criteria of PIs: to connect the repository to the heart of the research community of the institution and to match the institution's strategic goals.

In order to be able to compare repository metrics across institutions, the gathering and reporting of metrics needs to be standardized. While this is enabled through national repository networks in countries that have them, there is currently no solution in the United States that encompasses all repository platforms. As institutional repositories mature, the collection and reporting of meaningful, contextualized metrics will enable libraries to effectively demonstrate that repositories are a key service that supports the mission and goals of their host colleges and universities.

REFERENCES

Aguillo, I. F., Ortega, J. L., Fernandez, M., & Utrilla, A. M. (2010). Indicators for a webometric ranking of open access repositories. *Scientometrics, 82*(3), 477–486. http://dx.doi.org/10.1007/s11192-010-0183-y

Antelman, K. (2004). Do open access articles have a greater research impact? *College & Research Libraries, 65*(5), 372–382. Retrieved from http://crl.acrl .org/content/65/5/372.abstract

Bankier, J. (2013). *Modeling a shared national cross digital repository* (Charleston Conference Proceedings 2013, pp. 492–500). Retrieved from http://dx .doi.org/10.5703/1288284315312

Bruns, T., Knight-Davis, S., Corrigan, E., & Brantley, J. S. (2014). It takes a library: Building a robust institutional repository in two years. *College & Undergraduate Libraries, 21*(3/4), 244–262. http://dx.doi.org/10.1080/10691316.2014 .904207

Carr, L., & Brody, T. (2007). Size isn't everything: Sustainable repositories as evidenced by sustainable deposit profiles. *D-Lib Magazine, 13*(7/8). http://dx .doi.org/10.1045/july2007-carr

Cassella, M. (2010). Institutional repositories: An internal and external perspective on the value of IRs for researchers' communities. *Liber Quarterly, 20*(2), 210–223. Retrieved from http://liber.library.uu.nl/index.php/lq/article/view /7989

Dubinsky, E. (2014). A current snapshot of institutional repositories: Growth rate, disciplinary content and faculty contributions. *Journal of Librarianship and Scholarly Communication, 2*(3), eP1167. http://dx.doi.org/10.7710/2162-3309.1167

Eysenbach, G. (2006). Citation advantage of open access articles. *PLoS Biology, 4*(5): e157. http://dx.doi.org/10.371/journal.pbio.0040157

Gargouri, Y., Hajjem, C., Larivière, V., Gingras, Y., Carr, L., Brody, T., & Harnad, S. (2010). Self-selected or mandated, open access increases citation impact for higher quality research. *PLoS ONE, 5*(10): e13636. http://dx.doi.org/10.1371/journal.pone.0013636

Gibbons, S. (2004). Benefits of an institutional repository. *Library Technology Reports, 40*(4), 11–16. Heller, M. (2013, July). *Automating your way to easy faculty scholarship collection development.* Paper presented at the Digital Commons+ Great Lakes User Group annual conference, Bloomington, IL. Retrieved from http://digitalcommons.iwu.edu/dcglug/2013/breakout1/3/

Inefuku, H. (2013). *Digital repository @ Iowa State University—FY2013 annual report.* Retrieved from http://digitalcommons.bepress.com/collaboratory/63

Inefuku, H. (2013, July). *More than seeing what sticks: Aligning repository assessment with institutional priorities.* Poster presented at Open Repositories 2013, Charlottetown, Prince Edward Island, Canada. Retrieved from http://lib.dr.iastate.edu/digirep_conf/3/

Inefuku, H. (2014, August). *Baiting the hook: Generating faculty interest and excitement in institutional repositories.* Paper presented at the Digital Commons + Great Lakes User Group annual conference, Valparaiso, IN.

International Organization for Standardization. (2013). ISO 2789: Information and documentation—International library statistics.

Kelly, B., Sheppard, N., Delasalle, J., Dewey, M., Stephens, O., Johnson, G., & Taylor, S. (2012, July). *Open metrics for open repositories.* Paper presented at OR2012: The 7th International Conference on Open Repositories, Edinburgh, Scotland. Retrieved from http://opus.bath.ac.uk/30226/

Konkiel, S., & Scherer, D. (2013). New opportunities for repositories in the age of altmetrics. *Bulletin of the Association of Information Science and Technology, 39*(4), 22–26. http://dx.doi.org/10.1002/bult.2013.1720390408

Laakso, M., Welling, P., Bukvova, H., Nyman, L., Björk, B., & Hedlund, T. (2011). The development of open access journal publishing from 1993 to 2009. *PLoS ONE, 6*(6), e20961. http://dx.doi.org/10.1371/journal.pone.0020961

McDonald, R. H., & Thomas, C. (2008). The case for standardized reporting and assessment requirements for institutional repositories. *Journal of Electronic Resources Librarianship, 20*, 101–109. http://dx.doi.org/10.1080 /19411260802272743

Mercer, H., Rosenblum, B., & Emmett, A. (2007). A multifaceted approach to promote a university repository: The University of Kansas' experience. *OCLC Systems & Services: International Digital Library Perspectives, 23*(2), 190–203. http://dx.doi.org/10.1108/10650750710748496

Ochoa, M. N., Taylor, L. N., & Sullivan, M. V. (2014). *SPEC kit 341: Digital collections assessment and outreach*. Washington, DC: Association of Research Libraries.

Poll, R., & te Boekhorst, P. (Eds.). (2007). *Measuring quality: Performance measurement in libraries* (2nd rev. ed.). Munich: K. G. Saur.

Ranking Web of Repositories. (n.d.). Retrieved from http://repositories.webomet rics.info/en

Ranking Web of Repositories. (2014). Retrieved from http://repositories.webomet rics.info/en/node/26

Royster, P. (2014). *An alternative American approach to repositories*. Paper presented at Open Repositories 2014, Helsinki, Finland. Retrieved from http:// digitalcommons.unl.edu/library_talks/98/

Thomas, G. (2007). Evaluating the impact of the institutional repository, or positioning innovation between a rock and a hard place. *New Review of Information Networking, 13*(2), 133–146. http://dx.doi.org/10.1080/13614570802105992

Xia, J., Gilchrist, S. B., Smith, N. X. P., Kingery, J. A., Radecki, J. R., Wilhelm, M. L., . . . Mahn, A. J. (2012). A review of open access self-archiving mandate policies. *portal: Libraries and the Academy, 12*(1), 85–102. http://dx.doi.org /10.1353/pla.2012.0000

APPENDIX A
Crosswalk of Metrics, Purposes, Tools, and Audiences

Audience	Metric	Sources	Purpose
Granting agencies	Downloads	Platform-generated	Measure scholarly impact
	% of items with full-text availability	Platform-generated	Demonstrate compliance with open access mandates
Accrediting agencies	Downloads	Platform-generated	Measure scholarly impact
	Number of items Uploads	Platform-generated	Measure scholarly output
	Visitor locations	Web analytics	Demonstrate visibility and reach of scholarship
	Average number of downloads	Platform-generated	Demonstrate scholarly impact
	Average number of downloads for peer institutions	Repository network	Benchmarking against peer institutions
Governing board	Statistical highlights Top downloads	Platform-generated	Demonstrate scholarly impact; highlight scholarship with high usage
	Number of items Uploads	Platform generated	Measure scholarly output
	Average number of downloads	Platform-generated	Demonstrate scholarly impact
	Average number of downloads for peer institutions	Repository network	Benchmarking against peer institutions

Continued.

Audience	Metric	Sources	Purpose
University administration	Participating units	In-house	Measure repository uptake
	Participating faculty		
	% of faculty participating		
	Number of items	Platform-generated	Measure scholarly output
	Uploads		
	Visitor locations	Web analytics	Demonstrate visibility and reach of scholarship
	Average number of downloads	Platform-generated	Demonstrate scholarly impact
	Average number of downloads for peer institutions	Repository network	Benchmarking against peer institutions
Campus units	Participating faculty	In-house	Measure repository uptake
	% of faculty participating		
	% of faculty participating in other departments	In-house	Benchmarking against peer departments
	Downloads for unit	Platform-generated	Demonstrate impact of unit's scholarship
	Downloads per faculty	Platform-generated	Evaluate impact of faculty scholarship
	Number of items by unit	Platform-generated	Measure scholarly output of unit
	Uploads for unit		

This table is modified from Inefuku, H. (2013, July). *More than seeing what sticks: Aligning repository assessment with institutional priorities.* Poster presented at Open Repositories 2013, Charlottetown, Prince Edward Island, Canada.

Continued.

Audience	Metric	Sources	Purpose
Campus units—*cont'd.*	Number of items by faculty member	Platform-generated	Measure scholarly output of faculty; demonstrate compliance with campus open access mandates
	Uploads per faculty		
	Average number of downloads	Platform-generated	Demonstrate scholarly impact
	Average number of downloads for peer institutions	Repository network	Benchmarking against peer institutions
Authors	Downloads per item	Platform-generated	Demonstrate scholarly impact; promotion and tenure
	Uploads	Platform-generated	Demonstrate scholarly output; demonstrate compliance with campus open access mandates
	Altmetrics	Altmetrics sources	Demonstrate visibility and interest in research
	Number of citations	Citation measures	Demonstrate scholarly impact

Continued.

Audience	Metric	Sources	Purpose
Repository	All of the above	All of the above	Demonstrate success of the repository; recruit new participants; enumerate work done; improve services; benchmark with repositories at peer institutions
	Visitor demographics and behavior	Web analytics	Search engine optimization; improve visibility of repository; improve services

This table is modified from Inefuku, H. (2013, July). *More than seeing what sticks: Aligning repository assessment with institutional priorities.* Poster presented at Open Repositories 2013, Charlottetown, Prince Edward Island, Canada.

APPENDIX B
Lists of Performance Indicators

Source	Performance Indicators
Thomas (2007)	• Inputs • Outputs • Impact on end-users • Impact on the Institution

Cassella (2010)	• User Perspective
	  • Percentage of scholars depositing work
	  • Average number of items per scholar
	  • Number of communities
	  • Number of downloaded items annually/ monthly/daily
	• Internal Perspective
	  • Number of items deposited annually/daily
	  • Full-text availability of documents
	  • Full-text availability of articles
	  • Number of active collections
	  • Number of value-added services
	• Financial Perspective
	  • Cost per deposit
	  • Cost per download
	• Learning and Growth Perspective
	  • Number of FTE repository staff
	  • Expenditures on staff training

ISO 2789 (2013)	• Number of archives documents • Number of documents with unrestricted access • Number of documents added during the reporting period • Number of items that are metadata only • Number of records without documents added during the reporting period • Number of access to the repository • Number of downloads of units (full documents or parts of documents)

14 | Social Media Metrics as Indicators of Repository Impact

Kim Holmberg, Stefanie Haustein, and Daniel Beucke

The altmetrics movement has introduced user counts generated from social media platforms as crowdsourced filters of the relevance of scientific content and thus as broader and timelier measures of research impact than citations (Priem, Taraborelli, Groth, & Neylon, 2010). Various altmetrics, or social media metrics as a particular subset, might be useful for repositories to measure the visibility of their contents on social media and bookmarking platforms complementing download and citation metrics. This is particularly true for preprint repositories because activity on social media can keep up with the acceleration of the publication life cycle: opposed to citations, social media activity is visible in real time right after online availability. For example, tweets to scientific papers have been shown to peak shortly after online availability (Eysenbach, 2011; Shuai, Pepe, & Bollen, 2012). Thus, a significant share of Twitter activity is assumed to reference the preprint version in the repository rather than the published version in the journal of record (Haustein, Bowman, Macaluso, Sugimoto, & Larivière, 2014). Hence, repositories may be in an especially advantageous position to use altmetrics; however, altmetrics are not widely provided by repositories yet. Studies from Germany, Austria, and Switzerland have shown that out of 173 investigated repositories only one offered altmetrics as a value-added service (Kindling & Vierkant, 2014). This is likely to change as new tools and new services are being opened to help repositories integrate altmetrics. This chapter will provide an overview of various social media metrics and discuss possibilities and challenges in applying them in the context of online repositories.

THE VARIOUS TYPES AND SOURCES OF SOCIAL MEDIA COUNTS

In an environment where research is constantly being monitored and evaluated to optimize it, citations have come to play a substantial role in scholarly communication. Citation counts have often become a synonym for research impact and quality and are being used in funding and hiring decisions as a quick and simple way to obtain information about the impact and quality of earlier research and to provide a supposedly more objective substitute for peer assessment. This trend has caused protests in the scientific community to reduce the excessive use of simple and flawed citation indicators such as the h-index and the impact factor (see, for instance, the San Francisco Declaration on Research Assessment, DORA, at http://am.ascb.org/dora/), and also paved the way for altmetrics as a way to include other, broader forms of impact (e.g., bookmarks, online mentions and discussions, likes and shares) and output (e.g., blog articles, software, code, presentations). Some of these metrics have been shown to have at least some potential in measuring academic interest, impact, or attention from the general public, while others reflect mere online visibility. The term *altmetrics* is frequently used as an umbrella term that covers many different online sources for metrics about various scientific activities and products, but—since it is derived from "alternative metrics"—it is probably not a good name (Rousseau & Ye, 2013) for the new metrics, as it has already been shown that they do not provide an alternative to citations but rather are complementary (Costas, Zahedi, & Wouters, 2014; Haustein, Larivière, Thelwall, Amyot, & Peters, 2014; Haustein, Peters, Sugimoto, Thelwall, & Larivière, 2014; Thelwall, Haustein, Larivière, & Sugimoto, 2013).

Some altmetric data aggregators such as Impactstory and PLOS Article-Level Metrics (ALM) have introduced ad-hoc classifications of different social media platforms into types of impact (viewed, saved, discussed, recommended) onto different audiences (scholarly vs. general public). However, we refrain from a classification of social media metrics based on usage and audience type because we think that this approach is too simplistic. Tweeting a link to a scholarly article, for example, might range from plain diffusion of bibliographic information in the manner of an RSS feed or content alert to an in-depth discussion of an article's results by either a group of scientists or the general public. Since so far qualitative studies investigating the particular user behavior behind the counts are lacking—that is, identifying "tweeter motivations" parallel to "citer motivations"—we describe different types of platforms currently used for social media metrics, focusing on the most common sources: blogs, microblogs (Twitter), and social bookmarking (Mendeley).

Research Blogs

As scholarly blogs have been shown to be important in scholarly communication, at least for some researchers (Kjellberg, 2010), they could be an important source for altmetrics. It has been shown that the mentions, or the so-called blog citations, scientific articles receive from blogs can in fact predict future citations (Shema, Bar-Ilan, & Thelwall, 2014). It is, however, very difficult to monitor and aggregate the information from thousands or perhaps even millions of blogs that would be required to conduct analyses going beyond a small sample of articles or journals. Altmetric.com attempts to do so by automatically tracking mentions for a manually curated list of blogs. Based on this list, less than 2% of recent journal articles get mentioned in research blogs (Costas et al., 2014; Haustein, Costas, & Larivière, 2015), which is to be expected given the selectivity and effort involved in blog posts in contrast to other social media metrics.

Microblogs

Twitter has been shown to be one of the largest social media sources of scientific journal papers (Thelwall et al., 2013), and data from it are accessible with relative ease, given that tweets are constantly harvested through Twitter's Application Programming Interface (API). After an early study based on as few as 55 papers of the *Journal of Medical Internet Research* stating that tweets serve as an early indicator of citation impact (Eysenbach, 2011), more recent large-scale and systematic studies show that the correlations between tweet counts and citations have been very low or nonexistent (Costas et al., 2014; Haustein et al., 2015; Haustein, Larivière et al., 2014; Haustein, Peters et al., 2014). The scientific articles mentioned on Twitter have often reflected popular generic topics and curious titles and represent "the usual trilogy of sex, drugs, and rock and roll" (Neylon, 2014, para. 6), suggesting that the attention gained and created on Twitter mainly comes from the wider, general audience (Haustein, Peters et al., 2014). In other countries, other microblogging platforms are important, such as Weibo in China.

Social Bookmarking

Social bookmarking counts were among the first altmetrics before the term was even invented (Taraborelli, 2008). Supported by medium to high correlations, they are those of the new metrics most related to citations, which is to be expected given the academic user group compared to social media tools like Twitter. In fact, as social bookmarking has become an important part of the scholarly communication life cycle at least for some researchers, social bookmarking and reference manager counts might be most suitable as early indicators of citations. Mendeley is the prominent source of altmetrics data because of the availability of data; a technical dependency is, in fact, prevalent in all altmetrics. Other earlier tools such as CiteULike, Connotea, and BibSonomy (Haustein & Siebenlist, 2011) do not have actual relevance anymore because they could not accumulate the critical mass needed to be considered useful resources. Zotero could become an alternative source for reader counts, as they have announced that they will provide data via an API soon. Mendeley has shown moderate to high positive correlations with citations, indicating an academic interest (Haustein, Larivière et al., 2014; Li, Thelwall, & Giustini, 2011; Mohammadi & Thelwall, 2014; Mohammadi, Thelwall, Haustein, & Larivière, 2015). However, correlations are not high enough to consider Mendeley reader counts as alternatives to citations. There seems to be a higher focus on methodological papers, and also more general science papers have more readers than citations. Social reference/bookmarking counts seem promising as a metric that can reflect academic interests more broadly and slightly earlier than citations, although it is not yet clear how representative Mendeley is for the entire readership of scientific papers.

Other Types of Altmetrics

Other online resources have also been suggested as valuable sources of altmetrics about scientific activities, many of which have previously been completely uncredited or have been an invisible part of scholarly work. SlideShare, Figshare, Dryad, and GitHub aim to credit the creation of presentations, datasets, and code and provide metrics about how others have used them. Peer-review systems and journals such as F1000Research, Publons, and PubPeer and the expert recommendations on F1000Prime give credit to researchers about their reviewing tasks and could provide statistics about this previously hidden part of scholarly work. The reviews and comments to scientific articles on these platforms may provide some information about the perceived value of the articles. A clearly under-researched area of altmetrics is that of mainstream media and news. Scientific articles are mentioned and linked to in newspapers and other more traditional media sources. It should be noted that most of these altmetrics appear only for a small fraction of scientific papers—for example, less than 1% of recent Web of Science journal articles were cited in mainstream media tracked by Altmetric.com (Costas et al., 2014; Haustein et al., 2015)—either because the sources are particularly selective or because their uptake is still low.

SOCIAL MEDIA IMPACT FOR REPOSITORIES

Institutional repositories (IRs) are built to manage and disseminate digital content, such as research articles and datasets, created by the members of an institution. Their main job is to provide access to research carried out at the institution and to preserve it. Part of this work is to collect usage statistics, partly to provide researchers information about how their research is being used, but also partly to justify their own existence to university administrators. Ever since repositories came into existence, usage of their contents has been measured with tools such as Google Analytics or AWStats, which, for example, provide information about page views, unique visitors, and downloads. For some of the most common repository platforms, such as DSpace and EPrints, available plug-ins track download counts and display them both at item and collection level (Konkiel & Scherer, 2013). These metrics show content visibility and use and increase the repository's visibility. These advantages are, however, accompanied by challenges, such as a lack of transparency in the calculation of usage statistics as well as a lack of standardization, which make it difficult to compare different repositories. COUNTER (Counting Online Usage of Networked Electronic Resources) is a quasi-standard in the field of usage data for digital objects. The COUNTER initiative was originally established by publishers and libraries to set standards for collecting and reporting usage statistics of journals. In 2014, COUNTER published the *COUNTER Code of Practice for Articles* to provide a standard at the individual article level for IRs (http://www.projectcounter.org/counterarticles.html).

Social media metrics are the most recent addition to the metrics tool-box, monitoring and reflecting the impact of digital objects in repositories. These metrics are generated by users of various social media sites and usually collected through an API. Altmetrics aggregators, such as Altmetric.com and Plum Analytics, collect these user-generated mentions of scientific products from social media, use advanced algorithms to filter the data, and offer metrics—altmetrics—indicating the impact and visibility that the research products have gained in social media (Herb & Beucke, 2013). These companies offer altmetrics for different target groups and have somewhat different business models.

PlumX from Plum Analytics is a commercial tool that offers an impact dashboard for institutions. The tool aggregates data from different sources and divides the metrics into five categories: citations, usage, mentions, captures, and social media. It covers a lot of different formats of scientific output such as articles, books, datasets, posters, and many more. Subscribed institutions can embed the PlumX widget in their repository and present these metrics on the item level.

Impactstory is a commercial service for individual researchers to show what kind of impact and visibility their work has gained. Impactstory aggregates metrics for a researcher's online portfolio of scientific products and generates a type of CV showcasing various forms of impact. The data are open to reuse, but there are no plug-ins for repositories to integrate the metrics in their own services.

Altmetric.com is a start-up company collecting, aggregating, and providing scientific social media metrics. They provide various tools for different focus groups. On the one hand, they offer a subscription model for publishers and institutions to show the impact on the article and individual levels. On the other hand, Altmetric.com offers a free badge showing the altmetrics at article level for open access, noncommercial repositories.

As one of the early adopters of altmetrics, the Public Library of Science (PLOS) has its own software for aggregating article-level metrics. This software (Lagotto) is under an MIT license for free use. For now, publishers use the software to aggregate data, which are categorized in a similar manner as in PlumX (usage, citations, social bookmarking and dissemination activity, media and blog coverage, discussion activity, and ratings). For a single institutional repository it would be a huge effort to use this software because it has to harvest all the social media services and to store all the aggregated metrics.

While some of the services mentioned above operate with the same data, there are no standards for collecting, aggregating, or presenting altmetrics. Although the National Information Standards Organization has started an initiative to create standards for altmetrics (http://www.niso.org/topics/tl/altmetrics_initiative/), it seems premature to introduce standards of altmetrics before we know more about the meaning and validity of them. Currently most of the discussions about standards seem to be regarding basic technical definitions, as for example, how to collect tweets referring to scientific documents. Altmetrics can be collected from many different sources, some of which may provide indicators of scientific activities or broader societal impact and some that may not. This raises some caution for aggregating all the data available into a single score, which supposedly measures the impact of a scientific article or a researcher. More research is needed as to whether various social media metrics are valid indicators and what kind of impact they measure.

Currently, some institutional repositories include altmetrics as a value-added service for their users. In autumn of 2014, Altmetric.com provided its free badge to more than 30 institutional repositories, and this number can be expected to increase in the future. From a selection of badges displaying the altmetrics doughnut (a doughnut-shaped visualization demonstrating the sources for and their impact on the altmetric score), repositories can select which badge they want to display for each of the articles. Clicking on the badge will take the user to a page hosted at Altmetric.com, but pages can be customized to match the design of the repository. On this page the score is broken down by sources and the user can see from which social media sites the metrics originate. Instead of just showing the aggregated impact, the context in which the impact has been created can thus be explored. In fact, Altmetric.com emphasizes the value of exploring the details and stories behind the counts. Figure 14.1 provides an example of the implementation of the Altmetric.com badge by the open access scholarly publishing service bepress (http://digitalcommons.bepress.com/) for the institutional repository of the University of Massachusetts Medical School. They use the free altmetric badge and have a customized landing page on Altmetric.com (Figure 14.2).

Figure 14.1. Example article from the institutional repository of the University of Massachusetts Medical School.

Palmer (2013), who is an institutional repository manager at University of Massachusetts Medical School, states that the benefits of introducing altmetrics into the repository include the possibility of delivering impact measures for publications that have not been published in scientific journals, such as posters, dissertations, datasets, and books. Altmetrics can also help the repository managers to demonstrate the impact of open access, while providing the authors more information about the impact and attention their work has gained. In fact, Altmetric.com recently showed that there is an open access advantage in terms of social media activity (Adie, 2014).

An international interest group under the umbrella of COAR (Confederation of Open Access Repositories) has been set up to collect and enhance information about usage data and altmetrics for repositories. COAR is an international association whose aim is to enhance the visibility and application of research outputs through global networks of open access repositories. The interest group "Usage Data and Beyond" (https://www.coar-reposito ries.org/activities/repository-interoperability/usage-data-and-beyond/) gathers knowledge of repository managers that work together to collect, standardize, aggregate, and visualize metrics for repositories.

Figure 14.2. The landing page hosted by Altmetric.com showing the Twitter mentions of an article.

POSSIBILITIES AND CHALLENGES, FUTURE DIRECTIONS

As impact measures of scientific products and activities are increasingly being used as tools for administrative purposes, altmetrics in general and altmetrics in repositories in particular can be more useful in providing a broader view of the attention and impact than citations, which are limited to a particular use by citing authors. As social media metrics go beyond traditional impact measures (citations), usage measures (downloads) and measures of awareness (page views, unique visitors, etc.), together with these indicators can potentially give a more multifaceted view about where and how scientific output has left its traces. However, since a proof for the validity of various metrics is still lacking, one should be careful when using altmetrics and not apply them for evaluative purposes of scientific impact (yet).

Although the amount of research investigating the various social media metrics is constantly growing, studies are often restricted to quantitative approaches measuring the extent to which scientific content (mostly journal articles) is represented on different platforms (i.e., the percentage of items saved, tweeted, recommended, shared) and to what extent they correlate with citations as the common impact metric. Qualitative studies are fewer and mostly limited to surveys determining which social media platforms are used by academics (Pscheida, Albrecht, Herbst, Minet, & Köhler, 2013; Rowlands, Nicholas, Russell, Canty, & Watkinson, 2011; van Noorden, 2014). More research is clearly needed to gain a better understanding of the meaning of these counts and whether they are valid indicators of impact. However, altmetrics can already provide some interesting and useful information for authors, university libraries and institutional repositories, and university administrators from an exploratory point of view.

For authors altmetrics can help give credit where credit is due for activities and research products previously invisible. As researchers are able to see the online attention to their research, it may even have a positive impact on motivation and productivity. With the constantly increasing number of scientific publications it can be very difficult for researchers to keep themselves up-to-date in their field. Altmetrics may be able to help researchers in their information seeking by showing what is popular and what has gained most attention. For repositories, altmetrics may help to justify their existence and secure funding, as the use and impact of the articles (and data) in the repositories can be better communicated to administrators. Some researchers may see bringing their articles and data into repositories as unnecessary additional work, but as researchers learn more about the impact of their research their attitudes toward repositories may change.

There are, however, some challenges facing altmetrics. All the data are currently provided by third parties and neither the services aggregating altmetrics nor the authors or repositories using them would have anything to say if social media sites like Twitter or Mendeley decided to restrict the use of their APIs or close them completely. It is also important to acknowledge that a particular social media count relevant today may not be relevant in the future. Some of the technical challenges with altmetrics involve the complexity in correctly identifying research products, as there is no universal system to do so yet. Altmetric.com, for instance, can track the impact of an article as long as they can track its DOI, PubMed ID, arXiv ID, or Handle (other identification methods are likely to be included in the future).

Some of the challenges are more related to what these new metrics actually measure. In this context it is important to remind ourselves that altmetrics is an umbrella term that covers many different sources for data about the impact and visibility that research products have received in social media, and some of these may indicate scientific interest while others may not. Moreover, what is considered an altmetric is merely based on the technical feasibility and ease of collecting data rather than what is worth measuring. As stated above, more research is needed before we can fully understand what kind of impact various social media metrics are measuring and before we have proof of their validity. A correlation between specific social media counts and citations does not necessarily prove validity; it only proves a connection between the two measures. The validity of Twitter as impact metrics have in fact recently been questioned as the existence of scientific bots automatically tweeting arXiv submissions was detected (Haustein, Bowman, Holmberg, Tsou, Sugimoto, & Larivière, 2015).

CONCLUSION

The ease of collecting social media metrics as well as the discontent with citation-based measures (citation delay, misuse of impact factor as substitute for paper impact) have created a hype around altmetrics and led to the implementation of social media metrics on journal Web sites, in researchers' CVs (Piwowar & Priem, 2013), and in institutional repositories, and triggered the discussion in the community of research evaluators, scientific journals, and university libraries to consider these types of new metrics. As many altmetrics are accumulated in the days following the publication of a research product, repositories and altmetrics collected from repositories can fulfill the promises of timelier data about impact. The proposed benefits of showing altmetrics in institutional repositories include showing impact measures for research products that have not been published as articles in scientific journals, reporting the impact and visibility of their work to authors, demonstrating the impact of open access, and providing better and more diverse usage statistics of repository content. Other possible uses for altmetrics, such as highlighting popular articles in information retrieval, have also been suggested. There are, however, many challenges that need to be solved before altmetrics can be taken as a reliable impact measure, the greatest of which is determining which of the plethora of social media counts are valid indicators of research impact.

ACKNOWLEDGMENTS

This work was partly supported by the Alfred P. Sloan Foundation Grant #2014-3-25.

REFERENCES

Adie, E. (2014, October 23). Attention! A study of open access vs non-open access articles [Altmetric.com Web log post]. Retrieved from http://www.altmetric.com /blog/attentionoa/

Costas, R., Zahedi, Z., & Wouters, P. (2014). Do "altmetrics" correlate with citations? Extensive comparison of altmetric indicators with citations from a multidisciplinary perspective. *Journal of the Association for Information Science and Technology.* http://dx.doi,org/10.1002/asi.23309

Eysenbach, G. (2011). Can tweets predict citations? Metrics of social impact based on Twitter and correlation with traditional metrics of scientific impact. *Journal of Medical Internet Research, 13*(4), e123. http://dx.doi.org/10.2196 /jmir.2012

Haustein, S., Bowman, T. D., Holmberg, K., Tsou, A., Sugimoto, C. R., & Larivière, V. (2015). Tweets as impact indicators: Examining the implications of automated "bot" accounts on Twitter. *Journal of the Association for Information Science and Technology.* http://dx.doi.org/10.1002/asi.23456

Haustein, S., Bowman, T. D., Macaluso, B., Sugimoto, C. R., & Larivière, V. (2014). Measuring Twitter activity of arXiv e-prints and published papers. In *Altmetrics14: Expanding impacts and metrics. An ACM Web Science Conference 2014 Workshop.* Bloomington, IN. http://dx.doi.org/10.6084/m9.figshare .1041514

Haustein, S., Costas, R., & Larivière, V. (2015). Characterizing social media metrics of scholarly papers: The effect of document properties and collaboration patterns. *PLOS ONE, 10*(3), e0120495.

Haustein, S., Larivière, V., Thelwall, M., Amyot, D., & Peters, I. (2014). Tweets vs. Mendeley readers: How do these two social media metrics differ ? *Information Technology, 56*(5), 207–215. http://dx.doi.org/10.1515/itit-2014-1048

Haustein, S., Peters, I., Sugimoto, C. R., Thelwall, M., & Larivière, V. (2014). Tweeting biomedicine: An analysis of tweets and citations in the biomedical literature. *Journal of the American Society for Information Science and Technology, 65*(4), 656–669. http://dx.doi.org/10.1002/asi.23101

Haustein, S., & Siebenlist, T. (2011). Applying social bookmarking data to evaluate journal usage. *Journal of Informetrics, 5*(3), 446–457. http://dx.doi .org/10.1016/j.joi.2011.04.002

Herb, U., & Beucke, D. (2013). Die Zukunft der Impact-Messung. Social Media, Nutzung und Zitate Im World Wide Web. *Wissenschaftsmanagement. Zeitschrift für Innovation, 19*(4), 22–25.

Kindling, M., & Vierkant, P. (2014). *2014 census of open access repositories in Germany, Austria and Switzerland.* Presentation at Open Repositories 2014, Helsinki, Finland, June 9–13, 2014.

Kjellberg, S. (2010). *Scholarly blogs: Scholarly communication and knowledge production in the blogosphere.* Dissertation. University of Lund, 2010.

Konkiel, S., & Scherer, D. (2013). New opportunities for repositories in the age of altmetrics. *Bulletin of the American Society for Information Science and Technology, 39*(4), 22–26. http://dx.doi.org/10.1002/bult.2013.1720390408

Li, X., Thelwall, M., & Giustini, D. (2011). Validating online reference managers for scholarly impact measurement. *Scientometrics, 91*(2), 461–471. http://dx.doi .org/10.1007/s11192-011-0580-x

Mohammadi, E., & Thelwall, M. (2014). Mendeley readership altmetrics for the social sciences and humanities: Research evaluation and knowledge flows. *Journal of the Association for Information Science and Technology, 65(8),* 1627–1638. http://dx.doi.org/10.1002/asi.23071

Mohammadi, E., Thelwall, M., Haustein, S., & Larivière, V. (2015). Who reads research articles? An altmetrics analysis of Mendeley user categories. *Journal of the Association for Information Science and Technology, 66*(9), 1832–1846. http://dx.doi.org/10.1002/asi.23286

Neylon, C. (2014, October 3). Altmetrics: What are they good for? [*PLOS Opens* Web log post]. Retrieved from http://blogs.plos.org/opens/2014/10/03/alt metrics-what-are-they-good-for/

Palmer, L. A. (2013). *Altmetrics and institutional repositories: A health sciences library experiment.* University of Massachusetts Medical School. Library Publications and Presentations. Paper 142. Retrieved from http://escholarship .umassmed.edu/lib_articles/142

Piwowar, H., & Priem, J. (2013). The power of altmetrics on a CV. *Bulletin of*

Association for Infomation Science and Technology, 39(4), 10–13. Retrieved from http://asis.org/Bulletin/Apr-13/AprMay13_Piwowar_Priem.html

Priem, J., Taraborelli, D., Groth, P., & Neylon, C. (2010). Alt-metrics: A manifesto. Retrieved from http://altmetrics.org/manifesto

Pscheida, D., Albrecht, S., Herbst, S., Minet, C., & Köhler, T. (2013). Nutzung von Social Media und onlinebasierten Anwendungen in der Wissenschaft. Erste Ergebnisse des Science 2.0–Survey 2013 des Leibniz-Forschungsverbunds. *Science 2.0.* Retrieved from http://www.qucosa.de/fileadmin/data/qucosa /documents/13296/Science20_Datenreport_2013_PDF_A.pdf

Rousseau, R., & Ye, F. Y. (2013). A multi-metric approach for research evaluation. *Chinese Science Bulletin, 58*(26), 3288–3290. http://dx.doi.org/10.1007/s11 434-013-5939-3

Rowlands, I., Nicholas, D., Russell, B., Canty, N., & Watkinson, A. (2011). Social media use in the research workflow. *Learned Publishing, 24*(3), 183–195. http://dx.doi.org/10.1087/20110306

Shema, H., Bar-Ilan, J., & Thelwall, M. (2014). Do blog citations correlate with a higher number of future citations? Research blogs as a potential source for alternative metrics. *Journal of the American Society for Information Science and Technology, 65*(5), 1018–1027. http://dx.doi.org/10.1002/asi.23037

Shuai, X., Pepe, A., & Bollen, J. (2012). How the scientific community reacts to newly submitted preprints: Article downloads, Twitter mentions, and citations. *PLoS ONE, 7*(11), e47523. http://dx.doi.org/10.1371/journal.pone.0047523

Taraborelli, D. (2008). Soft peer review: Social software and distributed scientific evaluation. In *Proceedings of the 8th International Conference on the Design of Cooperative Systems* (pp. 99–110). COOP.

Thelwall, M., Haustein, S., Larivière, V., & Sugimoto, C. R. (2013). Do altmetrics work? Twitter and ten other candidates. *PLOS ONE, 8*(5), e64841. http://dx .doi.org/10.1371/journal.pone.0064841

Van Noorden, R. (2014). Online collaboration: Scientists and the social network. *Nature, 512*(7513), 126–129. http://dx.doi.org/10.1038/512126a

15 | Peer Review and Institutional Repositories

Burton Callicott

What role, if any, do institutional repositories (IRs) have in terms of scholarly peer review? Since the advent of the Royal Society in London in 1662 and the birth of a peer-review system, there has been debate on the efficacy and value of having scholarly oversight and a gatekeeper that determines what should and what should not be published in a given journal.[1] The open access (OA) movement coupled with a culture of immediate, open online commentary has intensified and changed the shape of the debate in recent years. The remarkable success of arXiv and other preprint, subject repositories coupled with the creation of numerous institution-based online "journals" and experiments with open, crowdsourced review processes have set the stage for what could be a radical shift in the way that scholarship is vetted. As Wheeler puts it, "Whether peer review will remain the mandated norm for scholarly recognition is not yet up for grabs: what is uncertain is the form it will take—more likely, the multiple forms it will take" (2011, p. 317). In a post to the SCHOLCOMM listserv, Glenn Hampson, director of the National Science Communication Institute, posits a potential major role for IRs in terms of peer review: "If research institutions could take it upon themselves to set up a peer review process and edit pieces so they are clear and readable and if the press offices of these institutions could help promote these works to the outside world (including immediately posting them on institution websites or OA resources), we are 99% of the way there. . . . The rest is just institutional inertia with regard to tenure" (2014). In addition to the glacial pace of change when it comes to the culture of academia and the Catch-22 nature of tenure review (those with the most at stake have the least amount of power to change the system), Hampson's vision ignores the difficulties smaller institutions with smaller departments would have to field a pool of reviewers deep and broad enough to provide an adequate sounding board, not to mention the myriad of potential personal biases that would crop up in such a system that would be far from anonymous and could easily silence objectively important contributions. However, if oriented and implemented properly, IRs have a serious and significant role to play in developing, directing, and shaping the evolution of scholarly peer review.

It has been well documented that institutional repositories have struggled to acquire scholarly content from academics. Of the various reasons for this, the fact that repositories provide little if any credentialing in the form of peer review is arguably the single biggest reason that scholars do not actively provide content to their home IR. At present the gold (and in many cases only) standard that tenure and promotion review committees value and count are publications in traditional peer-review journals and academic presses. A 2006 survey at the University of California, sponsored by the Center for Studies in Higher Education, concluded that "Peer review is *the* hallmark of quality that results from external and independent valuation. It also functions as an effective means of winnowing the papers that a researcher needs to examine in the course of his/her research" (King et al., 2006). Although many faculty members indicate in surveys and interviews that they value and support efforts to make scholarship available to those who do not have the means to access material published in traditional journals, they rarely take the time and effort to deposit material into their institution's repositories. Easy but legitimate excuses such as concerns about copyright infringement as well as clunky, difficult to use deposit interfaces belie the underlying reason: most faculty do not feel compelled to add to their IR because they do not see that it will have any effect on their tenure and promotion. In their 2008 study, "Institutional Repositories: Faculty Deposits, Marketing, and the Reform of Scholarly Communication," Jantz and Wilson remark on the remarkable lack of deposits and interest in IRs: "Given the lack of faculty participation, the obvious question is 'why the lack of interest?' The most likely answer is that faculty do not perceive any significant value of an IR to their scholarly endeavors. We believe this is due, in large part, to two factors: immaturity of the IR platform (both content and infrastructure) and the absence of any coherent articulation of how IRs can advance scholarship" (p. 194).

Faculty are busy and without a mandate to deposit, most will not take the time or put forth the effort to do so. Managers and ambassadors of IRs who are at institutions that do not have a deposit mandate have two things to offer faculty that can leverage tenure and promotion needs in order to increase participation: a place to gather and collate all scholarly impact measures and a platform for publishing and disseminating gray literature.

FROM GRAY TO WHITE

Because of its very nature, gray literature is tricky to define and, with the rise of open access and growth of the Web, it has already outgrown the 2010 "Prague definition" established at the 12th annual Conference on Grey Literature: "Grey literature stands for manifold document types produced on all levels of government, academics, business and industry in print and electronic formats that are protected by intellectual property rights, of sufficient quality to be collected and preserved by library holdings or institutional repositories, but not controlled by commercial publishers i.e., where publishing is not the primary activity of the producing body" (Schopfel, 2011, p. 15).With the myriad of ways to make information available electronically, what it means to publish something is not as obvious or straightforward as it once was. The key distinguishing term in the Prague definition is "commercial." Although many academic publishers are not huge money makers, they are ultimately commercial ventures. Despite the budgets and marketing that undergird any institution of higher learning, those that feature an IR or some other means of serving up scholarship nurture a free exchange of ideas, and that work done to make scholarship available to anyone with access to the Internet is done without commercial motivations—at least not in a direct way. This new, noncommercial institutional publishing space is tailor-made for gray literature, which typically does not seek or hold monetary value. Examples of gray literature include working papers, preprints, conference papers, technical reports, information sheets, datasets, honors essays, theses, and so on. In essence, gray literature describes anything of potential informational value that was either not intended to be published or was rejected by a traditional publisher. With the right configuration, IRs provide a natural home and a nouveau form of publication for this information that can transform it into something that can not only serve the academic mission of the institution but can also impact a tenure and promotion packet. For polished, fully formed scholarly work that was previously published or destined for a publication in an established journal, subject or disciplinary repositories make all the sense in the world. For everything else, including data that supplement published work, an IR provides the perfect home and complement to subject repositories.

In a 2003 ACRL report, Clifford Lynch outlines the true raison d'etre of IRs that can be seen to rest largely on gray literature:

> Institutional repositories can encourage the exploration and adoption of new forms of scholarly communication that exploit the digital medium in fundamental ways. This, to me, is perhaps the most important and exciting payoff: facilitating change not so much in the existing system of scholarly publishing but by opening up entire new forms of scholarly communication that will need to be legitimized and nurtured with guarantees of both short- and long-term accessibility. Institutional repositories can support new practices of scholarship that emphasize data as an integral part of the record and discourse of scholarship. They can structure and make effective otherwise diffuse efforts to capture and disseminate learning and teaching materials, symposia and performances, and related documentation of the intellectual life of universities. (p. 1)

Lynch's report has proved to be prophetic. IRs have been quietly and, in some cases, dramatically legitimizing and nurturing gray literature to the point that it has made an undeniable impact on scholarship. Because of a moratorium on making previously published literature available in its IR due to lack of in-house legal counsel, Purdue University originally only sought out and served up gray literature in their IR. Some IRs have reversed this process and have begun to pointedly shift focus from acquiring pre- and postprints to gray literature. In an effort to get out of a time-consuming copyright clearance quagmire, the director of the Digital Repository at the

University of Maryland (DRUM) began to phase out of a program geared toward populating its repository with previously published research and to engage in a new program designed to acquire gray literature: "Because much of this formally published research was most likely available on the journal website or in another repository, such as PubMed Central, the decision was made to discontinue the project [of acquiring preprints] and instead concentrate on acquiring and making available the unique gray literature produced at the University" (Owen, 2011, p. 154).

Those on the forefront of the open access movement will surely grimace at this quote as it reveals the way that those in large institutions are often comfortably unaware of the difficulty many scholars in smaller, less endowed institutions, especially those in small-market economies, have to simply get their hands on current scholarship. Without diminishing the potential role IRs have in expanding access to the ivory tower, it is important to put things in perspective. As is also implied in the quote, subject repositories provide the natural place for soon-to-be or "formally published" material—they provide the ontological community and logical place for discovery. As such, it can be argued that national and consortially based repositories have more leverage and are perhaps better suited to be on the forefront of the open access initiative. This is not to say that IRs do not have a role to play in terms of advocacy, education, and curation of the work itself but simply to say that IRs have a unique role in terms of providing a locale and access point for gray literature. In their 2010 study, "Authors' Awareness and Attitudes toward Open Access Repositories," Creaser and colleagues found that: "Although 46% of authors expressed a preference for depositing in subject-based repositories, compared to 22% preferring an institutional repository, only 37% of respondents knew of a suitable subject repository they could use" (p. 153).

Opposition to gray literature in IRs rests largely on two arguments: (1) that the potentially less scholarly work will contaminate and pollute repositories and turn faculty away, and (2) that by not making gray literature a primary focus of an IR, this will signal a defeat or at least provide a distraction from what proponents of the open access movement regard as the foremost responsibility of IRs: "The reason OA is urgent is that potential research uptake, usage, and impact—hence applications, progress and productivity—are being lost, daily, cumulatively, some of it probably irretrievably, because the only users with access to journal articles are those whose institutions can afford subscription access to the journals in which the articles are published" (Harnad, 2013, p. 5). The fear of contamination is largely due to miscommunication and paranoia. As Bankier and Smith note in their 2010 study of repository collection policies: "There appears to be little or no conclusive literature showing that faculty are dissuaded from participating in the IR simply because the repository might also publish less scholarly faculty endeavors or content from other groups on campus" (p. 247). Bankier and others conclude that as long as the IR hosting the material makes it clear whether or not a given item has gone through a peer-review process and has been previously (or will soon be) published, there is no logical or essential reason that the work would be confused or tainted by association with non-peer-reviewed material.

Harnad has been one of the most vocal and impassioned of the OA mandate camp. In a "counterpoint" to Kennison's essay "Institutional Repositories: So Much More Than Green OA," he contends that "all the evidence suggests that there is no point in just continuing to collect other kinds of contents [gray literature] in the hope that they will somehow lead to an OA mandate and compliance" (Kennison, Shreeves, & Harnad, 2013, p. 6). Harnad's arguments and conviction are convincing, but his proof by negation is unsupported by the experiences of most IR managers who have worked closely with faculty. Dave Scherer, who has been involved in Purdue's IR from inception, echoes the experience of most if not all IR managers: "Gray literature is an easy 'in' with faculty. There are fewer concerns on copyright and sharing and in most cases the copyright is either held by the university or the faculty member. It is a way to get them started with the IR and to experience the benefits. Once they've experienced it for some time it's a great way to lead into 'We can do this with your published work too'" (personal communication, October 30, 2014). Harnad rightfully points out that the number of schools with an OA mandate is growing slowly. However, the gospel is spreading on a grassroots level that may ultimately lead to an open access culture that is more organic and stronger than one that is mandated. The results of Creaser's study back up what many veteran IR managers are observing and reporting: "Of those authors surveyed who had deposited a stage-two manuscript, 70% reported that they did so voluntarily. The most frequently cited motivations to deposit included: suggestion from a colleague (12% of those who had deposited); invitation from the repository in question (11%); request from a co-author (10%); publisher invitation to deposit (8%); mandated by institution (8%); and funder mandate (3%)" (Creaser et al., 2010, p. 156).

Though it does not go through a traditional peer-review process, gray literature does have a legitimate role to play in scholarly communication. A chapter in *Scientific Communication for Natural Resource Professionals* addresses the importance of gray literature in the field: "Gray literature typically serves to formally document field projects, policy development initiatives, and other activities of government agencies and educational institutions, industry, or public institutes, and nongovernmental organizations. These documents provide supplemental information in a broad framework of knowledge within which researchers can place their work" (Eells, Vondracek, & Vondracek, 2012, p. 3). In their article "Grey Literature: A Growing Need for Good Practice," De Castro and Salinetti (2013) note, "Our recent search (May 2013) using PubMed . . . showed a massive increase in the number of times the term 'grey literature' occurred in titles and abstracts of articles indexed in the database in the last 20 years" (p. 66). Seymour (2010) makes an impassioned case for the importance and quality of gray literature in the field of archaeology in his "Sanctioned Inequality and Accessibility Issues in the Grey Literature in the United States." Because of the informal and unstructured way that gray literature has been circulated, it has been hard to find. As more and more of this material gets served up in IRs, more and more will be discovered and cited. These citations serve to record the importance and impact of the work and can be used to supplement and augment a tenure or promotion packet as well as raise the profile of the home institution. Those institutions that have strict collection development policies that may bar gray literature for reasons other than adequate digital space may be unwittingly suppressing valuable work that has the potential to impact the scholarly community, the tenure and promotion packets of scholars at their institution, as well as the prominence of the institution itself: "Some value is relatively explicit, as when previously inaccessible grey literature becomes freely available on the Web. Such is the view from the content-focused perspective: value is generated for the library, faculty member, and the university alike through open access dissemination of an ever-larger corpus of scholarship" (Palmer, Teffeau, & Newton, 2008, p. 255).

Due to the initial work of IRs to catalog, describe, house, and make gray literature available to Web crawlers, a growing number of these items are gaining acceptance, use, and citations—undoubtedly this work would previously have languished on a single hard drive or a cloud-based account shared with few if any. The now popular and frequently downloaded *Dictionary of Invertebrate Zoology* edited by Maggenti, Maggenti, and Gardner provides an illustrative example. After having been rejected by traditional publishers, the manuscript wound up in a departmental lab literally gathering dust until an IR coordinator at the University of Nebraska–Lincoln went to meet with faculty and saw the copy "lying on the shelves" (Giesecke, 2011, p. 537). After a brief discussion and some minimal editing, the manuscript was published in DigitalCommons@University of Nebraska–Lincoln. Due to the high number of downloads, a print-on-demand version of the dictionary was made available and can be purchased from Amazon and Barnes & Noble (p. 538). A study of the Cornell ILR repository underscores the positive feedback loop that can result from a liberal collection development policy that welcomes previously unpublished material: "In terms of content type, the Cornell ILR repository utilises a strategy of housing content relevant to the faculty's research. . . . It provides an example of materials of interest outside the post-print collection scope which serve an important purpose for faculty engagement, and are able to create more awareness and, in a circular fashion, bring in more content" (Bankier & Smith, 2010, p. 250).

The ability to record the number and frequency of downloads is where IRs can play a serious and potentially foundational role in terms of tenure and promotion and, by proxy, peer review. Evidence that work is being read and having an influence on the expansion of knowledge can add legitimacy to gray scholarship and function as a measure of importance and a form of peer review when it comes to tenure and promotion. "Many researchers include the JIF's [Journal Impact Factor] for journals in which they have published on their vitas when going up for tenure or promotion, as a means of documenting the impact of their work. By also including supplemental measure of impact (usage counts and altmetrics) for traditional publications as well as grey literature and other outputs deposited in IRs, faculty can more fully document the impact of their scholarship" (Konkiel & Scherer, 2013, p. 23). In their "Tenure and Promotion in the Age of Online Social Media," Gruzd, Staves, and Wilk conclude: "In sum, the idea of incorporating social media mentions/publications into scholars' overall scholarly impact is growing in popularity and acceptance" (2011, p. 8). Since this literature is rarely published anywhere else, IR managers have a responsibility to the scholarly community and in particular to scholars at their home institution to make it discoverable and consequently, to make its impact measurable: "They [IRs] have a major role to play in extending the metadata systems, and technical interoperability that will support regional and global subject access to repositories, that will bring them more into line with the needs of their academic communities" (Cullen & Chawner, 2011, p. 496).

After his article, "Twitter Mood Predicts the Stock Market," was rejected by numerous peer-reviewed journals, Johan Bollen made it available on arXiv. The subsequent attention and downloads that the article received led to it being accepted by the *Journal of Computational Science.* The remarkable response that Bollen received—73,000 downloads in the first week on arXiv—is unique if not unprecedented, but it does reveal not only the Achilles' heel of the traditional peer-review system but the potential reservoir of important work that may be languishing unread because it had been rejected by a publisher. Because the pool of reviewers is not only small but consists of established scholars with reputations to defend, they may be unable to see (or be afraid of) the implications of new takes on old arguments or new arguments altogether. IRs and subject repositories can be seen as the YouTube of scholarly communication. Though Justin Bieber and E. L. James, author of *50 Shades of Grey,* may not provide the best examples in terms of objective quality (and reveal the flip side of a more popular/democratic form of peer review), the success and subsequent recording and publishing deals that resulted from a popular response is an illustration of the way that a small number of experts can miss or reject important work. If not a means for uncovering scholarly rock stars, by accepting, properly tagging, and publishing rejected work, IRs can potentially legitimize faculty members who have tried and failed to find a publisher. Although the number of these lost gems may be small, given the amount of digital space most IRs have available, it makes no sense not to solicit and upload them to an IR. By increasing the number and the prominence of impactful scholarly work that found legitimacy through a more crowdsourced (and open sourced) means, repositories can provide the evidence and the mechanism to radically change and democratize the peer-review publication process.

In "The Invisible Hand of Peer Review," Harnad makes explicit what almost anyone who has published knows and in a lot of cases has experienced: "There is a hierarchy among journals, based on the rigor of their peer review, all the way down to an unrefereed vanity press at the bottom. Persistent authors can work their way down until their paper finds its own level, not without considerable wasting of time and resources along the way, including the editorial office budgets of the journals and the freely given time of the referees, who might find themselves called upon more than once to review the same paper, sometimes unchanged, for several different journals" (2004, p. 236). Like subject repositories, IRs can serve as a segue or stepping-stone toward the subversive proposal that Harnad first suggested in 1998 where "papers will be submitted in electronic form, and archived on the Web (in hidden referee-only sites, or publicly, in open-archive preprint sectors, depending on the author's preferences). . . . To distribute the load among referees more equitably the journal editor can formally approach a much larger population of selected, qualified experts about relevant papers they are invited to referee if they have the time and the inclination" (p. 240). With the right setup, IRs can password-protect or make publicly available draft essays. Librarians and authors can serve not so much as journal editors but as promoters or brokers who can match up interested readers for informal peer review/test audience services. Download statistics coupled with altmetrics as well as reader responses can funnel essays to the right journal and provide editors with valuable information about the potential impact of new work. As most journal editors know, there is a looming crisis of peer review that is due to a dramatic increase of scholarship that will tax the already overburdened stable of peer reviewers who do their work anonymously and free of charge: "With other countries such as Singapore and Brazil joining the fray, all of them adopting the same numbers-driven incentives for researchers to publish, and European countries and the United States exponentially increasing their publication outputs as well, a 'publication tsunami' appears likely in the next decade" (Baveye, 2010, p. 204). By employing IRs as lodestones that can naturally attract readers and document interest, they represent an easy and natural pathway for evolving the publishing model that can blunt the coming peer-review crisis, help authors (especially those without a strong publishing history), and provide a new role for librarians as partners in the publication process.

NOTE

1. See Lee, Sugimoto, Zhang, and Cronin (2013) and Shatz (2004).

REFERENCES

Bankier, J., & Smith, C. (2010). Repository collection policies: Is a liberal or inclusive policy helpful or harmful? *Australian Academic and Research Libraries, 41,* 245–259.

Bavaye, P. (2010). Sticker shock and looming tsunami: The high cost of academic serials. *Journal of Scholarly Publishing, 41,* 191–215.

Bollen, J., Mao, H., & Zeng, X. (2011). Twitter mood predicts the stock market. *Journal of Computational Science, 2,* 1–8.

Creaser, C., Fry, J., Greenwood, H., Oppenheim, C., Probets, S., Spezi, V., & White, S. (2010). Authors' awareness and attitudes toward open access repositories. *New Review of Academic Librarianship, 16*(S1), 145–161.

Cullen, R., & Chawner, B. (2011). Institutional repositories, open access, and scholarly communication: A study of conflicting paradigms. *The Journal of Academic Librarianship, 37,* 460–470.

De Castro, P., & Salinetti, S. (2013). Grey literature: A growing need for good practice. *European Science Editing, 39*(3), 65–68.

Eells, L., Vondracek, R., & Vondracek, B. (2012). Fishing the deep web: The search for information. In C. A. Jennings, T. E. Lauer, & B. Vondracek (Eds.), *Scientific Communication for Information Professionals.* Bethesda, MD: American Fisheries Society.

Giesecke, J. (2011). Institutional repositories: Keys to success. *Journal of Library Administration, 51,* 529–542.

Gruzd, A., Staves, K., & Wilk, A. (2011). Tenure and promotion in the age of online social media. *Proceedings of the American Society for Information Science and Technology, 48,* 1–9.

Hampson, G. (2014, August 28). Re: Version of record [Electronic mailing list message]. Retrieved from http://lists.ala.org/wws

Harnad, S. (2004). The invisible hand of peer review. In D. Shatz (Ed.), *Peer review: A critical commentary* (pp. 235–242). Oxford, UK: Rowman and Littlefield.

Harnad, S. (2013). Ordering institutional repositories vs breaking through open doors. *Journal of Librarianship and Scholarly Communication, 1*(4), eP1105. http://dx.doi.org/10.7710/2162-3309.1105.

Jantz, R. C., & M. C. Wilson, M. C. (2008). Institutional repositories: Faculty deposits, marketing, and the reform of scholarly communication. *Journal of Academic Librarianship, 34,* 186–195.

Kennison, R., Shreeves, S. L., & Harnad, S. (2013). Point and counterpoint: The purpose of institutional repositories: Green OA or beyond? *Journal of Librarianship and Scholarly Communication, 1*(4).

King, C. J., Harley, D., Earl-Novell, S., Arter, J., Lawrence, S., & Perciali, I. (2006). *Scholarly communication: Academic values and sustainable models.* Retrieved from http://www.cshe.berkeley.edu/publications/scholarly-communication-academic-values-and-sustainable-models

Konkiel, S., & Scherer, D. (2013). New opportunities for repositories in the age of altmetrics. *Bulletin of the Association for Information Science and Technology, 39*(4), 22–26.

Lee, C., Sugimoto, C., Zhang, G., & Cronin, B. (2013). Bias in peer review. *Journal of the American Society for Information Science and Technology, 64,* 2–17.

Lynch, C. (2003). Institutional repositories: Essential infrastructure for scholarship in the digital age. *ARL Bimonthly Report, 226,* 1–7.

Owen, T. (2011). Evolution of a digital repository: One institution's experience. *Journal of Electronic Resources Librarianship, 23*(2), 142–149.

Palmer, C., Teffeau, L., & Newton, M. (2008). Strategies for institutional repository development: A case study of three evolving initiatives. *Library Trends, 56,* 142–167.

Schopfel, J. (2011). Towards a Prague definition of grey literature. *The Grey Journal, 7*(1), 5–18.

Seymour, D. J. (2010). Sanctioned inequality and accessibility issues in the grey literature in the United States. *Archaeologies: Journal of the World Archaeological Congress, 6,* 233–269.

Shatz, D. (2004). *Peer review: A critical commentary.* Oxford, UK: Rowman and Littlefield.

Wheeler, B. (2011). The ontology of the scholarly journal and the place of peer review. *Journal of Scholarly Publishing, 42,* 307–322.

16 | Defining Success and Impact for Scholars, Department Chairs, and Administrators: Is There a Sweet Spot?

Marianne A. Buehler

Various academic stakeholders are concentrated in the scholarly communication milieu with their varied and similar needs to focus on their ongoing research investments. Scientists, scholars, department heads, and administrators are the primary constituencies that engage academic research investors, such as the university and college library, in academic library–created digital repositories. The initial and ongoing advantage in creating digital repositories has been the usefulness of making multiple scholarly item types (articles, postprints, preprints, theses/dissertations) available to meet researcher and reader needs. We are now embarking on the future of the digital repository that truly engages faculty and administrators, meets institutional goals, holds big datasets, and uses linked data to connect authors, institutional repositories, and global research.

INSTITUTIONAL REPOSITORIES: PUBLISHING MODELS AND GLOBAL RESEARCH VISIBILITY

The first institutional repositories (IRs) initially designed and produced in 2000 and 2001, respectively, utilizing newly constructed EPrints and DSpace software, were created to alleviate the high cost of academic libraries' journal subscriptions, ensure greater access to journal articles, and provide scholarly communication tools for researchers to showcase their work. Overall, academic libraries have been steady in employing an institution's repository to engage researchers' scholarship and make it globally visible for further use. Libraries' primary purpose in archiving faculty research was the motivation to cancel journal subscriptions and use institutional research budget funding to purchase materials not available through other channels. Recurring universal challenges included faculty unaware of an IR's existence, its benefits, and/or a preference to showcase their research in a subject repository such as the Social Sciences Research Network (SSRN) or arXiv. Faculty who are interested in depositing their work in both an IR and a disciplinary repository (also referred to as central or subject repository) either have librarians deposit in multiple locations or the researchers proxy or self-archive their respective papers.

SCHOLARLY COMMUNICATION DISRUPTION: INSTITUTIONAL REPOSITORIES

In creating and building the University of Nevada Las Vegas (UNLV) institutional repository (IR) using Digital Commons software, initially it was a basic interface created by faculty librarians for scholarship that was undefined. The newly hired repository administrator (the author) made decisions in concert with an advisory board of stakeholders from library departments: special collections, liaisons, digital collections, and a metadata specialist. Some of the early decisions included deciding on a strategic composition of board members, adding FAST (OCLC's Faceted Application of Subject Terminology) metadata, and employing a standard hierarchy for IR staff to follow. Two years later, an updated UNLV interface was necessary to comply with the university's new color and design guidelines. As the primary architect in concert with the libraries' upper management through a series of meetings that included the dean, associate dean, statistics head, the director of technical services, and the IR administrator, an improved interface was agreed upon. For optimum online visibility and findability, IR URLs should contain the university's acronym and the name of the repository, including the extension .edu, delineating an academic Web site.

The role of the IR has evolved in librarians' collaboration with faculty's data deposits. Supercomputers and IR administrators are considering joining forces to accommodate large datasets, and faculty aspire to a potential option of adding data article output, metadata, and a URL to link all of a research project's facets together simultaneously. Librarians' data management knowledge and documentation is rapidly moving more quickly than the data are being ingested in IRs.

Institutional repositories have the ability to engage in linked data to connect item URIs to more easily have item findability across multiple IRs. The linked data cloud is growing exponentially; IR administrators and metadata specialists educated in linked data are gradually expanding their new skills.

Academic libraries are playing a pivotal role in faculty, department chair, and administrator perspectives by how these researcher and scholarship interest groups are engaging the tools they require to showcase their work. At a minimum, to be successful, librarians (repository managers and subject liaisons) and library staff ranging from the dean to support staff must initially and continually show faculty support for depositing their research and open access (OA) ventures: how to get started, remain committed, and convinced that the open publishing model is *the* model for research impact success.

Subject liaisons typically have the academic pulse of their assigned colleges from collection development and reference positions to building new relationships in new forms of scholarly communication that encompass research workflows, impact measures, and the like. In these new liaison roles, there has been "no formal training, no assessment tools, and no measures of performance" and "the need to transcend vestiges of turf protection and work towards a collaborative model of scholarly support . . . addressing the changing nature of research and teaching" (Kenney, 2014). Making IRs work has embraced data tools (DMPTool), linked data, persistent personal identifiers, and depositing research in both subject and institutional repositories, leveraging processes across multiple platforms.

Most universities and colleges now have numerous Web pages developed on the topic of scholarly communication for librarians. In 2014 ACRL's Scholarly Communication Committee updated its Scholarly Communication Toolkit (http://acrl.ala.org/scholcomm/) resources to support librarians' work with administrators, department heads, and faculty.

Typically, there is ongoing turnover in faculty, department heads, and administration in an academic environment. Interim deans and other administrators do not make critical decisions while temporarily holding down their academic role. Once new department heads and administrators are hired and in place, it is time to set up an appointment to support their knowledge of the digital repository and garner curriculum vitae and full-text content. Without an academic mandate to archive articles and postprints (final approved papers) in an IR, repository administrators will need to build relationships.

The UNLV IR role has matured to incorporating IR metadata and full text to OAIster and WorldCat and by presenting the green and gold models to the Graduate College, College of Engineering, deans, associate deans, department heads, and faculty to create a greater understanding of what research article versions are journal copyright legal to deposit in an IR. Successful repository managers engage their library liaisons by offering workshops on researcher profile tools, such as SelectedWorks (bepress), to showcase faculty scholarship, updates on predatory publishing practices, researcher identifiers, and the current state of open access to research to provide library colleagues with tools to build effective programs on their campuses. ACRL's 2014 update on its Scholarly Communication Toolkit focuses on supportive librarian essential dialogue topics that include author's rights and licensing, digital repositories, journal economics, new models of publishing and scholarship, digital humanities, research data management, outreach and engagement actions, and realigning library resources, services, and practices. These are but a few of the essential tools that assist librarians in the service of facilitating and defining success and impact for faculty, department heads, and administrators.

SCHOLARLY COMMUNICATION SITUATION: THEN AND NOW

As an early adopter of an institutional repository, Cornell University's DSpace installation was primarily underused by faculty and consisted of empty or underpopulated research collections. Faculty had little motivation to migrate from disciplinary repositories or personal Web sites, and had concerns about redundancy with other dissemination tools, copyright confusion, plagiarism fears, having one's work scooped, and knowing what constitutes a published work using green and gold model definitions (Davis & Connolly, 2007). Six years later, Cornell's library continues expectations of faculty diligence in preserving their research and active dissemination, asking them to do more than they have been typically willing to be responsible for, as stated in the 2013 *White Paper: Institutional Repositories at Cornell.*

Another epiphany of hampered IR success was accountability by the University of Rochester (UR) Library's organizational culture. It was manifested by a set of protracted assumptions and complicated policies (modeled after MIT's) that faculty were expected to follow. UR Library intentions were principled and simultaneously misguided. The provost and library dean were interested in scholarly communication economics and e-theses/dissertations (ETDs). Their ethnographic study led to creating researcher profile pages and department communities when their success was clearly with individuals, and not bureaucratic decisions that included securing departmental agreements, levels of service, and form signing. UR librarians learned to stress the value of research sharing and preservation, especially for works that supplemented published materials, presentations, and gray literature that included high-demand musical scores (Lindahl, Bell, Gibbons, & Foster, 2007).

Dubinsky's (2014) mixed method study included two quantitative considerations: repository growth by IR item counts and IR content authored by faculty in the sciences, humanities, and social sciences. The author's two measures provided a recent picture of the growth and scope of IRs that reflected faculty participation using the Berkeley Electronic Press's Digital Commons repository system of 107 institutions of higher education academic repositories (whittled down from 214). IR administrator training, technologies, and strategies were used to engage faculty participation in IRs. Item counts included pre/postprints, metadata records only, full text, and gray literature.

This recent study presents a current assessment of the growth, scope, and successful strategies of increasing faculty participation, and an analysis of the IR's content. In the 107 repositories, there were 63,706 items primarily in the sciences. Faculty IR participation concerns included a lack of repository awareness, copyright concerns, preference for a disciplinary repository, perception of submission process difficulty, and plagiarism fears. Respondents planned to develop promotional and instructional tools and held a preference for direct and personal communication with faculty one to one and groups. IR administration survey responses to a mediated deposit method showed an inclination to spend the time promoting IRs instead of faculty deposit instruction. The rising numbers of faculty content items indicates that they are willing to participate in the OA "movement."

IR MAPPING: INSTITUTIONAL GOALS AS A WHOLE, DIFFERENT INTERESTS, AND INVESTMENTS

What is the sound of one e-print (a digital version of a research document, usually a journal article, but could also be a thesis, conference paper, book chapter, or a book that is accessible online—Wikipedia) downloading? Berkeley Electronic Press's Digital Commons has developed an online real-time readership activity map that answers the question nicely.

Each pin drop represents a reader. The map shows where the reader is located and the card shows the title of the downloaded article as well as the collection to which it belongs. The map successfully demonstrates the value of the IR investment for many academic libraries. As a library project, this in turn demonstrates the value of the library and the role it plays in fulfilling the goals of its academic institution. An example of the readership map in action is at Purdue University's institutional repository called e-Pubs: http://docs.lib.purdue.edu/readership_map.html#content.

On the scale that readers are discovering materials in repositories, readership statistics are difficult to conceptualize. This kind of visualization can finally demonstrate the impressive impact that the libraries are having with their IR initiatives. In addition, the real-time mapping is a compelling author investment instrument for faculty, department chairs, administrators, and graduate student scholars with the potential for greater research visibility, citations, and use impact. Where scholarly research impact success influences academic institutional goals, the reflection on the organization is magnified through the ability to obtain grants, book contracts, journal articles, and speaking engagements, to name a few.

WHAT MEASURES OF SUCCESS AND IMPACT MATTER TO SCHOLARS, DEPARTMENT CHAIRS, AND ADMINISTRATORS: EXAMPLES

Diverse constituents at academic institutions have related and at the same time, varied interests and investments in IRs. Approaches to assessment in this chapter will focus on academia where faculty, department chairs, and administrator contingents can acquire research output that meets their needs within their broader institutional goals.

Academia is increasingly interested in research statistics and other metrics that provide impact documentation for administrators to be accountable to their superiors, regents, or board. Institutional repositories are one of the multiple research archival tools that provide quantitative scholarly output usage statistics directly to faculty, department heads, administrators, graduate students, and to journal article authors. DSpace, EPrints, and Digital Commons, three of the most used institutional repository software packages, provide a variety of data. DSpace's and EPrints' administrators may make repository decisions to code in statistics, including the Open Access button for requesting an author's postprint. Digital Commons' "Discipline Commons" data and scholarly content downloads are e-mailed monthly to the repository manager. Each author receives download counts and the dashboard has referral URLs, search terms, university downloads (own university and others), a list of research and downloads, and a chart mapping downloads over time.

ALTERNATIVE METRICS

Altmetrics (alternative metrics), as listed above, is based on online scholarly communication activity that may include a variety of other tool options; please see the section on sustainable publishing and green and gold models below for more altmetrics choices. "Altmetrics can supplement existing usage statistics to provide a broader interpretation of research-output impact for the benefit of authors, library-based publishers and repository managers, and university administrators alike" (Konkiel & Scherer, 2013).

A best-practice assessment tool where department chairs and administrators can employ this data might encourage faculty scientists and scholars to build a virtual visible community of scholars to archive current and retrospective research in an IR. Academically showcasing research in multiple venues provides the opportunity to increase citation impact for globally prominent articles.

In highlighting academic internal and external stakeholders' supplementary standards of impact next to traditional metrics, trustees and state representatives are interested in the university's research significance within the state and beyond. Faculty tenure reviewers might request a faculty's scholarship IR report that shows supplemental impact measures to help the committee members understand the reach of the academic achievement (Konkiel & Scherer, 2013) beyond the Thompson-Reuters journal impact factor (JIF).

Scholarly and popular impact each have their own place of influence and value for the author and stakeholders. Services and Web sites track scholarship usage during the research life cycle. "As supplementary metrics, scholarly altmetrics can prove value for OA content, including content held by repositories" (Priem, Piwowar, & Hemminger, 2012).

Individual tweets that mention specific articles showcase who is reading and sharing the scholarship, in addition to what they are saying about it online. Altmetric.com's content dashboard showcases sophisticated demographic reports for its readers. Giving authors insight into their readership can help them better understand how their OA content archived in IRs is making an impact. The visual of how content is used and shared on which Web sites, by what demographics, and for what purposes is fascinating so we can know where our research's online works are used and cited (Konkiel & Scherer, 2013).

Harvard University's *Good Practices for University Open-Access Policies* project is a consultation service to assist other universities in developing their own open access policies. This pro bono resource is valuable for administrators to take advantage of, to support the success of their institutional scholars by engaging in spreading awareness of open access models to globally showcase faculty and scholars' research (Suber, 2014).

CREATION AND PRESERVATION

While librarians are focused on open research, faculty can distinguish this model as a nonissue in publishing within the status quo. Faculty overall are focused on creating but not necessarily preserving open knowledge. Stevan Harnad, University of Southampton, has argued that academics should publicly showcase their articles in digital repositories (Davis & Connolly, 2007; Harnad, 1994). International collective efforts would moderate power-wielding publishers that limit access to the scholarly literature. Additionally, Raym Crow conjectures that by increasing the dissemination of scholarship, open access research in repositories can "increase competition in the marketplace and reduce the monopoly power of journals" (Crow, 2002). Institutional repositories were not designed to simply host journal articles, but to preserve a variety of research material types that may encompass articles, theses and dissertations, datasets, institutional records, OA journals, and educational resources, among other scholarly content.

Research disciplines play a role in the dissemination of work that faculty are willing to deposit in an IR. Lawal's 2002 survey using nine disciplines across the United States and Canada solicited faculty participation to determine deposited articles in digital repositories. Results reported that the highest participants were physicists and astronomers, followed by computer scientists and mathematicians, engineers, psychologists and cognitive scientists, and biological scientists. There were no contributions from chemists. Participants cited "the dissemination of research results, visibility, and the author's exposure as reasons for depositing their work" (Lawal, 2002). This study conducted at the genesis of the open access to research progression demonstrates that scientists were already participating in open scholarship at some level.

PubMed Central's meager National Institutes of Health (NIH) faculty research paper archiving participation was a recommendation, not required at the time this chapter was written. Faculty who received grant monies overall were not participating in the article deposits. The low compliance rate resulted in the NIH holding funds back from researchers who did not comply with depositing the funded research articles in PubMed Central (Charbonneau & McGlone, 2014).

Cornell University faculty's lack of motivation and understanding of the advantages of open access research, the U.S. and Canadian survey that found no chemists participated in article deposits, and the NIH not receiving the contracted articles in return for grant monies all characterize the current faculty and publisher culture at some level. These few examples represent a multitude of research that is locked up behind subscriptions providing financial and paywall success to journal publishers. Stevan Harnad and Raym Crow both address increasing article dissemination methods that encourage open access to research. In what scholarly communication dimension can we define success for the creators that would include scholars, department chairs, and administrators?

AUTHOR IDENTIFIERS

Locating an article or an author's list of research papers can be a frustrating task unless the scholarship is deposited in a digital repository. Google and other search engines are typically able to locate works that are not locked up behind journal subscriptions. For those researchers with institutional library journal subscriptions, access is more probable and expensive whether paid for by interlibrary loan or journal holdings. An expanding list of metadata for rights' holder identifiers is being created to aid in identifying and locating researchers and their scholarship: DOIs, EZID, ORCID, ISNIs, CrossRef, and FundRef. Identifier discovery of scholarly works is an advantage for faculty and student scholars, department chairs, and administrators to acquire author and scholarship data that meets their individual and collective research needs.

SUSTAINABLE PUBLISHING: GREEN AND GOLD MODELS

Publishers are not encouraging scientists and scholars to self-archive—it is a responsibility of authors to manage their research output and support colleagues and graduate/undergraduate students in doing the same (Nature Web Focus, 2014). To enable researchers to take advantage of and make sense of the green and gold open access publishing model and avoid the failure of not globally showcasing their work, the author proposes a visual mapping of the scholarly communication methodology that encompasses a context of interpretation for faculty to garner a greater understanding and knowledge of how and why the green and the born open access (OA) and article publishing charge (APC) gold models provide open access to research.

University administrators should become familiar with the evolving academic scholarly communication landscape and offer their support in improving the dissemination and impact of research activities, especially those involving open access to the scholarship produced by their faculty. Open access policies will benefit authors by increased citations and the impact of their research, also providing access to scholarship for independent or underfunded researchers.

Benefits provided by an open access fund are clear to those who believe in and promote open access to their research. Authors can publish in open access journals with the knowledge that their institution, supported by administrators, department heads, and possibly the library will absorb the subsidized article publication charges. Readers will have free access to these articles in a timely manner. Discussions may result in a faculty member's use of and support for new services created by the library's scholarly communication initiatives. Some faculty will become advocates for introducing changes in the institution's strategy of disseminating locally generated scholarly content (ACRL Scholarly Communication ToolKit, 2014).

This is an opportunity for scholarly communication and liaison librarians to promote library services focused on faculty knowledge of IR advantages and how faculty can reposition their scholarship to be openly accessible and more successful in its findability. The green (postprint or preprint) and gold (born digital in an OA journal) publishing business models have been designed to advocate for and to utilize open research. Open access frameworks have exploited scholarly tools and applications, created greater awareness, and noted usage impact. Social media tools, such as download counts, referrer URLs, citations, and more, globally participate in circulating the OA research. Alternative metrics have also appeared in digital repository software (bepress's Digital Commons) and on publisher Web sites where an article publication charge (APC) is the norm, such as the Public Library of Science's (PLOS) policy.

A major hurdle in author awareness of consulting the SHERPA/RoMEO publisher tool is significant. Scholarly communication librarians and IR staff habitually use the publisher copyright policies and self-archiving in the course of their work. Scientists and scholars are typically not familiar with this essential tool that provides opportunities to link global visibility to a preprint or postprint archived in an institutional or subject repository. An author of a journal article who recently submitted a draft paper (preprint) to an editor has an accepted peer-reviewed paper (postprint) with at least a 70%-plus probability of depositing one of the manuscript versions in the library's institutional repository. For greater research visibility, calculate in advance to locate a journal that accepts a preprint or postprint paper version in SHERPA/RoMEO by consciously choosing to submit to a green or gold publisher that offers an OA paper opportunity to be archived in the author's IR. If there are multiple authors, the first author must be proactive to provide the preprint or postprint to all of the authors for their open access benefit, and also to archive in their own institutions' digital repositories (Buehler, 2013).

The green model also indicates that faculty and independent researchers have tangential scholarly communication tools available to alert their colleagues to their pre- or postprint research widely and publicly available for reuse, citation, and impact. The value proposition of increased visibility relates to researcher scholarship, sharing work with peers, and building upon the original research. Evidence of recent open access scholarship archived in an institutional repository has the potential to be found through online social networks that might include Twitter, commenting, citations, page views, Facebook, LinkedIn, blogging, and Instagram, to name a few. Engaging researchers to embrace the value of green and gold (open access journal) visibility publishing awareness has the opportunity to secure a broader societal impact and efficiency of ensuring open access to research across multiple stakeholders, because it matters. The green and gold journal publishing models are some of the most lucrative strategies that multiple publishers offer authors and the university's IR.

Another source of the green open access publishing terminology confusion for researchers are the terms *postprint* and *preprint*. The SHERPA/RoMEO website (http://www.sherpa.ac.uk/romeo/) explains what version of the green model (postprint or preprint) can be deposited in an institutional repository. Once an author locates the journal of his or her publishing choice by consulting SHERPA/RoMEO, all of the open access publishing colors' infrastructure options are visible, and authors can make their own research dissemination decisions based on consulting a publisher's preprint, postprint, and PDF version guidelines (see RoMEO Color Archiving Policy chart at http://www.sherpa.ac .uk/romeo/search.php?la=en&fIDnum=|&mode=simple).

The open access progression in the publishing infrastructure has experienced its successes and failures. The success of the gold and green publishing models has penetrated researchers who understand the value of open access and those who investigate alternative types of publishing to ensure global visibility and greater impact for their scholarship. Researchers who delve into the philosophical details of providing open access to their scholarship have a clear sense of the open access journal (gold model) and open access repository publishing (green model) intricacies that allow their scholarship to be open. These researchers are typically from institutions that were able to permeate the open access milieu to research through colleague champions to navigate their publisher contracts in the context of the green and born-digital gold model. Universities have employed mandates requiring articles to be archived in their academy's institutional repository (IR) by engaging their faculty senate or the equivalent to support a vote. Many of these polls required years of meetings and conversations to

Figure 16.1. A visual map of the gold and green publishing models for authors aspiring to self-archive their open access research in an institutional repository for global visibility. *(Copyright 2014 by Marianne A. Buehler. This work is licensed under a Creative Commons License. Attribution: CC BY.)*

negotiate final terms. Right now, we have tools that permit open access to research; it requires taking the initiative to grasp the practice.

There are multiple and new informational details in the green and gold open access archiving model for faculty to remember from a previous conversation or presentation. Distributing copies of the diagram in Figure 16.1 to scholars (faculty, department chairs, administrators, and graduate students) will simplify the archiving model process and engage a larger number of valued research articles in open access venues. In addition, offering clarification of the various publishing models for successful open access shows that benefits accrue for authors and readers: expedient dissemination, access to all materials in low-income countries and by independent researchers, a reduced cost of publication, and a new and better science (Rentier, 2013).

Use a visual model to engage scientists and scholars to comprehend the gold article and green postprint/preprint research route. They also must be able to envisage the model to more fully understand how it can deftly benefit their own and their colleagues' community of scholarship.

EARLY ADOPTION OF INSTITUTIONAL REPOSITORIES AND CURRENT CORRECTIONS

Institutional repositories (IRs) continue to evolve and grow as expanding tools with the capability to archive new item types, such as big data and essential metadata identifiers, and meeting the needs of researchers to garner their acceptance of an IR. After the initial waves of new repositories were established in the early 21st century, academic librarians began to evaluate exactly how researchers were using (or not) the repository archiving tool.

FUTURE OF INSTITUTIONAL REPOSITORIES: CONNECTING GLOBAL RESEARCH WITH LINKED DATA

Several advantages of institutional repository archived research benefits for authors and readers provides access and visibility to the Internet's scientific and scholarly production when consuming and publishing Linked Open Data. The W3C Library Linked Data Incubator Group 32 (2010–2011) mentioned in its recommendations to encourage libraries to participate in the Linked Data framework:

> The web of information should be embraced, both by making data available for use as Linked Data and by using the web of data in information services. Ideally, data should integrate fully with other resources on the Web. In engaging with the web of Linked Data, libraries can take on a leadership role grounded in their traditional activities: management of resources for current use and long term preservation; description of resources on the basis of agreed rules; and responding to the needs of information seekers. (Baker et al., 2011)

The Semantic Web's Linked Data is a set of best practices for publishing and connecting structured data on the Web. This particular scenario "first links html pages or documents, the second goes beyond the concept of a document and links structured data." Digital repositories have the ability to enhance the visibility and interoperability of data (articles, presentations, chapters, etc.) by linking their content to the wider Web of Data (Coalition of Open Access Repositories).

The Resource Description Framework (RDF) for metadata was developed on the Web by the W3C based on using resource expressions that follow the form subject-predicate-object, known as the RDF triple or statement. Within its URI (uniform resource identifier used in institutional repository links), but with a subject (person), the predicate (relationship to the subject), and the object related directly to the subject or another resource that establishes a relationship. The easiest method to facilitate establishing automatic linking between datasets is the use of standard vocabularies that includes describing data or metadata elements and indicating their values (Baker et al., 2011; Lampert & Southwick, 2013; Schreur, 2012). By utilizing URIs to link data (research), the Internet's network infrastructure and the Web's ability to access allows people and machines to explore information and additional research interconnections. The ability to easily acquire usable data that meets faculty's scholarly needs (as readers and authors) is essential for successful ongoing scholarly communication.

In making institutional repositories work for scholars, department chairs, and administrators, each of these groups share strategically relevant interests and research investments in the success of having these needs met. Academic library IR administrators have focused on the scholarly communication needs of faculty, department heads, administrators, and graduate student scholars to create a knowledgeable and understood environment that offers impact through altmetrics and scholarly communication. Linked Data holds the promise of connecting all repositories utilizing the RDF triple model with its association to the Semantic Web and scholarly applications to identify research content. Both Linked Data and IRs expand discoverability of our materials and place information where people are looking for it and where it helps bridge applications and systems (Lampert & Southwick, 2013; Schreur, 2012).

REFERENCES

Baker, T., et al. (2011). *7 things you should know about linked data*. Retrieved from https://www.coar-repositories.org/activities/repository-observatory/second

-edition-linked-open-data/7-things-you-should-know-about-open-data/

Buehler, M. (2013). *Demystifying the institutional repository for success*. Oxford, UK: Chandos/Elsevier.

Charbonneau, D., & McGlone, J. (2014). Faculty experiences with the National Institutes of Health (NIH) public access policy, compliance issues, and copyright practices. *Journal of the Medical Library Association, 101*(1): 21–25.

Coalition of Open Access Repositories (COAR). Retrieved from https://www .coar-repositories.org/activities/repository-observatory/second-edition -linked-open-data/7-things-you-should-know-about-open-data/

Crow, R. (2002). *SPARC institutional repository checklist & resource guide*. Scholarly Publishing & Academic Resources Coalition.

Davis, M., & Connolly, M. (2007, March/April). Institutional repositories: Evaluating the reasons for non-use of Cornell University's installation of DSpace. *D-Lib Magazine, 13*(3/4).

Dubinsky, E. (2014). A current snapshot of institutional repositories: Growth rate, disciplinary content and faculty contributions. *Journal of Librarianship and Scholarly Communication, 2*(3), eP1167. http://dx.doi.org/10.7710/2162-3309 .1167

Harnad, S. (1994). *The importance of requiring institutional repository deposit immediately upon acceptance for publication* [Web log]. Retrieved from http://openaccess.eprints.org/index.php?/archives/1119-DOE-The-Impor tance-of-Requiring-Institutional-Repository-Deposit-Immediately-Upon-Ac ceptance-for-Publication.html

Kenney, A. (2014). Leveraging the liaison model. *Ithaka S+R*. Retrieved from http://www.sr.ithaka.org/sites/default/files/files/SR_BriefingPaper_Ken ney_20140322.pdf

Konkiel, S., & Scherer, D. (2013, April/May). New opportunities for repositories in the age of altmetrics. *Association for Information Science and Technology Bulletin*.

Lampert, C., & Southwick, S. (2013, September). Leading to linking: Introducing linked data to academic library digital collections. *Journal of Library Metadata, 13*(2–3), 230–253. http://dx.doi.org/10.1080/19386389.2013.826-95

Lawal, I. (2002). Scholarly communication: The use and non-use of e-print archives for the dissemination of scientific information. *Issues in Science and Technology Librarianship, 36*.

Lindahl, D., Bell, S., Gibbons, S., & Foster, N. (2007). *Institutional repositories, policies, and disruption.* Retrieved from http://open.bu.edu/handle/2144/919

Nature Web Focus. (2014). The green and the gold roads to open access. Retrieved from http://www.nature.com/nature/focus/accessdebate/21.html

Priem, J., Piwowar, H., & Hemminger, B. (2012, March). *Altmetrics in the wild: Using social media to explore scholarly impact.* Retrieved from http://arxiv.org/html/1203.4745v1

Rentier, B. (2013). *Open access: Don't mistake the cherry for the cake.* Retrieved from http://recteur.blogs.ulg.ac.be/?p=1093

Schreur, P. (2012). *Linked data as transformation.* Paper presented at the Coalition for Networked Information semiannual meeting, April 3, 2012, Baltimore, MD.

Suber, P. (2014, Summer). Institutional policies for open access. *Information Standards Quarterly, 26*(2), 6–8.

Part 5

INSTITUTIONAL REPOSITORIES IN PRACTICE: CASE STUDIES

17 | Creating the IR Culture

Anne Langley and Yuan Li

This case study maps out the path we took to raise awareness of and support for an institutional repository at Princeton University. The creation of our institutional repository culture is a little different because before any repository work had been done, the open access policy was passed unanimously by the faculty. This is not the typical path for creation of an IR culture. Once the policy was passed, university partners in the library and the Office of Information Technology (OIT) collaborated to build a scholarly communications program, which included design and creation of the institutional repository. A librarian and a digital information architect (OIT) proposed a recommended path, specifying staffing, infrastructure, and legal requirements. The recommendation document was unanimously supported by administrators from the libraries and OIT and text from the recommendation was used to request funding from a university priorities committee. Based on the recommendations, a scholarly communications (SC) librarian and a digital repository programmer were hired; a working group was formed to design the repository workflow; and through collaboration with many university partners, outreach and education ventures are under way to increase campus awareness of the policy and the upcoming repository.

BRIEF DESCRIPTION OF INSTITUTION

Princeton University is one of the oldest institutions of higher learning in North America. Established in 1746, Princeton has a student body of 7,910: 5,244 undergraduates and 2,666 graduate students (2013–2014). It offers instruction in the humanities, social sciences, natural sciences, and engineering. Though it does not have medical, law, education, divinity, or business schools, it offers professional degrees through the Woodrow Wilson School of Public and International Affairs, the School of Engineering and Applied Science, the School of Architecture, and the Bendheim Center for Finance. In spring 2014, there were 1,175 full-time, part-time, and visiting faculty in 34 academic departments.

The Princeton University Library (PUL) and the Office of Information Technology (OIT) have a long history of working together. Though the digital information architect is based in OIT, a large majority of his projects are with library partners, most recently with university archives in providing a repository for electronic theses (including senior theses) and dissertations. There is a formal university committee on library and computing, and interoffice and departmental collaboration is encouraged and supported throughout the university.

Timeline of Open Access and Scholarly Communication Related Events

Late 2010—Dean of the faculty appoints ad-hoc faculty committee (includes the University Librarian) to study the question of open access (OA) to faculty publications.

March 2011—Ad-hoc committee adopts OA policy and writes report to explain the issues and interpret the policy.

September 19, 2011—Princeton faculty pass the OA policy.

October 2011—Princeton joins Coalition for Open Access Policy Institutions (COAPI); librarian assigned to scholarly communication planning attends COAPI meeting in Washington, DC.

November 2011—Library, dean of faculty, and OIT administrators meet to discuss policy implementation—the librarian and digital information architect (DIA) are charged with investigating options and writing a proposal for implementation.

May 2012—Librarian and DIA submit OA Policy Implementation Recommendation report.

Fall 2012—Library application to university funding committee for SC librarian in FY2013.

January 2013—University funding committee approves new SC librarian; provost funds new software developer (OIT) for three-year term position; DIA given title of associate director of Academic Technology Services, librarian named director of Scholarly Communications.

July 2013—Funds released for both new positions.

Summer 2013—Position descriptions finalized; search committees formed.

Fall 2013—Active searches for SC librarian and software developer.

December 2013—Software developer position is filled.

Winter 2014—SC librarian accepts position to begin April 21.

Spring 2014—Formation of the Princeton Open Access Repository Implementation Working Group (POARIWG) and the Scholarly Communications Outreach group; SC librarian begins meeting with subject liaisons.

Summer 2014—Design of the workflow is well under way, and plans for outreach are begun; SC librarian continues to meet with subject liaisons; the director and SC librarian write white paper for university provost on scholarly communication issues and open access.

Fall 2014—OA Week group formed and funding obtained for various OA Week activities; SC brochure designed; SC Office logo designed; SC website created and launched; POARIWG gains additional members in the areas of preservation and digital archives.

CAMPUS CONVERSATIONS—AD-HOC COMMITTEE AND OA POLICY ADOPTION

In late 2010, the dean of the faculty appointed an ad-hoc faculty committee, comprising professors from all the divisions of the university, to study the question of open access for faculty publications. The committee met several times in February and March 2011 and adopted a policy and report by unanimous vote. The policy was brought to the fall 2011 faculty meeting and passed by unanimous vote. Shortly after the policy was passed, the university librarian contacted Anne Langley, head librarian of Science and Technology libraries, whose job description included the responsibility to "advance campus conversations about scholarly communication and e-science, working collaboratively with other Princeton librarians, the University's Office of Information Technology, the Office of the Dean for Research, and special campus research centers such as the Princeton Institute for Computational Science and Engineering." Langley was asked to investigate what it would take to put the OA policy in place and to serve as the point person for the project.

INVESTIGATION OF POLICY IMPLEMENTATION

Langley was put in touch with colleagues at MIT to learn more about their OA policy and institutional repository. From MIT colleagues, Langley learned about an upcoming meeting of the Coalition of Open Access Policy Institutions (COAPI). COAPI brings together representatives from North American institutions with established faculty OA policies and those in the process of developing such policies. It was formed to share information and experiences and to illuminate opportunities for moving faculty-led open access forward at member institutions and advocating for open access nationally and internationally. Princeton asked to join COAPI, and Langley attended the October COAPI meeting. The meeting fortuitously focused on requirements for building a repository, and Langley came back armed with a solid understanding of what Princeton needed to implement the policy and establish a repository.

Shortly after returning from the COAPI meeting, Langley reported what she learned to administrators from the library, OIT, and the office of the dean of the faculty. At this meeting, Langley accepted the responsibility, with Mark Ratliff, the digital information architect, of investigating and recommending how to proceed. They were assigned a project manager, set up regular meetings, and created a project plan.

They established the following goals and assumptions to guide the approach they would propose in the recommendation document:

Goals

- To collect in the repository all Princeton University faculty journal articles and conference papers published since the Open Access Policy was passed on September 19, 2011. Approximately 1,200 faculty in 34 departments generate 4,000 scholarly articles each year. This number is derived from searches in Web of Science and SCOPUS for Princeton authors. In SCOPUS, the average for each year is about 3,500, and Web of Science was in the same ballpark. The total number of articles is expected to be greater, however, because these databases don't thoroughly index humanities publications.

- To minimize the amount of extra work that the Open Access Policy imposes on faculty.
- To enhance access to content held in the repository by making the content easily discoverable and downloadable.

Assumptions

- A new full-time position will be created to support Scholarly Communications.
- The library is the service owner and will manage promotion and submission.
- OIT will be an active partner and lead in technology and technical support.
- Existing staff in the library and in OIT will be assigned new responsibilities to support the acquisitions workflow.

For this last assumption, they suggested inserting the required tasks into existing staff workflows, both in the library and OIT, with oversight and coordination by the Scholarly Communications librarian in concert with Mark Ratliff.

MOVING FORWARD WITH RECOMMENDATIONS: GETTING FUNDING, BUILDING TEAMS, SETTING UP PROCESSES, AND MAKING ALLIES

For the first four months of 2012, Langley and Ratliff met with stakeholders on campus, staff at peer institutions that have implemented similar OA policies, faculty on the initial Open Access Policy ad-hoc committee, vendors offering technology solutions, library staff, and OIT staff. They solicited ideas from peers in higher education who are members of COAPI. They synthesized their findings and created implementation recommendations in the areas of legal requirements, operational services, functional requirements, and technical requirements.

After the recommendations were submitted, the university librarian and the CIO took the recommendations higher up in the organization to seek the necessary funding. In fall 2012, modified language from the recommendation report was used to apply for funding from a university committee called PRICOM, or the Priorities Committee, which is a committee of the Council of the Princeton University Community and advises the university president. The committee makes recommendations regarding the following year's operating budget. The provost chairs the committee, which also includes the dean of the faculty, the executive vice president, the treasurer, six faculty members, four undergraduates, two graduate students, and one member from one of the other groups represented on the council.

In January 2013, PRICOM approved funding, to begin in FY2014, to hire a Scholarly Communications librarian, and the provost designated separate funds for a software developer to design the ingest workflow for a three-year period. Money was set aside for the purchase of proprietary software that might be necessary for some portion of the workflow.

Once funding was released in July 2013, Langley and Ratliff wrote job descriptions and ads, formed search committees, and got the searches under way. Interviews were held for both positions in the fall of 2013, and by December the software developer position was filled; the developer began work right away. Hiring an SC librarian took a bit longer. Yuan Li accepted the SC librarian position in early 2014, and she began work in April 2014.

EARLY STAGES OF IMPLEMENTATION

Implementation began by focusing on three distinct areas: building formal and informal teams, designing the repository workflows, and making the Scholarly Communications Office and its services known to campus. With two new hires in place, the administrative bodies were created. In the library, the Scholarly Communications Office was created to implement the OA policy and to develop the accompanying Scholarly Communications services. The Scholarly Communications Office consists of the director (Langley), the Scholarly Communications librarian (Li), and the E-Science librarian (Willow Dressel), who is in charge of building the data management program. In the Office of Information Technology, there is the formal team consisting of the associate director for Academic Services (Ratliff), who is also the digital repository architect, and the software developer. Informally, there are three groups: an outreach planning group, a repository implementation working group, and a steering committee to guide and manage the work of the repository implementation working group.

Formation of the Repository Implementation Working Group

The Princeton Open Access Repository Implementation Working Group (POARIWG) has members from OIT, including the software developer and the associate director for Academic Technology; and members from various units of the library, including subject liaisons, cataloging and metadata librarians, a digital initiatives analyst, the E-Science librarian, the Scholarly Communications librarian, and the director of Scholarly Communications. The group was charged with designing and creating an ingest workflow process for the repository. Because it is a large group, the members wanted to ensure productive meetings so they created a steering committee. This committee meets five days before each POARIWG biweekly meeting to plan the agenda and work of the larger group.

POARIWG has been working diligently to identify workflow and system requirements for the repository. Langley and Ratliff have met with a variety of vendors who may be able to provide information to populate the repository ingest system, and they are working with colleagues at MIT to find areas where they can collaborate on workflow design. Li has served as a consultant during the software development process, solidifying the collaborative nature of the repository design.

Making Our Presence Known on Campus

Subject liaisons in the library are responsible for informing and promoting scholarly communication issues to campus scholars, including the university's OA policy for faculty research, so it was important to include them in the early culture-building work. Shortly after she began working at Princeton, Li started to meet individually with subject liaisons in the library to inform them of the plan and the progress that the Scholarly Communications team has made; to learn how well they understand open access and scholarly communication issues; to assess their interest in helping with campus outreach; and to learn about their expectations for the repository. This process took place in late spring and through the summer. By meeting with the liaisons, Li accomplished a variety of important things: she learned which liaisons were proponents of OA and, from that group, who would be willing to help with early outreach; she learned who needed more convincing and more time to process their new responsibilities; and she discovered names of faculty she could count on to be OA advocates.

In addition to meeting with individual subject liaisons, Li and Langley have made presentations to department head meetings and the Library Managers Group. A presentation to all library staff is scheduled in the late fall. Beyond the library, Li also met with various campus partners to create awareness of the OA program's presence and services, including the associate dean for Research, the general counsel for Copyright, the associate dean for the Digital Humanities Center, and the coordinator of the McGraw Center for Teaching and Learning. In early fall, Li gave a presentation about open access as part of the McGraw Center Productive Scholars Series. The session drew a full house and was a good start in terms of outreach to campus.

While the SC outreach team were developing outreach plans and making progress, the university librarian asked Li and Langley to write a short white paper on the economic drivers of open access for the provost to get him up to speed on the new program, and to prepare him for a fall meeting with other provosts. They had to craft a careful message that was informative and concise. It was a great opportunity to teach the university administration about the issues and our work. Completed in mid-August, the white paper was well received by the provost.

Another opportunity to make our presence known on campus and promote OA was 2014 OA Week, planned and organized by the 2014 OA Week Planning Group. We decided to focus on raising awareness in the library before doing systematic outreach to faculty. However, we set up an OA Week information table in the campus center to get a feel for where and how to do more outreach in the future, and also decided to organize an event for graduate students later in the fall, since OA Week fell during mid-term exams.

CONCLUSION

Creating our IR culture required building a strong base of support among allies from many areas of the university, primarily within the libraries and information technology; because so many areas of the university are affected, partners from all parts of the institution must be discovered and recruited. We needed to be able to tell the story of OA and describe the roles all allies must play in disseminating scholarly communication in a variety of ways, being very careful to shape our message to fit the audience. We asked: What are their motivations? What's in it for them? Why is it in their best interest, and/or in the best interest of the institution? Allies also want to see that we have invested time and effort into our program. There is a fine balance between building a program and recruiting allies. Culture creation is primarily about having a clear message and finding the most productive ways to share it.

18 | On Implementing an Open Source Institutional Repository

James Tyler Mobley

In 2005, in an attempt to streamline the graduate thesis submission and publication process, the Graduate School at the College of Charleston in Charleston, South Carolina, entered a contract with ProQuest/UMI Dissertation Publishing to use the ProQuest ETD Administrator platform for students to submit their works and have them made available online. Prior to this agreement, paper copies were submitted and processed directly by the Graduate School, and copies were later sent to the College of Charleston Libraries for cataloging. With the removal of the paper component of these thesis submissions, the library suddenly faced the question of how to pivot to preserving electronic copies and how to make them available for students and faculty in the long term. At the time, the library did not have a platform dedicated to electronic content created by the college's students and faculty. In fact, the library had almost no infrastructure to handle local storage of electronic content whatsoever.

The single "repository" of content within the library at this time was the Lowcountry Digital Library (LCDL). LCDL consisted of a CONTENTdm-based digital library created for the express purpose of digitizing and presenting cultural heritage materials from the Lowcountry region of South Carolina. This installation was hosted on servers maintained by the library acquired through grant funding. While this repository was not intended to house non-historical works, it was the only portal through which the library could effectively manage and present electronic materials, especially materials like theses that came with various access restrictions and embargoes. As such, a limited number of electronic theses received from ProQuest were processed by a library cataloger and placed into the Lowcountry Digital Library. Over the next few years, theses were sporadically added to LCDL, though a formal workflow was not in place.

In the spring of 2010, the Lowcountry Digital Library project initiated a migration from CONTENTdm to an open source digital library platform based on Fedora Commons. It was at this time that the library concurrently began considering options for an institutional repository (IR) system for the preservation and presentation of contemporary College of Charleston output like theses and other works by students and faculty. An institutional repository could potentially provide a long-term home not only for electronic theses but also the output of the college as a whole. Obstacles and considerations encountered during this search included a lack of dedicated funds, limited staff time and expertise, and uncertainty about the perceived demand for such a system.

Limited budget allocation for new software projects proved to be the greatest single obstacle while investigating options for an IR. The library has a limited annual budget, most of which goes to the collection and other essential expenses. There is not a dedicated fund for pilot software projects or other exploratory initiatives. Additionally, though it was agreed that a solution for handling theses and other content was greatly needed, library staff remained unsure about the potential use of and enthusiasm for such a system by the rest of the institution. We were hesitant to secure large amounts of money for an unproven concept that our students and faculty might not even want to use. Because of this, we knew from the outset that we would prefer an open source option if one existed with adequate features and community support.

In terms of staff capability, the library had four dedicated technology employees who could be considered relevant to installing and managing an IR. There were two Digital Services librarians, one Digital Scholarship librarian, and one server administrator, all of whom were tied up in a variety of tasks throughout the day supporting library technology as a whole. The library did not have its own internal IT, and campus IT are typically busy handling campus-wide applications and maintaining network security and coverage. Therefore, we needed a mostly packaged solution to implement. We were prepared to maintain existing systems, but we did not have the staff to dedicate to building new systems from scratch, especially alongside the digital library rebuild that was already in progress.

When we began to explore our options, one immediate thought was to leave the theses in the CONTENTdm installation that LCDL was leaving and continue the manual cataloging process. We could then add new materials from around campus into new collections in CONTENTdm. We would basically reset CONTENTdm as an IR. The library had, after all, already paid for a portion of the system, and it still functioned well overall. While this wasn't a popular idea, it was potentially at least more economical than others. However, after further evaluation, the ongoing annual maintenance fees for CONTENTdm and the looming cost of hardware replacements made even this option a substantial investment. Some investment would be necessary with whatever option we chose, but we preferred it at least be toward new and improved systems and services rather than maintenance on a process that already didn't work very well. With that in mind, we shelved this option and took a look at the upcoming digital library platform.

The new digital library platform is built on the Fedora Commons Repository, which offers a great deal of flexibility in storing and handling digital content. We briefly imagined placing new campus materials in this repository alongside LCDL's cultural heritage materials and accessing each set of content separately through different interfaces. This would allow us to keep heritage materials separate from general college materials within a single repository.

Unfortunately, staff expertise was limited when it came to separating pools of content within one Fedora Commons repository, and Fedora Commons does not include robust front-end features for access control or display. At the time, just the construction of the Lowcountry Digital Library as a Fedora Commons repository was proving difficult enough without adding another factor to the challenge. The digital library repository was thus abandoned as an option in favor of a new turnkey solution. Today, the Fedora Commons repository only houses cultural heritage materials for the Lowcountry Digital Library, and we do not have plans to further expand its scope in the near future.

Digital Commons from bepress quickly became a major option for us as a turnkey IR system once we abandoned hopes of leveraging existing internal systems. Clemson University had already purchased it for use with their campus materials, so it already had some buy-in among our state peers. Additionally, bepress provides a great deal of support to clients using Digital Commons. Dedicated support would be ideal for an institution like ours with limited staff.

Beyond support, Digital Commons offers a number of features that other solutions don't have by default and which would be very time-consuming to create in-house, including dedicated pages for faculty profiles and various custom theming options. User-friendly features like these made Digital Commons a very enticing option. It is very much a one-stop solution for an institutional repository.

Unsurprisingly, such a robust feature list and support system came with a cost. Given our previous concerns that the library and the college as a whole might not ultimately care for an IR in the long term, we could not commit to purchasing something like Digital Commons. Had we already noted an expressed demand for an IR system, our outcome might have been different. With this aversion to license agreements, we turned our gaze more firmly to the open source community.

While exploring digital library system options for the Lowcountry Digital Library migration, we had previously come across DSpace. DSpace is an open source IR application initially developed by MIT that, like Digital Commons, is meant to be mostly turnkey. DuraSpace, the same group that maintains the Fedora Commons repository, now curates it. For the purposes of LCDL and its largely visual cultural heritage materials, DSpace was not a perfect fit. However, when reevaluated in the context of institutional repositories, which is DSpace's intended use case, it immediately became a primary contender.

The open source DSpace immediately checked a large box in the cost department, at least in terms of licensing and contract fees. It would, of course, incur further costs in acquisition of server hardware and staff-hours, but it lacked a lump sum cost of entry. We could test, modify, break, and even soft launch DSpace on existing hardware with no consequence other than possibly wasted time.

However, open source alternately meant a higher barrier to entry in the form of technical expertise. DSpace is a Java-based application that, while very well documented and maintained, requires at least some personnel that can run, configure, and maintain such applications and the servers they need to operate. Additionally, all customization would have to be done in-house by existing staff.

Furthermore, as DSpace is not a vendor-hosted solution, storage and backup capabilities would have to be considered concurrently. We could not approach the campus with a solution that did not on some level promise long-term storage and preservation of its collective output. This would have been a consideration with any locally hosted option, however, so this was not a consideration unique to DSpace so much as to locally hosted solutions in general.

It became fairly clear when outlining an open source product alongside a proprietary system that the debate of cost was powerful but also misleading. We were not and are not able to lay down large sums of money for the purchase of new software for untested needs. However, the long-term cost in staff time and server hardware for an open source solution was not negligible either. Both solutions would incur costs, some more direct than others. In this case, the library already owned at least some existing hardware running various Web sites and services. Hardware acquisition and management would make even considering DSpace a difficult task for some institutions, but it fit well into our existing infrastructure. The prospect of hardware cost and maintenance was thus more palatable than software costs.

Despite these technical complications and storage needs, DSpace promised a huge list of features that rivaled a system like Digital Commons. User groups, access controls, batch item loading, search and discovery, and other features were available out of the box with some amount of configuration.

In addition to a wealth of native features, DSpace also had the benefit of a very active development community. In any investigation of open source software, one must consider the activity of the community surrounding it. As open source software does not comes with a license agreement for ongoing updates and support, it is vital to ascertain whether the application in question will see support from its own volunteer community over time. After all, you don't want your staff stuck maintaining abandoned code for years to come. Ultimately, we came to the decision that DSpace struck a healthy balance between cost and features for our initial trials.

After the decision to run DSpace as a pilot project for the IR, the application was briefly installed on a test server and run for staff demonstration and testing. After that period, the library was able to acquire new server hardware to provide adequate processing power and storage to this and other library projects. As previously mentioned, the library already maintained a number of servers hosting smaller, basic Web sites and some essential proprietary applications like interlibrary loan software. At this time, the library had gone a number of years without new hardware, and existing servers were both limited in space and nearing their end of life. The acquisition of new hardware allowed us to set up DSpace in a proper production environment. This was not an expected turn of events, but it greatly eased the process of implementation. This acquisition also benefited the aforementioned digital library project.

The actual installation process of DSpace on a virtual machine running Fedora Linux was fairly smooth thanks to documentation provided by DuraSpace. While the system takes a few extra steps to implement due to the nature of deploying Java applications to Web servers, the documentation provided a more than adequate guide for a user with intermediate server and application experience.

After this installation came a moderate amount of customization. How DSpace looks and operates is largely "up to you." There are a number of ways to approach your system, including two entirely different Web interfaces from which to choose. One is rendered in traditional JavaServer pages (the JSP interface), while Apache Cocoon powers the newer XMLUI interface. We opted for the XMLUI interface as it promised more flexibility and features moving forward. XMLUI, for example, was the first interface to have an integrated discovery interface built on Apache Solr.

DSpace also offered more than a few options for user authentication. The College of Charleston campus uses LDAP as a user authentication method, and DSpace provided an authentication plug-in to support LDAP by default. LDAP in conjunction with IP authentication fit very comfortably into our campus environment.

After the site was visually customized and allowed campus users to access it properly, we had to approach the issue of content organization. DSpace breaks content down into Communities and Collections. In our case, we decided to break college departments into Communities that could have their own Collections. Each of these Communities and Collections needed individually assigned access restrictions depending on the type of content.

Once this organization was complete, there came the matter of getting electronic thesis content, our initial test material, into the system. As a proof of concept, we batch loaded 32 electronic theses from ProQuest into the collection via DSpace's command-line batch processing interface. This content fit well within the native structure of DSpace's Community and Collection hierarchy, so we decided to move forward with a more streamlined submission and deposit process. Conveniently, DSpace supports the SWORD protocol for document deposits. ProQuest has recently implemented this protocol as well, so, after some communication with ProQuest technical support, electronic theses are now automatically deposited as complete items into DSpace by ProQuest. This workflow eliminates the process of retrieving a PDF and metadata file from ProQuest and manually processing it. Instead, catalogers can now simply check on the IR system when they receive notifications that new items have been deposited into the Electronic Theses & Dissertations Collection.

DSpace handily solved our initial use case for an institutional repository by giving our electronic theses a permanent home managed on our local servers. Now that we have an institutional repository in place, we will have to consider staffing allocation to handle the management of the application as well as workflows for new content from other sources. These details are currently under consideration by the library, and a faculty committee is drafting a formal policy for IR content. Additionally, the library will be hiring a dedicated metadata librarian, a large focus of whose role will be to directly oversee the institutional repository.

While these formal considerations and new positions are worked out, we have embarked on a few test projects using the system. We have worked with the College of Charleston Honors College on two projects that have allowed students to submit items via a submission form. These forms automatically submit items to the IR to appropriate collections. Both of these projects make use of the SWORD protocol alongside DSpace.

Small test projects like these have contributed to awareness on campus in small doses; however, the question of overall institutional interest in an IR remains. We believe that our IR built on DSpace can provide a home for the digital output of students and faculty at the College of Charleston.

However, we have to pursue faculty engagement to prove its value as a tool for preservation and presentation. Once we have formalized our internal processes, we will move forward with broader campus outreach.

What began as a question of where to house some PDF copies of electronic theses developed over the past few years into the construction of a potential home for the College of Charleston's scholarly output. The choice to go open source for this project let us experiment with new directions in our library systems without risking valuable annual library budgets or sinking too much staff time into developing homegrown applications. However, selection and implementation were only the beginning of a longer dialogue over the role of an academic library in preserving the collected academic output of its institution. At the College of Charleston, that dialogue is ongoing.

19 | Interlinking Institutional Repository Content and Enhancing User Experiences

David Scherer, Lisa Zilinski, and Kelley Kimm

In February 2013 the White House Office of Science and Technology Policy announced new requirements for government agencies that fund over $100 million worth of research: The results of funded projects (both the published research and underlying data) must be made publicly and openly available (Holdren, 2013). At Purdue University, the Libraries and the Joint Transportation Research Program (JTRP) are collaborating to produce and disseminate technical report publications and their underlying datasets. In 2014 these two campus partners developed a comprehensive workflow that intersects two separate workflows for gathering and producing these outputs. This new comprehensive workflow allows these interlinked research outputs to be deposited and made publicly available in two unique yet complementary institutional repositories: the Purdue e-Pubs repository and the Purdue University Research Repository (PURR). Although these outputs are deposited in separate repositories, this workflow allows these materials to be interlinked so that users are aware of the other's existence. This case study highlights the development of these two repositories and workflow models and the changes adopted to enhance the content presentation and user experience.

BACKGROUND

Formed in 1936, the Joint Transportation Research Program (JTRP; https://engineering.purdue.edu/JTRP) is a collaboration between the Indiana Department of Transportation and Purdue University Civil Engineering.

299

In a typical year JTRP produces 20 to 30 technical reports on a variety of transportation-related issues. These reports are published and made available as free PDF downloads from the JTRP collection (http://docs.lib .purdue.edu/jtrp/) on Purdue e-Pubs, the Purdue Libraries Publishing Division's online publishing platform. The process of publishing these technical reports has evolved through the years so that, beginning in 2006, JTRP began a partnership with the Purdue Libraries to produce and disseminate its technical report publications. In 2010 the partnership expanded further to the Purdue e-Pubs institutional repository, which became both the publishing platform and mode of dissemination.

Beginning in 2013–2014 the Libraries/JTRP partnership extended to include the use of the Purdue University Research Repository (PURR). PURR enables JTRP researchers to publish their datasets online and then link these data to their technical reports via digital object identifier (DOI) (Purdue University Research Repository; https://purr.purdue.edu/). After an initial implementation the workflow model was utilized in the publishing of the first interlinked technical report publication and datasets. It became apparent, however, that something was missing from this process. A means for previewing the datasets was needed to allow for users coming from a variety of platforms or devices (e.g., mobile- or tablet-based platforms) and to ensure a complementary user experience. By interlinking the unique workflows of both of these repositories and providing a common user experience, the repository administrators, research administrators, and editorial manager can coordinate the deposit process of the materials, develop the points of interlinkage, and further ensure that users' needs and experience expectations are being met by repository capabilities and metadata practices.

INSTITUTIONAL REPOSITORIES AT PURDUE UNIVERSITY

The Purdue e-Pubs Institutional Document Repository

In 2005, the Purdue University Libraries established the Purdue e-Pubs repository, a traditional institutional repository and online publishing platform for the Libraries Publishing Division. The repository, built upon the Digital Commons platform from bepress, provides free global online open access to scholarship and research authored by Purdue faculty, staff, and students. Since 2010, Purdue e-Pubs has been both the hosting repository and publishing platform for JTRP technical reports. This platform has provided for a holistic production process and standard processes for journal article production and publication. A production editor who manages the review process and production of the technical reports is supported by JTRP funds (Zilinski, Scherer, Bullock, Horton, & Matthews, 2014).

The Purdue University Research Repository (PURR)

The Purdue University Research Repository (PURR), in collaboration with the Office of the Vice President of Research (OVPR) and Information Technology at Purdue (ITaP), is the Libraries' data repository and was designed to assist Purdue researchers in meeting the data management plan (DMP) requirements of granting agencies. The PURR hub was built using Purdue's own HUBzero open source platform, which "support(s) collaborative development and dissemination of scientific models running in an infrastructure that leverages a 'cloud' of computing resources" (McLennan & Kennell, 2010). PURR was made operational in fall 2011, went live for Purdue users in January 2013, and extends the HUBzero capabilities by allowing users to publish data as scholarship with a DataCite DOI. Some examples of research data are spreadsheets, models, instrument or sensor readings, software source code, surveys, interview transcripts, images, and audiovisual files. In addition to housing and publishing research datasets, PURR allows researchers and graduate students to collaborate on research and create working project spaces.

COHESIVE MULTIREPOSITORY WORKFLOW MODEL

In 2012, Newton and colleagues reported that publishing and repository services and expertise could be leveraged to provide an enhanced publication with increased discoverability and accessibility. These efforts were further enhanced with the adoption of a second data-focused institutional repository and workflow, which could be used to provide access and disseminate the affiliated datasets. This part of the case study discusses the two workflows used to accomplish the linking of technical reports and datasets—the technical report publication workflow (including the peer-review process) and the PURR dataset publication workflow—and where they intersect.

Joint Transportation Research Program (JTRP)
Technical Report Publication Workflow

Purdue e-Pubs is both the hosting repository and the publishing platform for JTRP technical reports, as well as the vehicle for managing the peer-review process. The following is the path from initial report submission to publication:

1. The principal investigator (PI) submits the draft final report with metadata to Purdue e-Pubs.
2. Via e-Pubs, the production editor invites the Study Advisory Committee (SAC) members to review the report.
3. SAC members submit their reviews to e-Pubs.
4. The production editor sends reviews to the PI via e-Pubs.
5. The PI provides a revised report to the project administrator and business owner prior to the closeout SAC meeting.
6. Once the report is approved by the SAC, the PI submits the final report to e-Pubs.
7. The production editor sends the final report to the JTRP managing director, who obtains approval for publication from the Indiana Department of Transportation.
8. Upon approval, the production editor does the following to prepare the report for publication.
   a. Assigns report number and DOI.
   b. Performs light copyediting for consistency.
   c. *Ensures that the PURR DataCite DOI(s) are referenced in the report.*
   d. Manages the typesetting and proof revision process.
   e. Uploads the final typeset report to e-Pubs and completes metadata entry, *including PURR citation(s) with live DOI link(s) to one or more datasets.*
   f. Publishes the report on Purdue e-Pubs and registers the DOI with CrossRef.
   g. Provides the DOI link to the publication to the authors and other interested parties.
   h. Prepares the report to be made available via print on demand and in a free downloadable e-book format.

Purdue University Research Repository (PURR)
Dataset Publication Workflow

Most JTRP datasets published to date on PURR are videos linked to technical reports. While the ideal scenario is that the PI creates a DMP and publishes his or her data in PURR, then simply provides the minted DataCite DOI(s) to the production editor before the technical report is sent for typesetting (or includes them in the final report before submission), we are still in the early stages of implementing this workflow. At the time of this writing, what commonly occurs is that the PI provides the production editor with the dataset(s) and metadata, and the production editor publishes them in PURR and ensures that they are referenced properly in the technical report.

The remainder of this section discusses the PURR publication workflow when the PI provides the production editor with the dataset and metadata and requests that the production editor handle the submission and publication.

The production editor performs the following steps to publish a dataset in PURR:

1. Initiates a project in PURR.
   a. Enters a project title and description.
   b. Uploads one or more datasets to the project.
2. Starts a publication. Each dataset is its own publication, and each receives its own DataCite DOI. A project may contain several publications.
   a. Chooses the dataset to publish and makes it available as a downloadable file.
   b. Enters a synopsis.
   c. Enters the abstract text and, if the dataset is a video, a video streaming link. (With video datasets, because we want the video to stream easily on the PURR Web landing page, we upload the video to our YouTube channel and embed the YouTube link in the abstract field. Visitors can view the video immediately on the PURR site, and they can also download the MP4 file.)
   d. Adds authors and tags (key words).
   e. Chooses a publication license.

    f. Enters the citation for the related technical report to be published in Purdue e-Pubs.

3. Publishes the dataset.

    a. Reviews all metadata carefully; if the dataset is a video, ensures that it streams; submits the request to publish.

    b. Once PURR has published the dataset and the DataCite DOI is live (generally within 48 hours of request), *adds the citation to the technical report Web landing page on Purdue e-Pubs.*

COMBINING THE TWO WORKFLOWS: REPOSITORIES IN ACTION

Linking Publications to Datasets

In short, the production editor performs the following tasks to link a PI's data to his or her technical report:

1. Publishes the dataset in PURR (with a cross-reference to the technical report citation) and obtains the DataCite DOI.

2. Ensures that the PURR DataCite DOI is referenced in the technical report before it goes to typesetting.

3. Adds the PURR citation with DataCite DOI as metadata to the Purdue e-Pubs record for the technical report.

4. Publishes the technical report in Purdue e-Pubs; the landing page includes a cross-reference to the dataset citation.

Sometimes a PI will request linking a dataset to a report after the report has been published in Purdue e-Pubs, and the dataset has not been referenced in the report. In these cases the dataset is published in PURR with a cross-reference citation to the report; then the PURR citation with live DOI link to the dataset is added to the e-Pubs metadata record page.

Figure 19.1 shows the metadata record page for a technical report published on Purdue e-Pubs that is affiliated with a published dataset (in this case an MP4 video). The metadata record contains two citations: (1) a recommended citation for the technical report itself, and (2) a citation that cross-references the dataset. If this report referenced in more than one dataset, the citation for each would be included.

Figure 19.1. Purdue e-Pubs technical report record page.

Likewise, the PURR Web landing page for this dataset contains two citations: (1) a citation for the dataset itself (Figure 19.2), and (2) a cross-reference citation to the technical report (Figure 19.3). The DOI links are live in all citations.

Points of Intersection and Linkage

As illustrated in the two repository workflows (Zilinski et al., 2014), there are three primary points of intersection. The initial point of intersection occurs at the point when the PI develops the DMP (Figure 19.4). This ensures that the PI, repository administrators, and production editor are aware in the earliest stages of the research life cycle that a technical report publication will also have datasets. The second point is at the time the DataCite

Figure 19.2. PURR dataset record page: citation for the dataset.

Figure 19.3. PURR dataset record page: citation for the cross-referenced technical report.

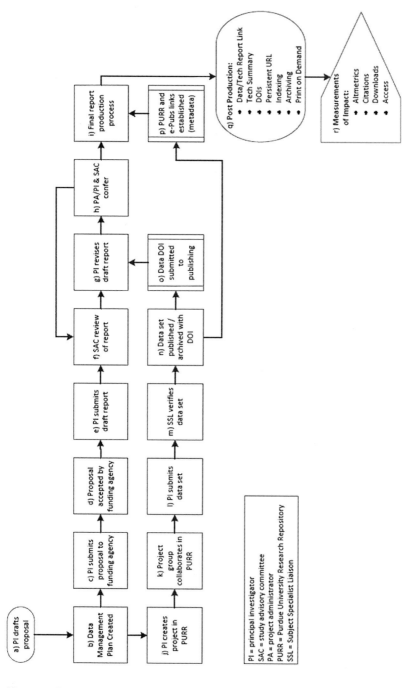

Figure 19.4. Purdue e-Pubs and PURR interlinked repository workflow for JTRP.

Figure 19.5. PURR embedded access-only dataset preview.

DOI is minted. This way the data citation with DOI can be added within the publication. And lastly, the citations and DOIs are embedded into the other objects' corresponding metadata record as a corresponding related object.

Enhancing the Users' Experiences

Once the integrated workflows were implemented and the technical report publication and datasets were being published and interlinked, it became apparent that another step was necessary. The publications in Purdue e-Pubs were being made available as a downloadable PDF to ensure the widest array of users could access the publications. The datasets for the given reports were in the form of MP4 videos. PURR provided the option for videos to be downloaded too, but the datasets remained in their native file format. This led to a potential issue of not providing users a means to quickly preview the datasets, or a means to play a dataset once it had been downloaded, and required users to have an appropriate video player program. A solution was then developed allowing users to play the dataset in line with their current browser window as a primary option instead of downloading the dataset. This also caused concerns for user experience. This solution required users to have the latest version of their browsers to ensure that the plug-ins created for the tool would play properly.

A final solution was created that would allow an access-only copy of the dataset to be added to an unlisted YouTube channel that could be played from within a wiki-enabled metadata field. Once the files are received the production editor is able to add the video to YouTube and the affiliated streaming linked macro to the wiki-enabled metadata field as described in step 2.C of the PURR workflow. With this new solution the access-only copy is available from the dataset's metadata record while the version of record can still be downloaded from the provided download button (Figure 19.5).

CONCLUSION

Scherer, Zilinski, and Matthews (2013) discussed several initial lessons learned from interlinking the data publication process with the traditional publication workflow:

1. Linking publishing and data workflows allows collaborators to coordinate resources and anticipate needs at each step of the process.
2. Early interaction with the data repository increases the likelihood that good data management principles and practices would be utilized.
3. Incorporating standard publication attributes increases the visibility and discoverability of the data and traditional publications.
4. Research usage and access metrics can be monitored and evaluated through the use of recognized publication attributes.

As the development of this integrated multirepository workflow model continues, additional lessons have been learned. First, with these new workflows being developed it's crucial to continue to evaluate them for possible revisions and additional steps to enhance the interlinkage of the publications. Second, it's important to involve all vested parties with workflow updates and additional enhancements. Without insight coming from research center administrators, authors, and users, there is no review of services or user experiences to evaluate what must be added or revised. And lastly, it's important that all of these changes are still in line with the overall goal of increasing access and visibility of the published technical report publications and published datasets. The new video dataset preview capability allows users to interact more fully with the dataset in a way that still allows the version of record to be downloaded for full data manipulation.

REFERENCES

Holdren, J. P. (2013, February 22). *Memorandum for the heads of executive departments and agencies* [Memorandum from the Executive Office of the President, Office of Science and Technology Policy]. Retrieved from https://www.whitehouse.gov/sites/default/files/microsites/ostp/ostp_public_access_memo_2013.pdf

McLennan, M., & Kennell R. (2010). HUBzero: A platform for dissemination and collaboration in computational science and engineering. *Computing in Science & Engineering, 12*(2), 48–53. http://dx.doi.org/10.1109/MCSE.2010.41

Newton, M. P., Bullock, D. M., Watkinson, C., Bracke, P. J., & Horton, D. (2012). Engaging new partners in transportation research: Integrating publishing, archiving, indexing of technical literature into the research process. *Transportation Research Record: Journal of the Transportation Research Board, 2291*, 111–123. http://dx.doi.org/10.3141/2291-13

Scherer, D. A., Zilinksi, L. D., & Matthews, C. E. (2013). *Opportunities and challenges of data publication: A case from Purdue* (Proceedings of the Charleston Library Conference). http://dx.doi.org/10.5703/1288284315319

Zilinski, L. D., Scherer, D. A., Bullock, D. M, Horton, D. K., & Matthews, C. E. (2014). Evolution of data creation, management, publication, and curation in the research process. *Transportation Research Record: Journal of the Transportation Research Board, 2414*, 9–19. http://dx.doi.org/10.3141/2414-02

20 Populating Your Institutional Repository and Promoting Your Students: IRs and Undergraduate Research

Betty Rozum and Becky Thoms

Establishing institutional repositories (IRs) and encouraging supportive faculty participation can be daunting. Gaining access to scholarly publications and other products that students produce, especially undergraduate researchers, can be an even more challenging task. Many IRs contain graduate theses and dissertations as well as undergraduate honors theses and the abstracts of work that students present at student research events or conferences. It is less common to find IRs whose compilers thoroughly collect student scholarship from all aspects of students' research activities, which can demonstrate the academic involvement of both a university's student population and the faculty who collaborate with their students (Barandiaran, Rozum, & Thoms, 2014). When an opportunity arose at Utah State University's Merrill-Cazier Library to begin such a process, a partnership was born that benefits students, faculty members, and the library. This case study describes the evolution and benefits of that partnership.

Utah State University's (USU's) IR was established in 2007, and it consisted solely of a small collection of theses and dissertations. This collection was made available using CONTENTdm, the software that USU was already using for its Digital Library. However, it quickly became clear that this was not a good fit, and after a review of the repository options available on the market, USU selected the bepress platform. DigitalCommons@ USU launched in October 2008 and was comprised primarily of the aforementioned theses and dissertations, a library newsletter, and a small selection of publications from academic departments. DigitalCommons quickly

Full-Text Documents in DigitalCommons@USU
Cumulative uploads by date

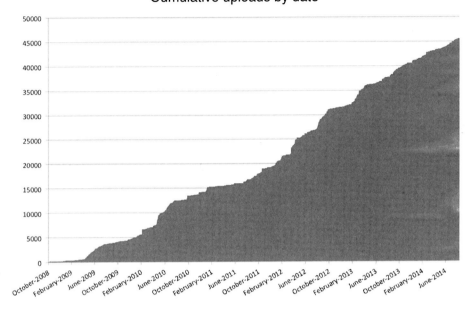

Figure 20.1. DigitalCommons@USU cumulative uploads by date, October 2008 through June 2014.

established itself and began to grow rapidly (see Figure 20.1). By the end of the first year, DigitalCommons had more than 10 distinct series, which included the Departments of Psychology and Animal, Dairy, and Veterinary Science as well the Quinney College of Natural Resources and the *Intermountain West Journal of Religious Studies,* in addition to the inaugural theses and dissertation and library content. As of September 2014, DigitalCommons holds more than 44,000 documents, which represent all of USU's nine colleges, six journals, products from myriad other research centers, events, and unique content.

All of this success has not come without its challenges. While some departments and faculty enthusiastically embraced DigitalCommons as a tool both to archive and expand the impact of their research, other USU units have required more convincing. Early on the Digital Initiatives Department made the decision to adopt a one-stop-shop approach to adding items to DigitalCommons, specifically faculty publications. This means that a faculty member need only submit a current curriculum vitae (CV), and DigitalCommons staff will use that to build a site (termed SelectedWorks in the bepress platform) for the individual, which will include entries for all of the scholarship noted on the faculty member's CV. These records are then used to populate the IR—specifically the series for that faculty member's home department. The next step is for DigitalCommons staff to research the copyright status of all of the publications on the CV—which is done primarily utilizing SHERPA/RoMEO, with additional research on individual publisher Web sites as needed. This information is collected into a document that clearly indicates which version (preprint, postprint, published version) can legally be added to the IR. Publisher versions, when allowed, are uploaded, and faculty are asked to submit other versions if they have them. This also serves to remind faculty of the importance of archiving versions of their papers. This model, which is very different from the self-deposit approach taken by many IRs, has contributed significantly to the flourishing of DigitalCommons@USU.

This hands-on approach provided opportunities to develop relationships with particular units on campus and to understand their research interests. In 2011, as DigitalCommons marked its third-year anniversary, the faculty of the USU Physics Department were becoming strong supporters, with well over half the department submitting their vitas for inclusion. Interest in the capabilities of the platform was at a peak, and the physics librarian and physics faculty began discussing some new ways to use DigitalCommons to promote faculty and student research.

It is fairly common to see institutional repositories arrange materials by producers of content along the lines of academic units or type of researcher. For example, the faculty scholarship is grouped together by department; graduate theses and dissertations are together, and so on. What we had not seen at USU was a gathering of scholarship from both faculty and students into one community, based on the research area of the scholarship, nor had we seen an intensive effort to collect student scholarship beyond graduate theses and dissertations and honors theses.

A member of the physics department was very interested in showcasing the research of his lab, which focuses on atmospheric physics. Locally known for the "green beam," which appears like a laser shooting into the night sky to collect data from the atmosphere, the Atmospheric LIDAR Observatory (ALO) has been measuring temperatures, densities, and waves in the mesosphere and looking for evidence of global warming since 1993. It has been upgraded to be the most powerful LIDAR in the world (Sox, Wickwar, Herron, Bingham, & Peterson, 2011).

The physicist in charge of the ALO recognized an opportunity to use DigitalCommons as a venue that would collect scholarship from all members of his research team, regardless of their status or the format of their research. Thus, this entry site would collate works from faculty as well as graduate and undergraduate students in the form of peer-reviewed articles, reports, conference publications, posters, presentations, and theses and dissertations. In addition to grouping the materials together in one area that would be easy to browse, such a collection would showcase the work of the research group and archive materials, some of which were scattered in computer files and print documents in offices around the university.

After establishing the structure in DigitalCommons, the physics librarian worked with the faculty member to gather materials and obtain permission to post them in the IR. The collection currently has 72 items that have received 3,870 downloads. Interestingly, the majority of downloads come from posters, presentations, and reports that would not be available through other venues (data as of September 2014).

At the same time that the library was working with the ALO group, the physics librarian was also working with the Physics Department head to outline options for a similar community for a student-led interdisciplinary research group on campus, the Get Away Special (GAS) Team. This student team was founded in 1976 at USU and has upheld the university's reputation for flying more experiments that include the work of student researchers into space than any other university in the world. Students participate from a number of departments on campus, drawing heavily from engineering and physics. The GAS program has been a rich part of the history of USU, and setting up a collection to promote the work of the students was in the best interests of all parties. The library worked closely with the student coordinator to gather materials and obtain permissions from students to post them. An additional benefit of this effort was that the library obtained the print archive that had been housed in the student lab, ensuring the records would be added to the university's Special Collections and Archives.

Some of the scholarship that students have produced, in particular the educational resources, is very popular. In fact, of the undergraduate research hosted in DigitalCommons, the four most frequently downloaded items come from the GAS program, with a total of more than 12,700 downloads among them. After a year, an exhibition was created in the library to showcase the GAS program and the research conducted through the years (Rozum, Wesolek, & Martin, 2012). This ultimately helped the library to secure additional archival materials pertaining to the early space program in Utah.

Working with the ALO group and the GAS Team paved the way to set up communities for other research groups. The physics librarian approached faculty members working with groups of undergraduate and graduate students in specific areas of physics. While a few wanted communities such as the ALO set up for them, no one took advantage of DigitalCommons to the extent that the Materials Physics Group (MPG) has. The MPG studies the effect of the space environment on aerospace materials. In addition to the lead faculty researcher, graduate and undergraduate students conduct research in this area. The faculty member has been diligent through the years about archiving article postprints and conference posters and presentations, and he came to the table with valuable resources in hand.

A community similar to the ALO was established for the MPG collection, and as time allowed, metadata and files were uploaded. As of September 2014, the site had just over 440 records, which have received more than 10,700 downloads. These include faculty publications, conference publications, reports, senior student reports, graduate theses and dissertations, posters, and presentations. As with the other sites, these are all grouped together—faculty with students—presenting a comprehensive view of the group's research to any visitor to the IR. A few MPG students began adding QR codes linking to DigitalCommons collections of materials to their posters so conference attendees could quickly discover more research.

Currently, all physics students, undergraduate and graduate, are encouraged to submit scholarship to the librarian for inclusion in Digital Commons. The community of Physics Student Research (http://digitalcom mons.usu.edu/phys_stures/), which does not include the capstone projects or theses and dissertations, collects all recent scholarship submitted. This community features just over 90 entries, as of September 2014, which have been downloaded more than 4,500 times. In 2014, the Physics Department began requiring undergraduates to submit their senior capstone projects to the IR as well (http://digitalcommons.usu.edu/phys_capstoneproject/). While only 16 documents have been uploaded as of September 2014, these have received a respectable 159 downloads.

Additionally, physics graduate students and undergraduates who are actively participating in DigitalCommons are provided with SelectedWorks sites. This affords students the opportunity to build an online presence with permanent links to their scholarship and to use this for graduate school, fellowship, scholarship, job, or other applications. Both faculty members and the physics librarian promote this service. The Physics Department links to the student research page and the graduate students' SelectedWorks sites from their departmental Web site, exposing visitors to their Web site and to the research and interests of their students and faculty. Although this is still a new effort, the department is beginning to see some positive recruitment effects, as evidenced by comments made by prospective graduate students who interview at USU. Students have commented on seeing research from other students and faculty through the department and DigitalCommons links.

Physics faculty feel that incorporating student research in DigitalCommons has concrete benefits. Including the senior capstone projects is very important to the department because it allows them to provide data for outcomes and assessment. This is being used as part of an accreditation process that requires students to demonstrate that they have reached a certain level of mastery in physics.

Faculty see a correlation between spikes in download activity in the MPG materials and the two major conferences for this group—the Spacecraft Charging Technology Conference and the Small Satellite Conference. At each conference, half a dozen people have approached members of the lab with unsolicited comments about research they discovered on the institutional repository site. At these conferences, students and faculty consistently place QR codes linking to the MPG site in DigitalCommons on business cards and presentations, which also boosts the visibility of their work.

Faculty also find that capturing the research from student poster presentations is very valuable as many of these posters contain significant research. After a particular conference, posters are generally tossed aside, or they may hang in the halls of the department. Capturing the posters and making the data accessible ensures the work does not disappear and allows students to point back to an archive of their scholarship. Student posters in DigitalCommons receive a fair amount of downloads.

Before attending important conferences, the faculty mentors for both ALO and MPG will touch base to make sure the most recent scholarship has been uploaded so that their students' and research groups' work can be readily available. The increased visibility of research conducted by the faculty and students has led to contacts by researchers from around the country to comment on papers. More significantly, the department has secured funding for two projects as a direct result of research that a private company discovered through the DigitalCommons. These projects will allow more students to participate in additional research, which again will be deposited in the IR.

What really has made the venture a success, according to conversations with faculty, has been the involvement of their librarian and the willingness of the library to offer expertise and staff to clear the copyright and enter records into DigitalCommons for both faculty and student scholarship. This allowed the faculty to overcome any fears or hesitations they might have had over legal issues or time commitment to participating in the IR.

The IR does raise a few concerns for the Physics Department, mainly with the nature of the SelectedWorks sites. The integration between the SelectedWorks sites (the author pages) and DigitalCommons is weak, resulting in inaccurate download statistics, added work for maintaining up-to-date sites for both, and confusion in explaining reports to faculty.

Another minor concern is the lack of control over the content of SelectedWorks sites. At USU, these sites, unlike the DigitalCommons side of the institutional repository, can be fully edited by the person to whom the page belongs. This means that students can add anything they wish, possibly claiming work done while at USU, adding a photo that is inappropriate, or posting other content that does not reflect well on the department or university. Several staff members in the library have full administrative rights to remove content so that they could remedy such situations, but it is an area, unfortunately, that librarians must think seriously about. Thankfully, these are relatively minor concerns and are more than offset by the significant benefit that the Physics Department and library have seen as a result of their efforts to incorporate faculty and student work in DigitalCommons.

This enormously successful project is the result of the unflagging efforts of a motivated subject librarian and faculty members in an extremely receptive and enthusiastic academic department. It is worth noting this work comprised only a small percentage of the librarian's time, demonstrating that a strategic investment of effort can have a major payoff. While at first glance it may seem unlikely that it could be replicated, early efforts to expand this initiative across campus have been positively received, and working in concert with the Office of Research and Graduate Studies, the library is making progress in expanding the successful physics model to other departments. Academic departments and disciplines have different needs, expectations, and concerns. There will not be a one-size-fits-all approach, but incorporating student work in DigitalCommons@USU has enormous potential benefit for faculty and students. USU's experience attests that a knowledgeable and enthusiastic team of librarians can work in concert with individual departments to find the unique blend of content and access that best highlights great local research accomplishments.

REFERENCES

Barandiaran, D., Rozum, B., & Thoms, B. (2014, November). Focusing on student research in the institutional repository. *C&RL News, 75*(10), 546–549. http://crln.acrl.org/content/75/10/546.full

Rozum, B., Wesolek, A., & Martin, P. (2012, Summer). *Merrill-Cazier Library GAS exhibition*. Exhbition, Merrill-Cazier Library, Utah State University, Logan, UT. Retrieved from http://digitalcommons.usu.edu/gas_educ/13/

Sox, L., Wickwar, V., Herron, J., Bingham, M., & Peterson, L. (2011). *The world's most sensitive Rayleigh-scatter lidar*. Presented at the CEDAR Workshop. Retrieved from http://digitalcommons.usu.edu/atmlidar_post/1

Part 6

CLOSING REFLECTIONS AND THE NEXT STEPS FOR INSTITUTIONAL REPOSITORIES

Institutional repositories were conceived and implemented by librarians who were concerned about an ever increasing commercial impact on scholarly communication. They sought a way to circumvent traditional publishers and increase access to scholarly work. Much of the early work was focused on building platforms and setting policies. Once the mechanics were in place, the next phase involved scholars and crafting ways to sell the idea of curating and increasing access to scholarly work in order to acquire content and encourage use. And yet, regardless of the philosophical or structural perspectives, the tools, resources, and services that are either built within the repository system or added as complementary components must be platform-agnostic.

Since the publishing of Raym Crow's position paper, IRs have been adopted ever more widely. However, an institutional repository is by definition siloed. In her summary conclusion on the future of institutional repositories, Heather Joseph argues for the need for developers to provide deeper and more meaningful levels of functional interoperability among repositories. This will require repositories to find mechanisms and organizations that will assist in binding repositories together, which, as Joseph alludes to, may include the increased adoption of repositories working with organizations like the Scholarly Publishing and Academic Resources Coalition (SPARC; http://sparc.arl.org/) or the Confederation of Open Access Repositories (COAR; https://www.coar-repositories.org/about/coar-ev/strategic-plan/).

In addition to a path toward total interoperability among repositories, Joseph points to an obligation among all those associated with repositories to think broadly about content and to work with scholars as well as students and community members about the ways that a repository can motivate a wide array of information and make it useful and impactful to scholars and laypersons alike. Repositories built to handle and serve datasets illustrate the way that repositories are not only expanding access to scholarship but expanding the very nature of what is considered scholarship. In order for repositories to reach their full potential, it is imperative that this expansion of the nature of scholarship and scholarly artifacts continue.

One final key for IRs to fully realize the dream that inspired their creation is to involve, if not indoctrinate, institutional leadership into the goals and aspirations of the project. The language and spirit of repositories needs to be woven into the mission and fabric of colleges and universities in a large-scale fashion. This work has begun and is gaining momentum, but has yet to hit critical mass. Steven Hyman, provost of Harvard University, provides a deceptively simple goal for the university that can serve as a model for all institutions: "The goal of university research is the creation, dissemination, and preservation of knowledge. At Harvard, where so much of our research is of global significance, we have an essential responsibility to distribute the fruits of our scholarship as widely as possible" (Hyman, 2010). As Joseph argues, for repositories to succeed, libraries will need to consider their repositories as integral components of their mission, and the broader mission of their institutions.

As evidenced by the contributions to this volume, much work has been done toward the development, implementation, and evaluation of repositories, which has led to their increasingly widespread adoption around the world. However, much work remains. Throughout this volume, we see the need to deeply understand the value of repository initiatives and demonstrate it to administrators as a key component of the mission of institutions of higher education. While this work must be contextualized on an institutional basis, together we need to promote interoperability with an eye toward not just changing cultural practices at our individual institutions, but profoundly changing the way scholarship is communicated in terms of access as well as content.

Finally, the continued success of institutional repositories and correlated open access to scholarship depends on scholars and practitioners speaking with a unified voice and acting with a unified vision. The legislative environment and byzantine publisher copyright transfer agreements are changing much more rapidly than a volume such as this can capture. To end on a warning: In addition to working toward more interoperable platforms, we must continue not only to follow these changes with a vigilant eye and speak out when they negatively impact openness, but to actively participate in the process. We must continue to develop and implement the infrastructure to archive and make scholarship openly available. However, we must also ensure that authors retain the rights to do so by actively pushing for openness at the highest levels of both government and commercial entities.

REFERENCE

Hyman, S. E. (2010). *Open access policies*. Harvard University.

21 | Next Steps for IRs and Open Access

Heather Joseph

Since their inception in the early 2000s, institutional repositories have carried the potential to play a key role in addressing key strategic issues facing higher education institutions. They hold the promise to fundamentally change the way scholarship is communicated by providing expanded access to scholarly research and raising the visibility of an institution's work. They can also provide an alternative to traditional publishing channels such as scholarly journals, introducing competition into a market where competition is sorely needed, and lessening the economic burden on academic and research libraries. Perhaps most critically, institutional repositories can provide an avenue for academic institutions to reassert control of the scholarly output that they produce—helping to broadly demonstrate the scientific, social, and economic value of the research, and raising the visibility and prestige of the institution as a whole.

However, as the earlier chapters in this volume clearly illustrate, this promise has so far been only partially realized—due in part to the natural complexities of introducing wholesale change into a system as large and as entrenched as the traditional scholarly communication system, but also to the lack of implementation of the *full* vision of what institutional repositories might be structured to achieve. To further complicate the picture, the world keeps on changing, and new technologies and economic and political exigencies have emerged that also put pressure on us to expand on the original vision of exactly what institutional repositories are, and how they might contribute to a new vision of sharing scientific and scholarly information.

In 2002, the Scholarly Publishing and Academic Resources Coalition (SPARC) published an important position paper titled "The Case for Institutional Repositories," in which Raym Crow examined the strategic roles that institutional repositories might play for colleges and universities. In this paper, institutional repositories were defined as digital collections that collect, preserve, and disseminate the intellectual output of a single- or multiuniversity community.

Crow placed a heavy emphasis on the potential of institutional repositories to play an immediate role in providing faculty with a convenient local mechanism to support the growing desire of authors to be able to share their scholarly work online at various stages of the research and publication process, as well as to ensure that access to these works be as nearly universal and perpetual as possible. This function has proven appealing to a growing segment of the faculty, student, and research community that chose to house their research outputs in repositories. It has also received a boost from institutional leadership, as a growing number of colleges and universities enact policies affirming that locally generated content logically should be housed in the institution's repository, in order to accrue the benefits of greater visibility and reach.

Looking across the current landscape of institutional repositories, this portion of the vision has been implemented to a reasonable degree. However, in the same paper, Crow was careful to emphasize that the rationale for implementing IRs extended far beyond the benefits that might accrue to individual authors at a single institution. The impetus was twofold: to generate direct and immediate benefits to individual institutions, of course, but also to ensure that repositories are effectively networked to create a global, interoperable system to benefit institutions—and stakeholders—collectively. The full power of repositories, Crow argued, lay in the creation of a robust infrastructure that would provide stakeholders in the academic community with the opportunity to reimagine—and reconstruct—the current scholarly communication system by offering options for where and when traditional components of the system (registration, certification, dissemination) could take place.

This notion of disaggregating (or unbundling) the system embodied by academic journal publishing further extended the potential benefits of IRs by presenting the possibility for real market efficiencies to be introduced through the creation of competitive, university-based publishing services—a particularly attractive proposition given the persistent economic pressures facing libraries.

Yet the reality is, while thousands of repositories have been successfully established on college and university campuses around the globe, and care has been taken to ensure that the majority of these are built using open source software platforms and using open communications protocols, with a few exceptions (most notably, the OpenAIRE initiative in the European Union), we have not yet seen the type of universal interoperability among these IRs implemented as originally envisioned. And while some new academy-based publishing services are beginning to emerge, the growth has been slow and has not yet been established on the scale needed to provide truly transformative change.

What does this mean for the future prospects of institutional repositories? As noted earlier, this somewhat slow pace of change is largely to be expected. Creating wholesale change to a long-established structure like the current scholarly publishing model is neither simple nor quick to accomplish. But a foundation for such change has been effectively established. The challenge now is for the community to take stock of the results of the significant collective investments made to date in the infrastructure of institutional repositories and to strategically move to strengthen the opportunities for this investment to realize its full potential. The chapters in this book surface many key opportunities that merit serious consideration, but there are three in particular that I would like to highlight here.

First, the need to provide a deeper and more meaningful level of functional interoperability among repositories stands out. No man is an island, and it is increasingly clear that this holds true for repositories as well. In order for the vision of a seamless, openly accessible global database of research and scholarship to come to fruition, a focused effort to address the nontrivial task of ensuring technical interoperability among as great a number of international repositories as possible must be supported by the community. The Confederation of Open Access Repositories (COAR) eloquently notes the need—and some of the potential outcomes—of such a large-scale effort in its mission statement, calling for repositories to develop the ability to "communicate with each other and pass information back and forth in a usable format. Interoperability allows us to exploit today's computational power so that we can aggregate, data mine, create new tools and services, and generate new knowledge from repository content." Such an effort will require significant additional investment, but the potential returns to the community are also significant and will be amplified by the collective nature of this endeavor.

A second key strategic opportunity is also alluded to in the COAR mission statement above, and requires broadly rethinking the kinds of content that repositories might hold and the activities that can be facilitated around various content types. While the original emphasis of institutional repositories lent itself to thinking about the infrastructure as primarily supporting a communications and preservation channel, we are beginning to see an important shift to thinking about repositories as a dynamic workspace for scholars and researchers as well. As institutions—and scholars—become more comfortable with the digital environment, repositories offer an increasingly attractive option for works-in-progress and collaborative or large-scale projects to be created, nurtured, and ultimately housed. This shift in focus also opens up new possibilities for active collaborations with other entities on campus, from university presses to individual labs or departments that have an interest in leveraging local, cost-effective infrastructure for sharing scholarly research outputs.

This is a particularly crucial development, as it holds the potential to further amplify the value of the repository to individual institutions, as scholars turn to this locally provided resource to surface and communicate information about their work at new and earlier stages in the research process, as well as to the global community, as collaboration across boundaries is facilitated in real time. It also presents the opportunity consider expanding the utility of the materials in the repository for other critical campus uses, particularly in terms of integration as teaching materials for classroom use.

Finally, it also seems increasingly clear that for institutional repositories to succeed on any scale, they must be considered as integral to the mission of the larger body in which they are housed and be able to demonstrate their clear value. Many efforts to date have focused on raising the number of objects—mainly articles, manuscripts, and dissertations—housed in the repository and have emphasized the increased use/visibility these objects—and their authors—received as a result. While this is an important strategy, it should not be the sole focus of communicating the value of a repository. These objects represent the tip of the iceberg in terms of the repository's potential value, and effectively communicating the additional benefits that can accrue as repositories are networked and increasingly utilized by scholars as active workspaces is an important message to send throughout the academy.

These are just a handful of the strategic opportunities to consider as the community looks forward to forging the next steps in the evolution of the scholarly communication system. The scope of the challenges are global, large-scale, and systemic, and they require focused, collective action to address effectively, but the ultimate result—a system of communicating research and scholarship that directly and equitably serves the needs of all stakeholders—remains well worth the effort.

About the Contributors

Kenning Arlitsch is a dean at Montana State University, where he leads a progressive research library that is committed to student success and the research enterprise. Prior to moving to Montana he spent 18 years at the University of Utah, serving as associate dean for IT services for the last five years. Arlitsch is the founder of several notable programs, including the Mountain West Digital Library and the Utah Digital Newspapers, and he is co-founder of the Acoustic Atlas. His funded research for the past four years has focused on search engine and Semantic Web optimization for digital repositories, and he and his research team have given numerous presentations and published widely on the topic.

Meghan Banach Bergin is the bibliographic access and metadata coordinator at the University of Massachusetts Amherst. In addition to providing leadership for the Bibliographic Access and Metadata Unit of the Information Resources Management Department, she is a member of the UMass Amherst Scholarly Communication Team and focuses primarily on the management of electronic theses and dissertations in the institutional repository. Her research interests center on managing, preserving, and providing access to digital materials. Bergin holds an MLIS with an archives management concentration from the Simmons College Graduate School of Library and Information Science and a BA in history from Mount Holyoke College.

Daniel Beucke is project manager at Göttingen State and University Library. He works on several digital library projects. Current tasks focus on open access, electronic publishing, bibliometrics, and altmetrics. He is chairing the COAR Interest Group on Usage Data and Beyond, and he is a member of the DINI working groups Electronic Publishing and CRIS. Beucke holds a master's degree in library and information science from Humboldt-Universität zu Berlin, Germany.

Todd Bruns is the institutional repository librarian at Eastern Illinois University (EIU). He manages the EIU institutional repository, The Keep (http://thekeep.eiu.edu), one of the fastest growing institutional repositories in the Midwest. He was recently honored by receiving the 2014 Berkeley Electronic Press Digital Commons Institutional Repository All-Star award. Bruns has several publications to his credit, including "It Takes a Library: Growing a Robust Institutional Repository in Two Years" in *College and Undergraduate Libraries*, volume 21, issue 3/4, and "Scholarly Communication Coaching: Liaison Librarians' Changing Roles," a book chapter in *Partnerships and New Roles in the 21st Century Academic Library: Collaborating, Embedding, and Cross-Training for the Future,* published in October 2015. Additionally he chairs the EIU Booth Library Web Resources Committee, runs the annual Edible Book Festival, and has regularly presented at several national conferences including the United States Electronic Theses and Dissertations Association, American Library Association Midwinter, and the Association of College and Research Libraries annual conferences.

Marianne A. Buehler was most recently an academic faculty at the University of Nevada, Las Vegas. Previously the libraries' digital scholarship administrator, her work has centered on leadership in scholarly communication and expertise in institutional repositories, digital publishing, author rights, and copyright. She formerly directed a publishing and scholarship center at Rochester Institute of Technology and was the managing editor of three open access publications: *Journal of Applied Science & Engineering Technology,* the *Scholarship@RIT* newsletter, and the *Promise of Sustainability* anthology. Her monograph, *Demystifying the Institutional Repository for Success,* was published in December 2013. Buehler has presented at national conferences and also publishes in areas of sustainability. She received a BA in English from the University of Maine and an MA in information resources and library science at the University of Arizona.

Sam Byrd is digital collections systems librarian at Virginia Commonwealth University. He has worked with digital projects and initiatives since 1996 at VCU and before that at the Library of Virginia.

Burton Callicott is a reference librarian at the College of Charleston, South Carolina, where he coordinates library instruction and serves on the Scholarly Communications Committee which oversees the Charleston ARC—the nascent College of Charleston institutional repository.

Jason A. Clark is currently an associate professor and head of library informatics and computing at Montana State University Libraries, where he builds digital library applications and sets digital content strategies. He writes and presents on a broad range of topics including Semantic Web development, metadata and data modeling, Web services and APIs, search engine optimization, and interface design. Clark holds an MLIS from the University of Wisconsin and an MA in English from the University of Vermont.

Hillary Corbett is the director of scholarly communication and digital publishing at Northeastern University in Boston. From 2007 to 2014 she managed the institutional repository; she now oversees the Library's publishing program. She also serves as the university copyright officer, providing assistance to faculty, staff, and students on issues of intellectual property, copyright, and fair use. She has served as co-chair of the Association of College and Research Libraries New England Chapter's Scholarly Communication Interest Group. Corbett received bachelor's degrees in English and history from the University of Massachusetts at Amherst, a master's degree in information and library studies from the University of Michigan, and a master's degree in American studies from the University of Massachusetts at Boston.

Stephanie Davis-Kahl is the scholarly communications librarian and associate professor at the Ames Library at Illinois Wesleyan University, where she provides leadership for scholarly communication programs, including

Digital Commons @ IWU. She is the liaison to the Economics, Educational Studies, and Psychology departments at IWU, and serves as the managing faculty co-editor of the *Undergraduate Economic Review*. Davis-Kahl is a facilitator for the ACRL Scholarly Communication Roadshow and is a member of the ACRL Intersections of Information Literacy and Scholarly Communication Task Force. She earned her BA in East Asian studies from Oberlin College and her MS in library science from the University of Illinois at Urbana-Champaign. In 2014 she was named a Mover & Shaker by *Library Journal* and was awarded the Education & Behavioral Sciences Section Distinguished Librarian Award.

Ellen Finnie Duranceau is the program manager for the MIT Libraries' Office of Scholarly Publishing, Copyright & Licensing, a position she has held since 2006. She leads the MIT Libraries' outreach efforts to faculty in support of scholarly publication reform and open access activities at MIT, including overseeing implementation of the MIT Faculty Open Access Policy. In addition, she acts as the MIT Libraries' chief resource for copyright issues and for content licensing policy and negotiations. She has written and spoken widely on digital acquisitions, repositories, licensing, and open access. Duranceau received an AB degree in psychology from Princeton University, an MS in library and information science from Simmons College, and an MA in English literature from Northeastern University.

Jimmy Ghaphery is associate professor and head of digital technologies at Virginia Commonwealth University Libraries. He is responsible for leading IT operations including Web systems, enterprise systems, desktop support, and digital collections. Over the past year he has been deeply involved in the launch of VCU's new institutional repository, Scholars Compass.

Isaac Gilman is associate professor and scholarly communication and publishing services librarian at Pacific University (Oregon). He manages Pacific's institutional repository, CommonKnowledge, as well as the university libraries' journal and monograph publishing services. His personal scholarship focuses on the roles and responsibilities of libraries in supporting and distributing original work, and he has taught courses on both journal publishing and research methods. He is the author of *Library*

Scholarly Communication Programs: Legal and Ethical Considerations, was a founding co-editor of *the Journal of Librarianship and Scholarly Communication,* and currently serves on the board of the Library Publishing Coalition. Gilman received a bachelor's degree in English from Kenyon College and an MLIS from the University of British Columbia.

Stefanie Haustein is a postdoctoral researcher at the Canada Research Chair on the Transformations of Scholarly Communication with Professor Vincent Larivière at the University of Montreal and a visiting lecturer at Heinrich Heine University Düsseldorf. Her current research focuses on social media in scholarly communication and altmetrics. She is a co-PI on a grant funded by the Alfred P. Sloan Foundation "to support greater understanding of social media in scholarly communication and the actual meaning of various altmetrics." Haustein holds a master's degree in history, American linguistics and literature, and information science and a PhD in information science from Heinrich Heine University Düsseldorf. Her doctoral work focused on the multidimensional evaluation of scholarly journals and was awarded the Eugene Garfield doctoral dissertation scholarship in 2011. Haustein previously worked as a research analyst at Science-Metrix in Montreal, Canada, and on the bibliometrics team at Forschungszentrum Jülich, Germany.

Kim Holmberg is a research associate at the Research Unit for the Sociology of Education at the University of Turku, Finland. He is also an honorary research fellow at the University of Wolverhampton, UK, and an adjunct professor in informetrics at Åbo Akademi University, Finland. His research interests are in altmetrics, webometrics, bibliometrics, informetrics, social media, and social network analysis. On these topics he has published numerous peer-reviewed articles and held over 100 invited talks and seminars. Currently Holmberg's main focus is on investigating the meaning of altmetrics.

Harrison W. Inefuku joined the Iowa State University Library as digital repository coordinator in 2012, where he oversees the growth and development of Digital Repository @ Iowa State University, the university's institutional repository. He holds bachelor's degrees in graphic design and visual culture from the University of the Pacific, and master's degrees in archival studies and library and information studies from the University of British Columbia.

Heather Joseph serves as the executive director of the Scholarly Publishing and Academic Resources Coalition (SPARC), an international coalition of academic and research libraries working to expand the global, cost-effective digital communication of research results. As SPARC's director since 2005, she leads the strategic and operational activities of the organization and has focused SPARC's efforts on supporting emerging open access communications models for digital articles, data, and educational resources. Prior to joining SPARC, Joseph spent 15 years as a publishing executive in both commercial and not-for-profit publishing organizations.

Kelley Kimm is the production editor for the Joint Transportation Research Program, a collaboration between Purdue University Civil Engineering and the Indiana Department of Transportation. She produces the JTRP technical report series, making the reports available on Purdue e-Pubs, the Purdue University Libraries Publishing Division's online publishing platform, and works with the Purdue University Research Repository to link researchers' datasets to their technical reports via digital object identifier (DOI). Kimm is also a production editor at Purdue University Press, where she edits, designs, and typesets books.

Sue Kriegsman is the associate director for the Berkman Center for Internet & Society at Harvard University, a research program founded to explore cyberspace, share in its study, and help pioneer its development. Her research focus is on open access and library innovation programs. Prior to joining Berkman she was the program manager for the Harvard Library Office for Scholarly Communication, where she identified and pioneered open access initiatives and ways for Harvard to open, share, and preserve scholarship. Kriegsman has written and spoken about open access, library innovation, digital libraries, and the Harvard-Google book digitization project. She holds an MLIS in archives management from Simmons College and a BA in English from Alfred University.

Anne Langley is the associate dean for research, collections, and scholarly communications in the University Libraries at Penn State. She worked previously at Princeton University as the director of scholarly communications and head librarian for the Science and Technology Libraries. Langley held several positions in the Duke University Libraries, including serving as head of the chemistry library, coordinator for the science and engineering libraries, and coordinator for public services assessment. She also held positions at North Carolina State University and the University of Tennessee. She has presented and written on a wide range of topics that have focused on collaboration, planning, and assessment among other topics. She is active professionally and is the current past chair for the Coalition for Open Access Policy Institutions (COAPI) and a member of the advisory board for the University of Tennessee's School of Information Science. Langley earned an MA in library science from the University of Tennessee and a BA in English and creative writing from Georgia State University. She did additional undergraduate work in chemical engineering at the Georgia Institute of Technology and work in chemistry and general engineering at Santa Monica College.

Yuan Li is the scholarly communications librarian at Princeton University, where she manages the Princeton University Library's efforts to support scholarly publication innovations and reforms, and supervises and coordinates activities related to the Princeton Open Access Policy and the Princeton institutional repository. Prior to joining Princeton, she served as the scholarly communication librarian at Syracuse University, the digital initiatives librarian at University of Rhode Island, and the digital repository librarian at University of Massachusetts Amherst. She was a guest editor for the *Code4Lib Journal* special issue on diversity in library technology. She is currently serving on ACRL's Research and Scholarly Environmental Committee (2015–2017). Li has a master's degree in library and information science from the University of Rhode Island, a master of engineering degree in applied computer science from the National Computer System Engineering Research Institute of China, and a bachelor of engineering degree in computer science and technology from Yanshan University, China.

Gail McMillan is the director of scholarly communication at Virginia Tech's University Libraries. Named the director of the Scholarly Communications Project (SCP) in 1994, she led the development of online services and resources. In 2011 VTechWorks was established under her direction to host and make publicly available the university's scholarship and research. McMillan is a founding member and serves on the steering committees of both the Networked Digital Library of Theses and Dissertations and the MetaArchive Cooperative, which broke new ground in 2004 when it began its distributed digital preservation strategy. She is currently focusing on library publishing and is regularly invited throughout the world to make presentations and publish about Virginia Tech's scholarly communications initiatives.

Katherine McNeill is the research data and economics librarian at the Massachusetts Institute of Technology (MIT). She is the convener of the Libraries' team that provides its research data management services, which supports the management and curation of research data produced at MIT. She also leads the Social Science Data Services program, which facilitates access to and use of secondary research data in the social sciences. McNeill is MIT's representative on the Data Documentation Initiative (DDI) Alliance Expert Committee and its official representative to the Interuniversity Consortium for Political and Social Research (ICPSR). In addition, she is a member of the Administrative Committee of the International Association for Social Science Information Services & Technology (IASSIST).

Catherine Mitchell serves as the director of the Access & Publishing Group at the California Digital Library, University of California. As such, she is responsible for overseeing the strategic planning, development, and operational management of the Publishing and the Digital Special Collections programs. The Publishing Group provides the University of California scholarly community with open access publication and distribution services through the development of advanced technologies and creative partnerships. The Digital Special Collections Program (DSC) supports collaboration between libraries, archives, and museums throughout the state of California to provide access to a world-class digital collection that serves an array of end users, from researchers and scholars to K–12 students. Mitchell is also operations director of UC's Office of Scholarly Communication. Her experience in scholarly publishing includes time spent on the other side of the academic house as a scholar of 19th-century British literature. She has a PhD in English literature from UC Berkeley.

Jeffrey K. Mixter is a recent graduate of Kent State University, having earned an MLIS and an MS degree in information architecture and knowledge management. His master's thesis demonstrated how to convert an existing flat data model into a detailed ontology that is interoperable with search engine aggregating services. As a research assistant at OCLC, Jeff worked with Dr. Ed O'Neill in developing the OCLC FAST controlled vocabulary. He is now working as a software engineer at OCLC with collaborators from Montana State University on the IMLS-funded project "Measuring Up: Assessing Accuracy of Reported Use and Impact of Digital Repositories." Kenning Arlitsch, dean of Libraries at Montana State, is the principal investigator. Mixter's role in the project is to serve as a data modeling expert, taking the lead in the development of an ontology for modeling items found in institutional repositories and digital collections in a form that can be discovered and indexed by Google and other major search engines.

James Tyler Mobley is a digital services librarian for College of Charleston Libraries. He graduated with his MLIS from the University of South Carolina, where he focused his studies on digital libraries and systems. He is the technical coordinator for both the South Carolina Digital Library and the Lowcountry Digital Library, and he develops and manages library applications and systems. Mobley has presented nationally at conferences on open source software implementations in libraries.

Mark Newton is the production manager at the Center for Digital Research and Scholarship (CDRS), a unit of the Columbia University Libraries/Information Services. At CDRS, his work focuses on the development of the library's scholarly publications partnership program, the Academic Commons institutional repository, and a variety of faculty- and student-led digital scholarship projects.

Patrick OBrien is the Semantic Web research director at the Montana State University Library. He is an expert in business strategy, Semantic Web technologies, predictive analytics and their application for improving data integration quality, discovering new relationships, and turning diverse data stores into conceptual knowledge. OBrien has more than 15 years of experience implementing data-driven marketing and risk management strategies in the pharmaceutical, biotechnology, health care, financial services, and telecommunications industries. His funded research for the past four years has been on search engine and Semantic Web optimization for digital repositories. OBrien holds a BA in economics from UCLA and an MBA in marketing and finance from The University of Chicago–Booth School of Business.

Charlotte Roh is the scholarly communication resident librarian at the University of Massachusetts Amherst, where she participates in a broad spectrum of scholarly communication efforts, including open education, copyright and fair use, library publishing, and the administration of the institutional repository. Her background is in academic publishing and she continues to freelance as an editor.

Paul Royster is coordinator of scholarly communications for the University of Nebraska–Lincoln Libraries, where for the past 10 years he has managed the institutional repository http://digitalcommons.unl.edu and served as publisher for the Zea Books digital monograph imprint. He has published a number of articles on repository management, library publishing, and issues involving copyright and open access. A veteran of more than 25 years in the publishing industry with the Library of America, Barron's Educational Series, Yale University Press, and the University of Nebraska Press, Royster holds an AB from Princeton University, an MA from the University of Michigan, and a PhD from Columbia University.

Betty Rozum is the associate dean for technical services and the physics librarian at Merrill-Cazier Library at Utah State University. Her scholarship focuses on scholarly communication and institutional repositories. She is currently working on examining the benefits and barriers to exposing student research via institutional repositories. Partnering with and serving the needs of the physics students and faculty provide the greatest job satisfaction. Rozum has a BS in biology from San Francisco State University and an MILS from the University of Michigan. Her work can be found at http://works.bepress.com/betty_rozum/

Simone Sacchi is the research and scholarship initiatives manager at the Center of Digital Research and Scholarship, Columbia University. His role is to research, develop, and promote the scholarly communication life cycle, tools, and services that support the research mission of Columbia University. As program manager, Sacchi oversees Columbia's Scholarly Communication Program, supervises the team managing Academic Commons—Columbia's institutional repository—and Columbia's Promoting Access to Research and Collaboration (Columbia PARC) program—an integrated CRIS in its piloting stage. He also conducts research in the area of open science and scholarship, digital stewardship, and data curation, with emphasis on the practical implications of their conceptual and modeling foundations. Sacchi holds a PhD in library and information science from the University of Illinois at Urbana–Champaign, an MS in LIS from the University of Parma, Italy, and a postgraduate specialization in free and open source software project management from the University of Bologna, Italy.

David Scherer is the assistant to the dean of libraries at Carnegie Mellon University. Previously, David was the scholarly repository specialist with the Purdue University Libraries. In that role he oversaw Purdue's primary institutional repository, Purdue e-Pubs, and educated faculty on open access and author rights, new models of publishing, and opportunities for open access publishing. Alongside his colleagues at the Purdue University Press, he was a member of the Purdue University Libraries Publishing Division, expanding library-led publishing opportunities across Purdue's campus. Scherer is also professionally active in library-based and open access publishing. Currently he is an associate editor for the Directory of Open Access Journals (DOAJ), evaluating applications and journals. He holds an MSLIS and an MA in history from Simmons College.

Lisa Schiff is the technical lead for the publishing program at the California Digital Library, University of California. Prior to joining the CDL, she was an information engineer at Interwoven. She received her PhD in library and information studies from the University of California, Berkeley, and is the author of *Informed Consent: Information Production and Ideology*, published by Scarecrow Press. Schiff is on the editorial board of the *Journal of Librarianship and Scholarly Communication* and is co-chair of the ORCID Business Steering Group.

Leila Sterman is the scholarly communication librarian at Montana State University. She manages MSU's institutional repository, ScholarWorks, consults on intellectual property, and edits the *Pacific Northwest Library Association Quarterly* journal. Her research focuses on collaborative initiatives between repositories, new uses of citation data, and repository workflows. Sterman has an MILS from Pratt Institute.

Becky Thoms is the head of the Digital Initiatives Department at the Merrill-Cazier Library at Utah State University and also serves as the scholarly communication and copyright librarian. She manages both the digital library and the institutional repository, DigitalCommons@USU. Her work focuses on the role of the library in the development of open educational resources, library provision of data management services, and student research in institutional repositories. Thoms received bachelor's degrees in political science and Spanish from the College of St. Benedict and an MA in library and information science from The University of Iowa.

Andrew Wesolek currently serves as head of digital scholarship at Clemson University. In this role, he oversees a new and increasingly robust institutional repository, serves as a copyright officer for the Libraries, educates faculty on new modes of scholarly publishing, and oversees the digitization of unique cultural heritage items. Wesolek is professionally active in library-based publishing efforts and open access initiatives. He currently manages a team of associate editors in evaluating applications and journals for the Directory of Open Access Journals (DOAJ) and serves as the past chair of the Coalition of Open Access Policy Institutions (COAPI).

Lauren Work is the digital collections librarian at Virginia Commonwealth University. She is responsible for the production, preservation, access, and discovery of VCU Libraries' digital assets. She received a bachelor's degree in geology and environmental science from the College of William and Mary and her master of science in library and information studies from the University of Washington.

Lisa Zilinski is the Carnegie Mellon University Libraries data services librarian. As part of the Scholarly Publishing, Archives, and Data Services Division, she works with library faculty to identity data literacy opportunities, develop learning plans and tools for data education, and investigate and develop programmatic and sustainable data services for the Libraries. Her research experience focuses on research data management education and literacy principles, integration of data services into the research process, and assessment and impact of data services and activities. Zilinski is a co-PI on an NSF DIBBs grant and serves on numerous boards and committees, including the Committee on Library and Information Science for Transportation (LIST) for TRB of the National Academies, the Information Science Education Committee for ASIS&T, and the Science & Technology Section (STS) of ACRL. She earned her master of science in library and information studies from Florida State University, School of Information.

Index